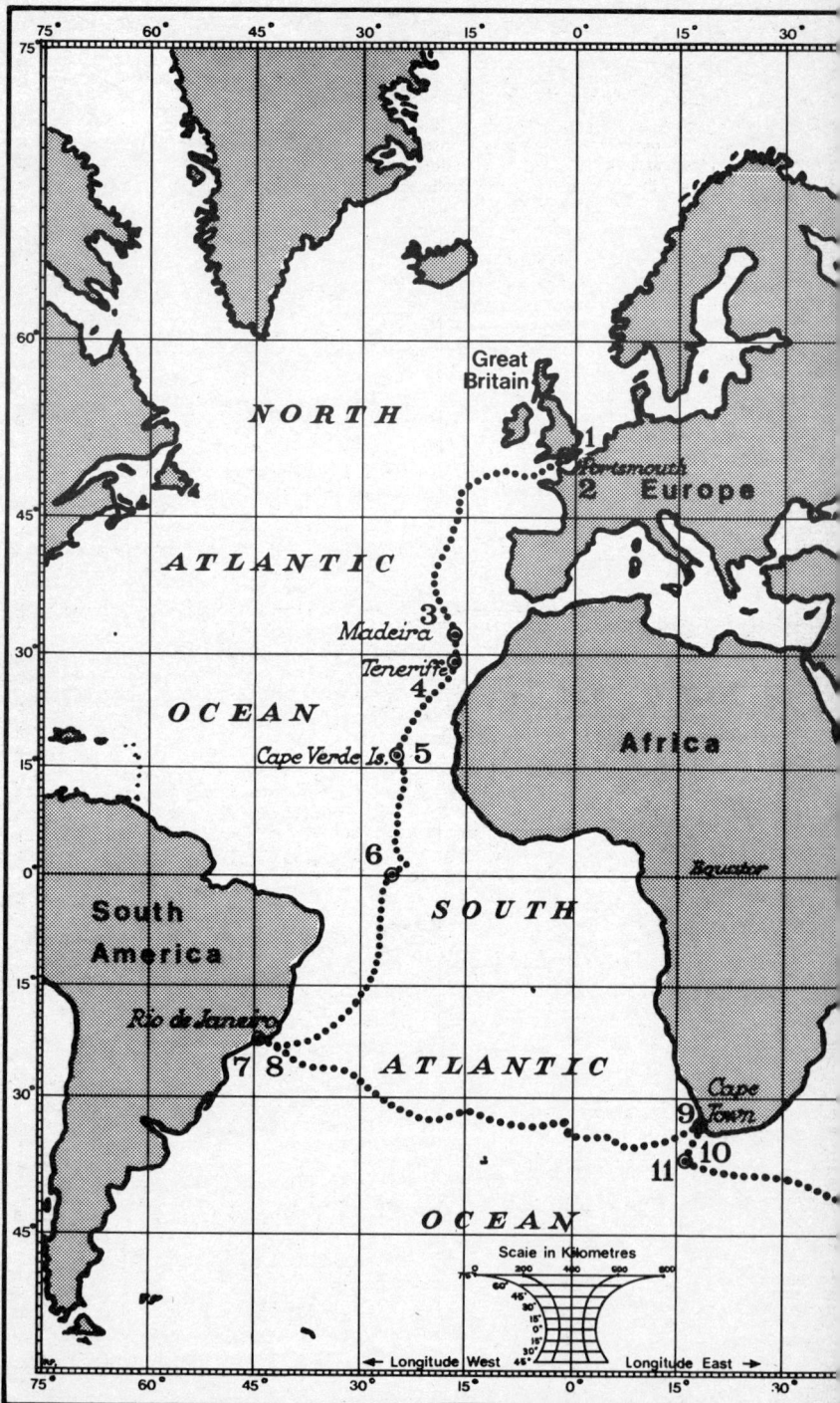

75°   60°   45°   30°   15°   0°   15°   30°

75°

NORTH

60°

Great
Britain

1
Portsmouth
2   Europe

45°

ATLANTIC

3
Madeira
Teneriffe
4

30°

OCEAN

Africa

Cape Verde Is. 5

15°

6

0°

SOUTH

South
America

Equator

Rio de Janeiro

15°

7 8   *ATLANTIC*

Cape
Town
9

30°

10

11

OCEAN

45°

Scale in Kilometres
200   400   600   800

← Longitude West   Longitude East →

75°   60°   45°   30°   15°   0°   15°   30°

The Voyage Of The First Fleet.

rom a map prepared by Mr Dudley Everingham, Eastwood, that shows track of the Transport *Scar-*
orough, in which Matthew Everingham was transported. Dates apply to all ships until Capetown.
.fter that the Fleet divided, Captain Phillip transferred to faster ship, *H.M. Supply* and went ahead
ith *Scarborough* and others. Diary of Private John Easty used for *Scarborough* dates. Bearings to
apetown, Lt Wm. Bradley, *H.M.S. Sirius.*

7.

1arch 4 — Sunday, 185 convicts taken aboard *Scar-*
  borough. (Everingham probably among them.)

1ay 13 — Sunday, 4 am. First Fleet departs from
  Portsmouth.

1ay 30 — Arrival at Madeira for water and stores.

une 4 — Teneriffe.

une 18 — Arrival at Cape Verde Islands. Unable to re-
  enter and revictual because of contrary winds.

uly 14 — Crossed the Equator.

ugust 6 — Arrived to Rio de Janiero. Stayed a month to
  revictual and repair sails, also to check instruments.

eptember 4 — Departed from Rio de Janiero. Had good
  breezes and made quick crossing to Table Bay.

)ctober 14 — 4 pm. Arrived at Table Bay [Capetown].
  Stayed one month to take on livestock and to water.

November 12 — Left Capetown. Sailed south to pick up
  Roaring Forties.

November 20 — Turning point at 37°30'S., 14°10'.,
  sailed east to round southern coast of Australian
  Continent.

12. *December 11* — Tuesday, 41°70'S., 38°12'E. spoke
  Friendship.

13. *December 25* — Christmas Day, in the middle of the
  Indian Ocean, 43°16'5., 100°18'E.

1788.

14. *January 1* — Tuesday, New Year's Day.44°25'S.,
  135°41'E.

15. *January 5* — Sighted Van Diemen's Land, (Tasmania).
  [Existence of Bass Strait unknown.]

16. *January 19* — Saturday, Arrived at Botany Bay, 8 am.

17. *January 26* — The First Fleet sailed into Port Jackson.
  All in Sydney Cove by 7.30 pm. Captain Phillip and
  officers went ashore, ran up the flag and drank a
  toast to the success of the Colony.

18. *January 27* — Sunday. A party of convicts sent ashore
  from the *Scarborough* to cut down trees and put up
  tents.

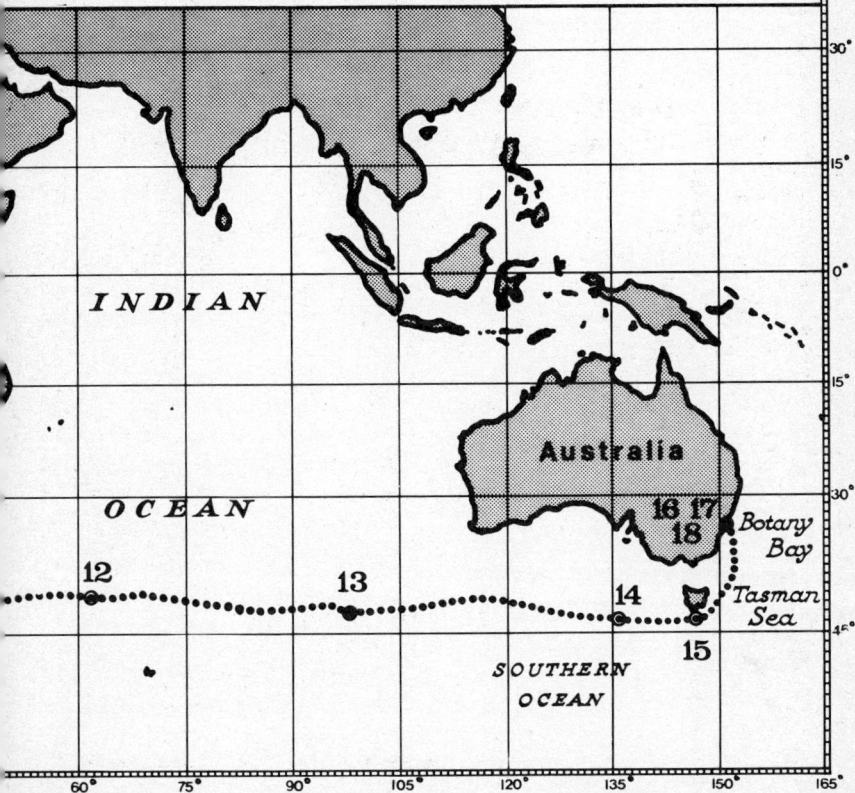

The First Fleet enters Port Jackson on the evening of January 26, 1788.

John Allcot O.B.E., F.R.A.S.

Matthew Everingham

A First Fleeter and his Times

Valerie Ross

Library of Australian History
Sydney
1988

LIBRARY OF AUSTRALIAN HISTORY — Publishers
17 Mitchell Street, NORTH SYDNEY, NSW. 2060

First Published 1980
Reprinted with Corrigenda 1988
ISBN 0 908120 37 0

Text © 1980,1986 Valerie Ross
Index © 1980 Library of Australian History

Printed in Australia by The Book Printer, Lane Cove, NSW. 2066

CONTENTS

ILLUSTRATIONS

PHOTOGRAPHIC PLATES

MAPS AND DIAGRAMS

ACKNOWLEDGMENTS

My thanks are due to all the family and to many residents of the Hawkesbury district. In addition, I would like to thank Mesdames Mary Thompson, Heather Everingham, E. McAllister and Jan Carver, Messrs. D.G. Bowd, Jim Bowden, Geoff Davis, Ken Luker, John McCullagh, Max Percival and Austin Woodbury, Dr. S. Devenish Meares, Dr. T.G. Parsons, Associate Professors David Bollen, K.J. Cable and Brian Fletcher.

I would like to acknowledge the help of the Royal Australian Historical Society, The Fellowship of First Fleeters and the Society of Australian Genealogists.

It has been a pleasure working with the publishers, the Library of Australian History. Mrs Una Fitzhardinge has provided valuable advice on the manuscript as have my family, John, Anne, Verity and Jennifer Ross.

For permission to reproduce drawings, pictures, manuscripts and maps, I wish to thank the following people and institutions: The British Museum, the National Maritime Museum and the Guildhall Library, London, the National Library of Australia, Canberra, the Council of the City of Sydney, the Church of St John, Parramatta, Norton Smith & Co., the Allcot Trust, Paul Hamlyn Pty. Ltd., Messrs. Frank Everingham and Monty Wedd, the State Library of New South Wales and the Archives Office of New South Wales. A special debt is owed to the staffs of the Mitchell Library and the Archives Office, who have been unfailingly courteous and helpful throughout.

During the course of writing, Matthew Everingham's grave has been restored. Foremost in this project was Mr Amos Everingham with the aid of donees to a fund, — Misses Victoria, Kathleen and L.M. Everingham, Messrs. Dudley, Frank, Garnsey, Robert, Graden, Colin, Herman C. and L.R. Everingham, Dr. Clarence Everingham, Mesdames Doris Hunziker, Violet Duck, V. Musgrave, Perram, Carita Naylor, Leone Cook, Frances Wonderley, L.M. Prince, Dulcie Clarke, Sue Benson, Julie Collier, Merilyn Hayward, Betty Beard, M. Hoeben, C. Bernath, Jill Mills, Clair Gledhill, Daphne Ryce, Beth Elton and Carmel Junner, Messrs. N.R. Lambert, Austin J. and Herbert Woodbury, J. Bowden, Keith Jennings, John Ross, L. Stephen, M.O. Humphries, Drs. H. Uren and D. O'Sullivan.

PREFACE

Frank Everingham's help is not mentioned in the Acknowledgments. That is because there have been times over the last six years when I have not known whether I should be thanking him or otherwise. However, Frank it was who first set me on my way 'to finding out more about Matthew Everingham'.

It was in 1970 that my daughters and I were on our way to Willow Park, Wilberforce, where they were to spend a riding holiday. Having read about Matthew's grave in the burial ground of St John's Church of England in D.G. Bowd's *Macquarie Country,* I decided to have a look at it. We also had a quick look inside the church and it was there that Jenny, typically, began to read the Visitors' Book and saw Frank Everingham's signature as President of the Fellowship of First Fleeters, the discovery that led to this work.

A slim volume was all that was at first intended but the book proved to have a life of its own. The stories which introduce each chapter are imaginary though based on fact. Their inclusion helped to fill the gaps one meets when writing the biographies of those who might be termed nonentities.

They were not nonentities, of course, because they were the many.

VAL ROSS
St Ives, N.S.W.
November 15, 1979.

PREFACE TO REPRINT

About two years after the appearance of this book, a notebook containing copies of three letters written by Matthew Everingham in 1789, 1792 and 1795 came to light. This notebook was published in 1985 as *The Everingham Letterbook* by the Anvil Press in association with the Royal Australian Historical Society.

The *Letterbook* contains much new material on Everingham, as recounted in his own words. Particularly interesting is an attempted crossing of the Blue Mountains in 1795 with First Fleeters, William Reid and John Ramsay.

However, very little has had to be changed in the original biography and the two books complement each other. The few changes appear as a corrigenda and addenda — see pp.166,167.

VAL ROSS,
Avoca Beach, N.S.W.
January, 1987

To my Mother and Uncle Dudley

BOOK ONE

A First Fleeter and His Times

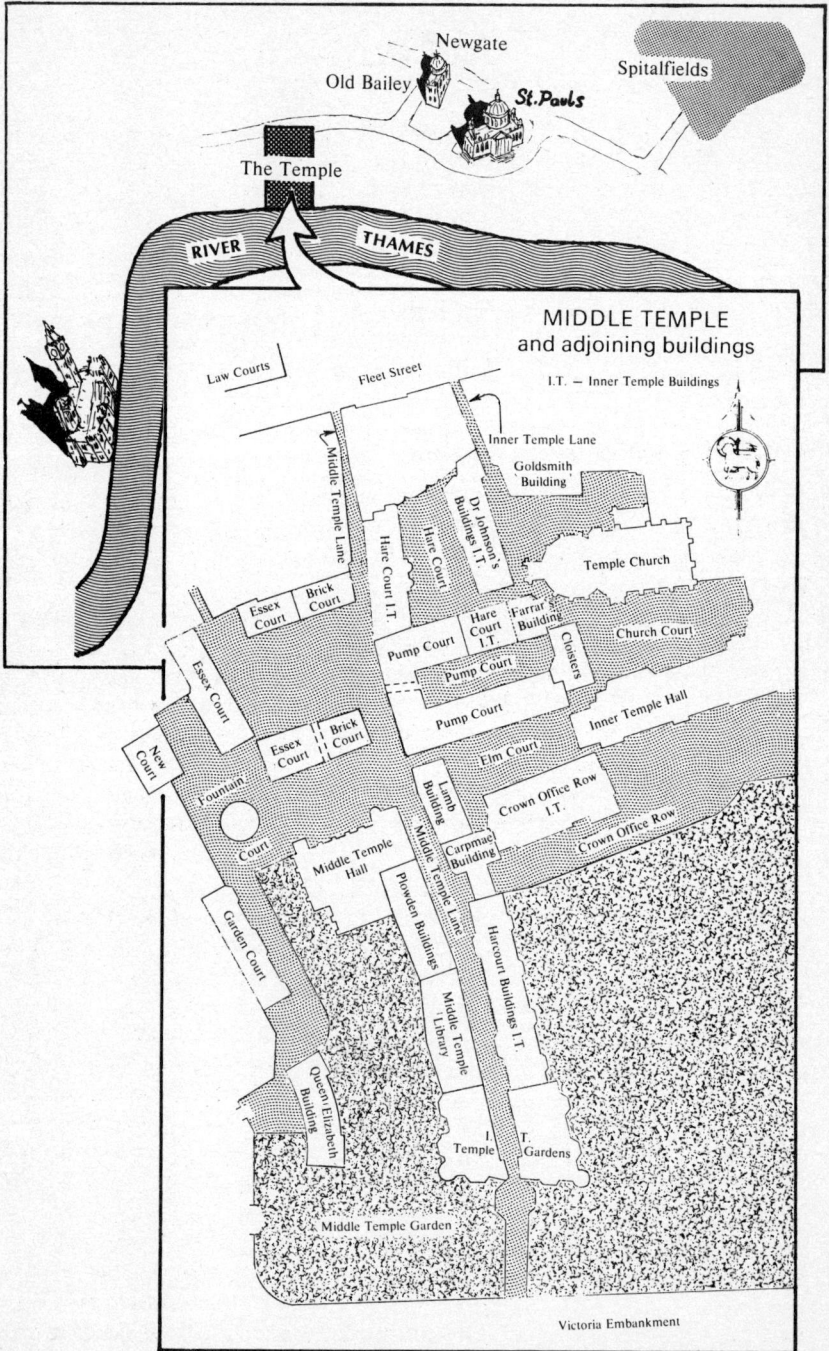

Newgate

Old Bailey

St. Pauls

Spitalfields

The Temple

RIVER THAMES

MIDDLE TEMPLE
and adjoining buildings

I.T. — Inner Temple Buildings

Law Courts

Fleet Street

Inner Temple Lane

Middle Temple Lane

Goldsmith Building

Dr. Johnson's Buildings I.T.

Hare Court

Hare Court I.T.

Temple Church

Essex Court

Brick Court

Pump Court

Hare Court I.T.

Farrar Building

Cloisters

Church Court

Pump Court

Essex Court

Pump Court

Inner Temple Hall

Essex Court

Brick Court

Elm Court

New Court

Fountain Court

Lamb Building

Crown Office Row I.T.

Crown Office Row

Middle Temple Hall

Middle Temple Lane

Carpmae Building

Plowden Buildings

Garden Court

Harcourt Buildings I.T.

Middle Temple Library

Queen Elizabeth Building

I.T. Temple Gardens

Middle Temple Garden

Victoria Embankment

CHAPTER ONE

Old Bailey

MATTHEW STOOD BEFORE the Bar and listened to the recital of his crime. He had been waiting for hours, not that any of the trials took long, but because there were so many like his own, petty thefts of one kind or another. It was almost a relief that his own turn had come.

The weather was warm and His Lordship, bespectacled and be wigged, had to struggle to keep awake, so tediously alike were the cases brought before him. One by one the prisoners had shuffled up to undergo their examinations, most of them poorly dressed, some gaudily — as befitted their calling of tout or doxy, but all of them stinking with the grime and sweat of Newgate, whence they had come that morning and where they had lingered these three weeks past, waiting for the Summer Sessions to begin.

The Judge had seen many younger defendants than the boy who now stood before him. Perhaps the features of his face were more finely cast, for the high forehead suggested intelligence and the heavy brows, determination.... but this was probably the mask of cunning, His Lordship reflected, for it was crystal clear that the lad was guilty. Shepherd of Pump Court had preferred the charge and the boy had been caught red-handed. So His Lordship stifled a yawn and nodded to the Clerk to proceed.

The witnesses to each case presented their evidence in a monotonous chant and so it was with Owen Owens, Attorney Shepherd's lackey, who now began to speak:

'I am a servant to Mr Shepherd. I was servant to him on the seventeenth of June last....'

Yet Matthew could see that Owens disliked giving testimony against him, for he and Owens had come to know each other over the past year and had been on good terms. In his mind, while the clerk testified and was cross examined, Matthew went back over the events that had led to his being here.

Clermont, the attorney with whom he lived and worked as a copy clerk and messenger boy, had dismissed him for some alleged fault, though Matthew believed it was because there was insufficient work — Clermont could not bear to see anyone idle for a moment. Then Matthew had had to leave Elm Street in the Temple and had taken lodgings in a dingy building near Chancery Lane, hoping to get work as assistant to one of the copy clerks to whom the overworked attorneys let out copying on a casual basis. But he had caught the ague, had been sick abed and had fallen behind with his rent. The woman who owned the lodgings and who, herself, needed the money had pressed him so that, weak and hungry, he had wandered the streets of the Temple wondering what to do.

He had been dawdling along Bell Yard and gazing into the window of Bannister's bookshop, when he had conceived a plan to free himself of his troubles. The window was full of volumes of all kinds, sets of statute books with peeling leather, bought cheap from some deceased and defunct practice, that would give a new man's rooms the necessary air of erudition and dependability. There were ink stands, scissors and pen knives, obviously from the same quarter — pocket books, diaries and almanacs, now going at sale price because it was the middle of the year. And then there were the reference books, such as Burn's Justice and Compton's Practice, that no indentured clerk could afford to be without, ready sellers, though much thumbed and keeping their value at five shillings apiece. It was upon seeing these that a course of action had suggested itself; and his eyes now turned momentarily to the table in the court room where identical copies of these books lay as exhibits in his trial.

So he had made his way across Fleet Street, back into the Temple to Pump Court and up the stairs that led to Shepherd's rooms. Haltingly, he had presented Mr Clermont's compliments and had told Owens, the clerk, that some of his erstwhile master's books had been mislaid by a servant girl and that Clermont had need of Burn's Justice or Compton's Practice.

'Well, now, Matthew,' Owens had said in his lilting Welsh voice, 'it's a long time since we've seen you surely?' So he had told Owens the tale of his illness, which was true enough. 'Well, the weather has been so changeable it's a wonder we're not all ill — and that's the truth of it,' Owens had said as he brought out both the books.

Hating himself for the deception, Matthew had nevertheless felt relieved that the worst was now over. He was thus surprised when he got to the bookshop to find that the old bookseller did not at once accept his story and was suspicious about the books.

So he had gone back to his lodgings, creeping in so that the woman would not know he had returned and had borrowed pen, ink and parchment from the copyist whose room was at the end of the passage. Conscious all the while that he was sinking deeper and deeper into evil ways, he had nevertheless put all his skill into producing a letter, whose writing and style had the maturity and courtesy he had observed in the missives of his master. Then he had gone back to the shop with the bow window, diffidently pushing open the door and starting at the bell which tinkled a warning to the bookseller that he had a customer. Even now old Bannister, seedy and austere in black, was in the box, telling the story of what followed:

'I said: 'My lad, I can give you five shillings for them but you must produce some authority or I shall detain the books.' He said, he, himself, lived in Elm Court, Temple, upon which he went away and returned and brought me a letter, on the authority of which I bought them; I thought it might be some distressed member of the law that wanted money, I could not tell.'

Matthew now felt acutely embarrassed, for the old man was the only one who took any time over his testimony or seemed regretful that one so young as he should be here. Clermont, his old employer, had testified as briefly as possible and had been out of the box in no time to return to a practice where time was money.

Now the Judge himself was thinking over what the bookseller had said, while Matthew's eyes travelled to the timber panelling in the high chamber, to the tall windows and the ornamentation above the seat of Justice. The youth's eyes closed and he swayed with the effort of standing still for so long. Then the Judge cleared his throat, peered down at Matthew over his spectacles and asked: 'And what have you to say to this charge?'

Reluctantly, the boy raised his eyes to those of the Judge to give the answer which they both knew would avail him little:

'I was in great distress....'

* * *

MATTHEW EVERINGHAM was not indicted, like so many of his companions for theft but for 'unlawfully by false pretences defrauding Samuel Shepherd, Esq. of goods value 10s. against the Statute etc.' The jury pronounced him guilty and could hardly have done otherwise, whereupon he was sentenced to transportation to America for the term of seven years. He was not immediately transported but before we see what happened to him in the intervening period, there are some aspects of his story which deserve attention and the first of these is his background.

Various family legends surround the parentage of Matthew but because they are legends, they are more appropriately dealt with in the chapter on the 'Everingham Millions', a fortune hunt which occurred as a direct result of their perpetration. Here we are dealing with facts and unfortunately, the names of Matthew's parents are unknown.

If the age given for him on his headstone and in the register of deaths for the Parish of St Matthew, Windsor, is correct, that is, forty-eight in 1817, then Matthew was born in 1769, which would make him fourteen or fifteen at the time of this trial in 1784. This age accords with the fatherly way in which Bannister, the bookseller, addressed him, as shown in the evidence of the trial, a facsimile of which is reproduced. Neither do we know where Matthew was born. All that we can reasonably say is that he had been living and working in the Temple area of London for a period of perhaps a year before his trial.[1]

Did we know Matthew's place of birth, there would be some chance of discovering his parentage. Although the registration of births did not become compulsory in England until 1837, many baptismal records prior to that date survive. These include not only parish records of the

Church of England but also records kept by the Roman Catholics, the Jews and Non-Conformist denominations. In each case, however, it is necessary to have an idea of the location in which the birth took place.

The Church of Jesus Christ of Latter Day Saints have used the records they possess to compile what is known as the Computer File Index, which is arranged on microfiche sheets by county; but this is by no means exhaustive and does not contain the name of any Everingham with the Christian name 'Matthew'.

Of course, before and after 1837, parents have been under no obligation to have their children baptized. But because there seemed every likelihood that Matthew had been baptized and possibly in the Church of England, efforts have been made to obtain details of his birth from parish records. Even though an authoritative guess places the number of parishes in England at eight and a half thousand at the time of Matthew's birth in 1769, one felt that some attempt should be made.

Accordingly and because it seemed logical to commence any search close to the place where we know Matthew had lived, the records of the Temple Church were searched, but without success. Then those of the village of Everingham in Yorkshire were examined but upon receipt of a negative result I wondered which of the two hundred parishes in the East Riding of Yorkshire would be the next best to try.[2]

Another avenue of investigation was suggested by the circumstance of Matthew's education. It was clear from a letter in his own handwriting, discovered in the State Archives of New South Wales, that he was not merely literate but had a natural and grammatical flow of language, which could only have been acquired in his boyhood prior to leaving England. Thus a remark made in a letter from one of his grandsons, Abel Everingham, that he had once heard of his grandfather attending 'the Blue Coat School' seemed worth pursuing. This would account for the quality of Matthew's education, would tie in with the suspicion that he may have been an orphan, and with the circumstance of his employment as servant to an attorney. Christ's Hospital or the 'Blue Coat School' was a charity school located not far from the Temple. Here the boys received an excellent education, Coleridge, Charles Lamb and Leigh Hunt were pupils over the years — and many went from there into the legal profession.[3]

However, a search of sixteen years (from 1769 to 1785) of the register for Christ's Hospital, which is held by the Guildhall Library, failed to show Matthew's name. In his reply to the enquiry, the Keeper of Manuscripts stated that there were several other schools in various parts of England, modelled on Christ's Hospital and adopting its distinctive apparel which were also known as 'Blue Coat Schools', but that his department had no information regarding the survival or whereabouts of records of such foundations. Further enquiry revealed that there had been such a school at York, the closest city to village of Everingham; but when the monthly committee meetings regarding the admission of scholars between January 1776 and December 1784, the

drawers they were not locked, in one of which I found this piece of silk.

JOHN ARMSTRONG *sworn.*

I am an officer; I went with the last witness, on the 17th of June, to this woman's lodgings, she was at the outside of the street door, she unlocked the door, and we went in and we found this silk in the drawers.

Prisoner. Have not you since had a person in custody that that room did belong to, and she has been discharged?——No, we did take up another woman for receiving, and we were informed, there was two women lived in the room, and she was discharged, there was no appearance of any things of any other woman.

Prisoner. Whether that Gentleman did not take a pair of stays off the bed, belonging to this other woman that has been in custody, since I was taken?——No, there was a pocket book, and a pair of breeches belonging to a man that is gone away.

Prisoner. The room did not belong to me, I did not take the room, pay no rent, nor receive no key.

NOT GUILTY.

Tried by the London Jury before Mr. ROSE.

---

775. MATTHEW JAMES EVERINGHAM was indicted, for that he being a profligate person, on the 17th of June did falsly pretend to Owen Owens servant to Samuel Shepherd, Esq; in the Middle Temple, that he was sent to Mr. Shepherd, from Mr. Clermont's for Burn's Justice or Compton's Practice meaning certain books, by which he obtained the same books, value 10s. the property of the said Samuel Shepherd, whereas he was not sent with that message.

OWEN OWENS *sworn.*

I am servant to Mr. Shepherd, I was servant to him on the 17th of June last, the prisoner came to me on the 17th of June in the morning, about ten or close he came with Mr. Clermont's compliments to Mr. Shepherd, and he would be obliged to him, if he would lend him Burn's Justice or Compton's Practice, I gave him the books, and asked him whether he lived with Mr. Clermont's or not, he said yes, he did, and he had had the fever and ague, and was come back again.

——— CLERMONT, Esq. *sworn.*

The prisoner at the bar was my servant, but not on the 17th of June.

Did you send him any where?——I did not send him any where.

RICHARD BANNISTER *sworn.*

I am a bookseller in Bell-yard, Temple-bar, the prisoner came to me about the middle of June, I did not take any particular notice then of the time, he brought to me to sell Compton's Practice, I gave him five shillings for it, if it had been the last edition of the book it would have been worth more, but not being the last, it was the full value of it.

What does the last edition sell for?——Sixteen shillings; I asked him whose they were, he asked me but three shillings, I said my lad I can give you five shillings for them, but you must produce me some authority, or I shall detain the books, he said he himself lived in Elm Court, Temple, upon which he went away, and returned and brought me a letter, on the authority of which I bought them; I thought it might be some distressed member of the law that wanted money, I could not tell.

PRISONER's DEFENCE.

I was in great distress.

Court to Owen Owens. Were Mr. Shepherd and Mr. Clermont acquainted?—Yes, they were.

GUILTY.

Transported for seven years.

Tried by the London Jury before Mr. ROSE.
WILLIAM

Trial (No.775) of Matthew James Everingham — entry in Old Bailey Sessions Papers
[see p15]

'Bell Alley, Fenchurch Street, Chancery Lane, May 4, 1818' *[see p17]*

relevant period, were examined, there was no entry at all for the surname 'Everingham'.[4]

A letter to a vicar in Kent, where the parish churchyard contained a tombstone with an epitaph similar to Matthew's revealed that the person had been interred after Matthew left England and that the surname of Everingham was unknown in those parts.

A few other leads, such as a search of Boyd's Marriage Index and of the parish records of several London churches were unsuccessful too. All this illustrates the problems which attend research into the backgrounds of Matthew Everingham and other convicts mentioned in this book.

We must therefore work on what we have, which, in Matthew's case, is a good account of the trial, being grateful that he was a 'London tried man' and had his trial recorded in the Old Bailey Sessions Papers.

What is apparent from the trial is that Matthew was familiar with the area known as Legal London. Elm Court, where he had lived with his employer Clermont, and Pump Court, where the attorney Shepherd from whom Matthew obtained the books had his rooms, and Bell Yard, where the bookseller Bannister had his shop, can still be seen on a present day map of London. They are in and about the area known as the Temple, which had been the legal centre of London for hundreds of years and which was and is one of the most historically interesting parts of the city.

The Temple was originally the seat in England of the famous Order of Knights Templars, who fought in the Crusades. On the dissolution of the order in 1312, the Temple passed to Crown and later into the possession of the Knights Hospitallers of St John, who leased it in the reign of Edward III to certain professors of the common law. The Temple is the general name covering two Inns of Court, the Middle and the Inner Temple. Nearby are Lincoln's Inn and Gray's Inn, these four great Inns of Court having the exclusive right of calling persons to the English Bar. Here to this day are the offices of many leading solicitors. Legal London is crossed from South to North by Chancery Lane which begins in Fleet Street, nearly opposite the Temple, and ends at Holborn near Gray's Inn. Charles Lamb was born near the Inner Temple, while Isaak Walton, Oliver Goldsmith and Dr Johnson all lived in the area. Shakespeare used the Middle Temple Gardens for the setting of that scene in Henry VI where the white rose of York and the red rose of Lancaster were plucked, symbolizing the opposing sides in the Wars of the Roses.[5]

The Old Bailey, or Central Criminal Court, where Matthew was tried, can be seen a little to the right on the map, the 'bailey' being part of the wall of the old Roman city between Lud Gate and New Gate. Newgate prison, where Matthew would have been imprisoned, while waiting for his trial, was the site of one of the ancient entrances to the city, it being customary to use the gates as prisons from earliest times. When excavations for a new Sessions House were made in 1907, traces of a Roman gate, the city wall and a surrounding ditch were found.[6]

The place names mentioned in the preceding two paragraphs occur frequently in the writings of Charles Dickens, who, like Matthew, was employed as office boy to a solicitor. Dickens was born in 1812 but things did not change very much in the forty years between Matthew Everingham's and Charles Dickens's residence in London. It was the great theme of Dickens's writing, propounded with humour in 'The Pickwick Papers' and by tragedy in 'Bleak House' that regrettably, neither the outward appearance nor the intrinsic character of Legal London had altered for generations. These novels and 'Great Expectations' are full of the kind of places Matthew had known. One thinks of Mr Jaggers' office, of Mr Perker, of the wily Dodson and Fogg and of the rows of clerks on stools who toiled for long hours copying documents before the days of carbon paper and the photo-copying machine, of the dark offices and dingy dwellings of those who lived on the fringe of the legal profession in Chancery Lane.[7]

There are some aspects of Matthew's trial and about the way in which offenders generally were brought to trial in the late eighteenth century which deserve attention. In most cases, when an offender was caught, he was taken before a magistrate, formerly charged and if there were enough evidence, detained for trial at the Old Bailey. Otherwise, he was convicted summarily by the Justice sitting alone to a period in a House of Correction. If he were to be tried at the Old Bailey, he was sent to gaol, (in Matthew's case, it would be Newgate), to await trial.[8]

The offender's appearance before a superior court depended on the circumstances of the theft, on whether the offender was recognized as one who had been before the police and magistrates before, and particularly, on the willingness of the prosecutor to carry the case forward. For there were no public prosecutors and the individual who had suffered loss had to collect his own witnesses and until 1818, could not recover costs. In these circumstances 'no one had an interest to convict' and much crime went unpunished. It is thus strange that the attorney, Shepherd, should have spent the time and trouble to prosecute Matthew when he could only hope to regain his books valued at ten shillings. Perhaps it was a matter of principle to him that thieving should not go unpunished or he felt that so cunning a boy as Matthew, who had not only 'falsely pretended' but forged a letter, might make greater mischief if left at large.[9]

That Matthew received the sentence of transportation also requires some comment. For it is known that the judges and juries who administered the laws, though bound by statutes which were severe and barbaric until the reforms of the middle nineteenth century, frequently exercised tolerance, restraint and generosity. Judges did not usually transport first offenders though Matthew must have been one, for the attorney, Clermont, would never have employed a boy with a record.[10]

In the published record of the Old Bailey Sessions Papers, Matthew's trial appears under the heading, 'Misdemeanours', to distinguish cases less serious than felonies. And although the value of the property concerned in his case was estimated at ten shillings and the death penalty, nearly always commuted to transportation, applied to thefts greater than twelve pence, it would have been within the judge's power to be less severe.

For instance, Ann Foster, (Trial No. 764), was found guilty of stealing goods to the value of seventeen shillings and sixpence. Perhaps because she brought a witness to testify to her character, she was sentenced to twelve months' hard labour in a House of Correction. John Young, (Trial No. 769), found guilty of stealing goods worth seven shillings, received a public whipping and six months' hard labour in a House of Correction; while Thomas Porter, (Trial No. 772), who stole goods to the value of thirty-five shillings — three and half times the value of the books falsely obtained by Matthew — was sentenced to a public whipping and to seventeen months' hard labour in a House of Correction. It is therefore puzzling that Matthew, fourteen or fifteen years old and seemingly a first offender should have been sentenced to transportation for seven years.[11]

It is interesting that the full name, Matthew James Everingham, is given in the Sessions Papers, whereas, in other papers dealing with the trial and transportation, the middle name is omitted. Not many convicts had two names and this suggests that he had not merely been given a name to distinghish him but was 'called after' someone. Yet there is no evidence of his having any friends or family to come forward to give a character reference at the time of his trial.

It will be noticed that Matthew was not employed by Clermont at the time of the commission of his crime, June 17, 1784. He is described as a 'former' 'servant' to Clermont and while, because of his literacy, one assumes that this involved the copying of documents, there is no record of Matthew having been an attorney's clerk in the sense of a trainee solicitor. The Law Society of London was not formed until 1825 and although it possesses historical material prior to this date, it has no information on Matthew Everingham nor any indenture record for him. There is no record of Clermont, Matthew's employer in the London Attorneys' section of the Law List during the years 1782-1788, which would cover the time, 1784, when Matthew was employed by him. But there are entries in 1785 and 1787 for Samuel Shepherd at Pump Court, Middle Temple, from whose office Matthew obtained the law books.[12]

After his trial, Matthew was returned to Newgate prison where he remained until September, 1784. Incorrectly listed as Matthew 'John' Everingham, he was, in that month, described as a 'prisoner upon orders' awaiting transportation. Then he is noted as 'delivered' which meant that he had been delivered out of the custody of Richard Akerman, the Keeper of Newgate to another prison, which was almost certainly one of the hulks on the Thames at Woolwich. Unfortunately, only three lists of prisoners delivered by Akerman to such prisons survive, the earliest of which is December, 1785, so it is impossible to be more precise in this matter.

He would now actually be living on the water, the Thames being the first of three rivers which figure in this story. From the time we first hear of Matthew to the very moment of his death, he lived near water. The sound which is most characteristic of his life and that of all his children is the swishing of oars.

To which particular hulk he was sent is unknown but it would have been much the same as the one depicted and the existence to which he now came would be harsh and dreary.

The idea of using old naval vessels as prisons had been adopted as a temporary expedient when the War of American Independence precluded the transportation of convicts to that country in 1776. In that year, Duncan Campbell, a contractor who had previously been engaged in transportation to the American colonies, bought two vessels, the *Justitia* of two hundred and sixty tons and the *Censor,* an old frigate, from the Admiralty, dismantled them of rigging and moored them in the stream of the Thames between Gallions' Reach and Barking Reach at Woolwich.[13]

As the condition of the bed and foreshores of the Thames — and thus the entry to the great port of London, had become befouled, employment was found for the convicts in cleansing it and in converting the banks of 'The Warren' into docks, quays and yards for the Royal Arsenal at Woolwich. The illustration shows the *Justitia* (and another vessel on the extreme right) and the work in full swing at 'Campbell's Academy' as it was wryly called. The date of this drawing is May, 1777, but the way in which the convicts were employed would have been much the same when Matthew arrived there in 1784.[14]

He would perhaps be put to work wheeling barrows of ballast and screening it, as seen in the picture, or bringing it out of the lighters in baskets to the wharf which was under construction by other convicts. One can see by the pile-driving machine and the windlass for getting the ballast on board that the methods used in the work were primitive. The simple charm of the drawing reminds one of Mediaeval woodcuts and stone carvings but a close view reveals the misery and hopelessness of the toilers. On the extreme right of the drawing and at centre back can be seen seven or eight overseers, cutlasses drawn to deal instantly with mutiny or escape. The convicts, ironed, as close observation shows, dared hardly speak to each other and were afraid to be caught slacking, for the overseers, men of the lowest class and underpaid, worked the convicts at their own discretion and not by turn.[15]

During the first two years of the hulk system, one hundred and seventy-six prisoners out of six hundred and thirty-two, or one in three, died — for gaol fever, (typhoid), dysentery, scurvy and venereal disease were rife. Doctors commented that the inmates included men over seventy, the blind, the crippled and the mad; and that in the first three years, 'eight boys not yet fifteen years old' were taken on board, but Matthew was this age.[16]

The clothing Campbell issued when the prisoners' own clothes wore out was a checked linen shirt, a brown jacket and a pair of breeches and this was worn until it almost dropped off and the owner resembled a scarecrow.[17]

The food was ox cheek, either boiled or made into soup, pease (boiled peas), bread and biscuit but on two days, 'Burgoo days', meat was replaced by oatmeal and cheese. There were six men to a mess and each mess received one undressed ox cheek, two pounds of cheese, three pints of pease or oatmeal and fourteen and a half to six pounds of biscuit or bread, which came in bags of crumbs and was frequently mouldy or green. River water was imperfectly filtered for drinking and on four days of the week, they had small (or inferior quality) beer. Friends were stopped from supplementing the food because so many knives, files and other tools had been smuggled in thus disguised.

The port holes on the river side of the vessel were left open but those on the shore side were blocked up, so the air became fetid, in addition to which, by 1787, the space allowed for each man's hammock had been reduced to an area six feet long by twenty inches wide. Visiting reformers were appalled at the conditions and the morality of the convicts.[18]

While Matthew was imprisoned on the hulk, he must have wondered what life on board had been like during the vessel's heyday at sea. He must also have wondered whether the sentence of transportation would ever be carried out and if he would be placed on a sailing ship bound for the American colonies. Though life here was hard, he may have learnt from some of the older convicts that transportation was an even more uncertain fate. The authorities had formerly paid contractors such as Campbell just to get rid of the convicts and had exercised no control over their disposal to masters in America.[19]

Until 1783, when the war was lost and the King acknowledged the existence of the United States, it had been hoped that transportation would resume. And even afterwards, until 1784, it had been hoped that the planters in the southern states would buy convicts, which possibly accounts for Matthew, as late as July 1784, being given the outdated sentence of transportation to America.

He could not have known that during his imprisonment, the authorities were considering alternative places for transportation. He would live his life from day to day and may even have lost track of the date, for he had no way of knowing that there was anything ahead but this soul destroying existence until his sentence expired.

As he saw others become ill and die, he might wonder whether he would survive his seven years' term. In any case, he would know that when his time finished, he would have little hope of obtaining employment; for those who survived imprisonment returned to a life of poverty and crime. In the circumstances, he might well have been as apathetic and demoralized as the convicts whom Dickens, surely from his own experience in the marsh country, described Pip, of *Great Expectations,* seeing:

'The boat had returned, and his guard were ready, so we followed him to the landing-place made of rough stakes and stones, and saw him put into the boat, which was rowed by a crew of convicts like himself. No one seemed surprised to see him, or interested in seeing him, or glad to see him, or sorry to see him, or spoke a word, except that somebody in the boat growled as if to dogs, 'Give way, you!' which was the signal for the dip of oars. By the light of the torches, we saw the black Hulk lying out a little way from the mud of the shore, like a wicked Noah's ark. Cribbed and barred and moored by massive rusty chains, the prison-ship seemed in my young eyes to be ironed like the prisoners. We saw the boat go alongside, and we saw him taken up the side and disappear. Then, the ends of the torches were flung hissing into the water, and went out, as if it were all over for him!'[20]

In this atmosphere did Matthew spend nearly three years of his life, from the age of fifteen to eighteen. Among those with whom he lived would be criminals of all types for there was no segregation accordiing to crime or age. The most violent men, rapists and thieves lay side by side and it is to be expected that, as a boy among men who had been away from women for long periods, he would have been subject to intimidation.

At last, as escapes from the hulks became more frequent and a source of danger and infection to the people of London and as the hulks became more overcrowded, the authorities were forced into the decision of establishing a penal settlement at Botany Bay.

How news came to Matthew that he was selected to be transported in the First Fleet is unknown, nor do we know what he thought of it. The Reverend Richard Johnson, who was to accompany the Fleet as Chaplain, visited intended transportees on the hulk, *Leviathan,* at Woolwich, in the months prior to the departure. But not even he knew very much about New Holland, because no one had been there since Captain James Cook's brief visit seventeen years before.[21]

After three years' imprisonment, Matthew can have retained little optimism. But perhaps it would be natural, as he and others climbed into the waggons that were to take them overland to Portsmouth, to look back at the hulks and to feel that any change could only be for the better.

CHAPTER TWO

The Voyage

IT WAS THE middle of the night when he was awakened and until he heard the creak of timbers and the whoosh of passing water behind his head, Matthew wondered where he could be. Someone was shaking his shoulder and at the same time, telling him not to make a noise.

'Matt, lad,' said the man, 'come on over! The boys here have got some business they want ye to hear of!'

This sounded like trouble but Matthew had learnt not to make enemies, so he shook the sleepiness out of his body and edged, as best he could in the confined space of the 'tweendecks, across to the group of squatting figures. As he drew nearer, he could see, even by the dim light, that all the trouble-makers on the ship were here. Two of them in particular, Philip Farrell, a sailor previously involved in a mutiny on the *Goliath* and Thomas Griffiths, who had once been a pirate, were malcontents and dangerous men. Black Jemmy, a negro, had barely escaped hanging and was the most reckless man Matthew had ever met.

'We'll come straight to the point, lad,' said Farrell 'we mean to take the ship'.

'God Almighty!' Matthew could not help saying, 'you must be mad!'

'No, matey,' said Ned, the little pick-pocket who had wakened him, 'we've got it planned. Phil here has been a bosun's mate and he reckons on taking the ship into one of them places in the Mediterrainy, where we could all just disappear.'

'Aye,' said Farrell, 'but we need a few more young coves to make the rush. And Ned here, suggested you.'

'No,' said Matthew, 'I'm not for that. You'd never get past the marines and then there'd be the seamen. I'd rather take my chance in New Holland.'

'Do ye think this ship will ever get that far?' asked Farrell and then went on. 'You heard the way she shuddered when we had that rough patch before and there's far worse to come.'

'And my Gawd,' said Ned, who had been terribly seasick at the time, 'I ain't about to go through all that again only to work me guts out farming at Botany Bay or get 'et by savages.'

'We'll never make it,' said Farrell, 'I've heard them seas are full of reefs. We've got a good chance now that our irons are off. So what do you say?'.

'No,' said Matthew, 'we'd be dead men. I'd rather risk the storms and Botany Bay than try it. And if you do, we'll all get a flogging.... or be starved.'

While Matthew tried to reason with them, a wily old lag named Sam had crawled behind him. At a sign from Griffiths he made a lunge at Matthew while the ex-pirate himself drew a knife from his shoe and held it to Matthew's throat.

'Perhaps we can persuade you to change your mind, son,' he said, 'for ye know too much now and might squawk!'

'Listen, Griffiths,' said Matthew, when he could speak, 'I'm past being scared. I just don't want trouble, but I won't talk either.'

'Let him go,' said Farrell after this. 'He's no good to us if he has to be scared into it. And Ned here says he'll keep his mouth buttoned.'

Sullenly they released him and he crept stealthily back to his berth, for the skirmish had already caused some of the sleeping convicts to stir. But for a long time he lay awake, his senses too stimulated for him to sleep. He wondered whether Farrell was right about them never getting there, for Farrell was a sailor after all. Then he thought of the grim picture Ned had painted of life at Botany Bay and wondered if it would be like America. At last, because this part of the future was too inconceivable even for his young imagination, he gave it up, rolled over and went to sleep.

* * *

THE INTENDED mutiny on the transport, *Scarborough* never took place for, on May 20, 1787, a week after the First Fleet had left Portsmouth, an unnamed informer told the Commandant of Marines of the convicts' plan to take the ship. Philip Farrell and Thomas Griffiths, suspected of being the ringleaders, were taken aboard the flagship, *Sirius,* given twenty-four lashes each and then transferred to the *Prince of Wales,* while some of the remaining convicts on the *Scarborough* were double-ironed.[22]

Whether Matthew knew of the mutiny or what he thought of it is unknown, the incident described in the story being imaginary. For we are still at a point in his history where information is scant, limited to the recording of his name on the victualling lists and the indent of the ship. But from the store of historical records we now possess such as despatches, journals, diaries and letters, it is possible to form a general picture of the voyage from the transportees' point of view and even to narrow it down to Matthew's particular experience on the *Scarborough.*[23]

The story shows the kind of men in whose company Matthew travelled for, as on the hulks, convicts of all types were placed together. The commander of the expedition, Governor Arthur Phillip, had asked for a list of the names, crimes and ages of the convicts, intending to put the worst together so that they might be more easily guarded and to prevent them having a bad influence on the others, but the list failed to arrive prior to departure. Phillip and the officers were later to lament that because of this, the best soon became as vicious as the worst. Yet there was remarkably little trouble during the voyage and the attempted mutiny provided one of the few dramatic moments.[24]

There were some prisoners, like Matthew, who, having endured the hellish existence of the hulks, would respond to the changed environment at Portsmouth and have become resigned, if not optimistic about their fate. Matthew's outlook was shown to be changed in the opening tale so now let us go back eleven weeks to see how this may have come about.

From the journal of Lieutenant William Bradley, First Lieutenant on the *Sirius,* we know that on March 4, 1787, two hundred and ten convicts arrived at Portsmouth, having travelled overland by waggon. One hundred and eighty-five were taken aboard the *Scarborough* transport the next day. In all, two hundred and eight male convicts travelled on this ship. There were no females on either it or the *Alexander.* The majority of convicts who arrived would seem to have come from the hulks on the Thames and this assumption is supported by the fact that most were London tried men and had been convicted at least two years.[25]

Under these circumstances it is surprising that, as Surgeon Arthur Bowes, who travelled on the *Lady Penrhyn* reports, the convicts taken aboard the *Scarborough* were all healthy. What Bowes meant was that none were actually ailing, as were those on the *Alexander.* On their former diet, they could hardly have been healthy by modern standards. Phillip had earlier refused to embark sick convicts, so perhaps the most healthy had been selected, which was fortunate for Matthew.[26]

As soon as they arrived on board the transports at Portsmouth the convicts were given soap with which to wash and a new set of clothes. The soap was borrowed from the marines and later paid back when the Fleet reached Teneriffe, while the clothing came from the stores of the *Sirius,* as we know from a letter Phillip wrote to the Home Office about its replacement. (In the same letter, Phillip reiterated his opinion that there would be epidemics if these things were not done, which would result in the sailors deserting or the Fleet being refused entry to a foreign port.) The convicts would then be examined by a surgeon, probably the Surgeon-General, John White, who insisted on the same standards of cleanliness as Phillip. The quarters in which the convicts were placed had been whitewashed with quick lime and disinfected by the explosion of gunpowder, while each man had a bed of his own. Spithead at Portsmouth had been chosen for the assembly of the seven hundred and fifty felons, so that although ironed, they could be allowed on deck during the Fleet's preparation for departure. The ten weeks confinement was monotonous but it was preferable to the labour of the hulks, while the marine guards were a better class of men than the convicts' former tyrannous overseers and were constantly supervised by officers.[27]

Most importantly, the food was much better. Instead of a scant diet of oxcheek soup, pease, oatmeal, dried-out cheese and mouldy bread or biscuit, each convict now had two thirds of the weekly allowance for seamen in the navy: that was seven pounds of bread, four pounds of beef, two pounds of pork, two pints of pease, two pints of oatmeal, six ounces of butter, three quarters of a pound of cheese and a half-pint of vinegar. Bowes said that few marines going out of England were ever so amply provided for as these convicts. The meat provided was mainly salted but Phillip did his best to see that both they and the marines should have some fresh meat in Portsmouth as well as fresh vegetables.[28]

By the date of departure, the ships of the Fleet were laden in every part with provisions, implements of agriculture, blacksmithing tools, camp equipment, clothing and baggage. It would have been impossible for the convicts not to have heard or seen something of the stowing operations or to have been unaware of the atmosphere of preparation and purpose that surrounded the undertaking.[29]

Thus it must slowly have become apparent to them that more interest was being taken in the manner of their exile by the country that despised them than had ever been shown, or was likely to be shown, while they remained on its doorstep. The explanation for this seeming paradox will shortly be discussed but, suffice it to say that Matthew and many others were now better off than they had been for years. And while, like Ned in the story, they might be apprehensive about the long sailing voyage and an unknown country, they would be reassured by the sight of the Governor, officers, marines and their wives preparing to accompany them in the expectation of arriving safely. That many were actually pleased to be departing we know from Captain Watkin Tench of the Marines, who was travelling on the *Charlotte* and who strolled down among the convicts just after the Fleet sailed. Some, he said, were sad to be separated perhaps forever, from their native land, but most faces showed a high degree of satisfaction.[30]

The First Fleet had finally set sail from Portsmouth on Sunday, May 13, 1787 and numbered eleven vessels. Two of these, the flagship, *H.M.S. Sirius* (540 tons,) and the armed tender *H.M. Brig Supply* (170 tons) were naval ships and were to remain in New South Wales until the colony was established. The other nine were privately owned merchantmen, being in order of size, *Alexander,* (448 tons), *Scarborough,* (420 tons), *Fishburn,* (378 tons), *Golden Grove,* (353 tons), *Charlotte,* (339 tons), *Prince of Wales,* (334 tons), *Lady Penrhyn,* (331 tons), *Friendship,* (276 tons) and *Borrowdale,* (274 tons). These were specially chartered to carry convicts and stores and once they had arrived and unloaded, their contract with the British Government would cease and they could make their way homeward or elsewhere by whatever route they pleased.[31]

Each convict vessel carried a number of marines, all under the command of Major Robert Ross, who was to be Lieutenant Governor in New South Wales. The Fleet as a whole was under the command of a naval captain, Arthur Phillip, who had been appointed Governor General and Commander in Chief of the colonizing expedition. Captain John Hunter of the *Sirius* was second-in-command at sea and was to become Acting Governor of the colony in the event of Phillip's illness, absence or death.

The success of the voyage and survival of the infant colony owed much to Phillip's leadership and the naval character of the whole project. At this time, the British Navy was a service which had no superior, for its discipline was excellent and both seamen and officers were trained, many since childhood, to a high degree of efficiency. Bravery, loyalty and duty were a way of life to such men as the Governor's supporting officers, Captain Hunter and Lieutenant Philip Gidley King, (both of whom later became Governors of New South Wales), Lieutenants William Bradley and Henry Ball. Of the Marines, Captains David Collins and Watkin Tench and Lieutenant William Dawes would later distinguish themselves.

When Phillip had received his appointment on October 12, 1786, his first Commission had been short and vague. He immediately began to think out the problems connected with the voyage and settlement, although hindered by the little information available about the country of the Fleet's destination; and his second Commission of April, 1787, seems to have embodied many of the ideas he had formulated and suggested. The scope of his vision will become apparent to the reader as we go on but it is interesting to us, who are following Matthew's experience, to see what plans Phillip and the Home Government had in mind for him and the other convicts.[32]

The prime object of the proposed colony at Botany Bay was to solve the problem of overcrowded gaols. Its remoteness made escape difficult, while its climate was thought to be healthy and its soil fertile, which would enable the convicts, after a year or two, to maintain themselves with no expense to the mother country. It was thought that the colony might one day be of strategic importance to Britain and it was hoped that the settlement of nearby Norfolk Island would provide naval stores such as flax for sailcloth and pine masts. Though England feared depopulation, it was also anticipated that, as time went by, some free settlers would come to the colony.[33]

Phillip stressed that he 'would not wish convicts to lay the foundations of an empire'. They would always remain separate from the garrison and free settlers, even after the seven or fourteen years for which they had been transported had expired. But they would be settled on land grants of their own and live in a free country under the protection of laws similar to those of the mother country, in which free country, 'there could be no slavery'. While social discrimination shows Phillip to have been a man of his times, in more important matters his ideas were well ahead of them. His humane treatment of the convicts was such that Lieutenant Ralph Clark on the *Friendship* was to remark at the end of the voyage that they had been treated more like children than prisoners.[34]

Matthew and the rest of the convicts were to come only gradually to a knowledge of Phillip's character and of his concept of their future. The removal of their irons, ordered by the Governor immediately they had set sail, would be welcomed and after the mutiny scare, they would probably hear by the 'grapevine' that, although Phillip had been quick to act, he had handled the punishment of the suspects himself and it had been light for the nature of the crime. The marines on the *Scarborough* were from time to time, sentenced to between fifty and one hundred lashes and were often placed in irons. The convicts would also be grateful for the efficient way in which their water was distributed, with always a marine officer present, but would see that there was another side to this efficiency. Lieutenant John Shortland came on board on May 25 to list their names and occupations so that each man could be put to the best use when they arrived at Botany Bay. Phillip had particularly asked that the prisoners who were initially sent should be artisans such as carpenters or farmers, but his request was not met and the majority turned out to be Londoners without a trade or training of any kind.[35]

But to the convicts whose names were taken and to the Governor who ordered the procedure, there were more immediate problems. Soon after they left Portsmouth and just prior to the affair on the *Scarborough,* the sea was so rough that many people became seasick. Phillip was also anxious about the navigational hazards of the Channel, but they reached the Atlantic safely. Then, at a point about two hundred miles west of the Scilly Islands, their escort, the man-of-war, *Hyaena,* exchanged three hearty cheers and left them; and they felt as if they were really on their way.[36]

The voyage would take eight and a half months, during which time Matthew would become very familiar with his surroundings on the *Scarborough,* so let us take a closer look at the vessel. John Allcot's painting of the 'The First Fleet' helps us to do so, for the *Scarborough,* always in the van, might well be the merchantman that follows the flagship, *Sirius,* into Port Jackson.

Here we see a three-masted, two decked vessel, rigged as a barque which in actual fact, was about the same tonnage as a small Manly Ferry. Like the other transports, she was blunt-nosed and round-bodied having an extreme length of 111 feet 6 inches, and extreme breadth of 30 feet 2 inches, while the height between decks was 4 feet 5 inches, not enough for the convicts to stand upright. Despite the fears imagined to have been held by Philip Farrell that she might succumb to the Southern Ocean, the *Scarborough* was one of the best sailers. She was fast, shipped less water than the others and was reasonably modern, having been built in the port in Yorkshire from which she derived her name in 1782.[37]

Inside, none of the ships of the First Fleet had the floating gaol appearance, with iron bars and cage like cells that one sees in drawing of the later convict ships. Lieutenant P.G. King tells us that the transports were fitted up in the same manner as for carrying troops except for strong thick bulkheads, filled with nails, run across 'tween decks from side to side abaft the mainmast, with loopholes through which to fire in case of trouble. The hatches were well secured by cross bars, bolts and locks and were railed round from deck to deck with oak stanchions. A penalty of £40-0-0 was payable by the captain of each transport for any convict who escaped but the actual guarding of the prisoners was left to the marines. There were sentinels at the different hatch-ways and a guard always under arms on the quarterdeck.[38]

One of the marines, Private John Easty, was to keep a diary, which though badly spelt and written in a cramped fashion in a small book is of particular interest to us. It is from Easty that we have the background information on the mutineers, many details of day to day activities and the sail changes and position of the *Scarborough*. Over Easty and the other thirty-four marine privates were three corporals, two lieutenants, Robert Kellow and William Dawes, (who was to set up the observatory on Dawes Point), while the whole were commanded by Captain John Shea who was consumptive during the voyage and died in the colony.[39]

The surgeon on board the *Scarborough* was Dennis Considen, who would be First Assistant to Surgeon John White in the colony. Considen was later to be a pioneer of Australian medicine by his use of bush herbs and gums to control the scurvy which broke out in the colony owing to a shortage of green vegetables and citrus fruits. But this was a long way off and at present, his charges were steadily improving in health as the result of good food, fresh air and the daily exercise on deck that the convicts were now allowed. Though a three feet high barricade had been erected to keep the prisoners apart, they would see the marines walking about and some of the thirty-five sailors at their tasks. And they might also catch a glimpse of the ship's captain, Captain John Marshall, with his Newfoundland dog, Hector, at his heels. In the Channel they would also have seen many other ships going to and fro but now the eleven ships were alone. Once in the Atlantic, the convoy was ordered to stay close together and at night time, the flagship, *Sirius*, carried a conspicuous light in her mainmast.[40]

To grasp the feeling of the voyage, we need to remember that wind was to that world what oil is today. Usually, the North East Trade is not encountered until latitude 27° but the Fleet was lucky enough to pick up a nor-easter on May 26, thirteen days out of Portsmouth and it carried them all the way to Teneriffe, the largest of the Canary Islands. It was ideal for the little square riggers to have the wind on their quarter so that, for days on end, only minor sail adjustments would be necessary. Even incurable land lubbers must have felt the exhilaration of being aboard ship as she bowled along in a fine breeze. And to a Londoner such as Matthew, it would be a novelty to find himself on deck, hearing the mast creak, looking up to the billowing squaresails and the figure in the lookout high above — and then out over the swell to the other ships and far up ahead to the little pathfinder, *Supply*, almost lost in the haze.[41]

As day succeeded day, and week, week, they settled down into a routine which had been much the same on sailing ships for centuries. On so small a vessel, everyone would feel a part of the life and acquire an interest in what was going on around them. They would hear the mate's orders, called from man to man and later on, when he tacked the ship, they would see it all and become familiar with what at first seemed strange language, the calls of: 'Helm's alee!' 'Haul, Mainsail, Haul!' and 'Full and bye!' as the bow came round to a new course. They would hear the sailors singing as they heaved on the capstan to raise the anchor and every half-hour through the watches, they would hear the sound of bells. There would be smells that Matthew would remember all his life, the gunpowder that was exploded below to purify the air, the pitch, oakum and wet ropes but most of all, the salty tang of the wind.[42]

But now their first landfall was due and they presently saw blue peaks, which were the tops of old volcanoes, rising from the ocean. On June 3, they entered the harbour of Santa Cruz in the island of Teneriffe, where they were to take on supplies of fresh meat, vegetables and water. It would be the first time that most of the convicts had seen a foreign port and they stayed there a week. In later years perhaps, Matthew would describe this and the other ports of call to his children, places that not one of them was ever destined to see. He would tell of the fort they passed on the way in and of the rows of white houses leading down to the water, of the dark skinned Portuguese who came out to the ship to sell their vegetables, figs and mulberries.[43]

He would perhaps always remember that it was at Teneriffe where he had seen Governor Phillip for the first time when he came on board to inspect the convicts. They would see a small insignificant man with a large nose, whose presence, nevertheless, immediately commanded respect and inspired confidence. For his part, Phillip wrote that he found the convicts quiet and contented but noticed some 'compleat villains' among them. It is probable that he now told them, as he had earlier stated his intention of doing, that their happiness or misery was in their own hands. They would learn that those who behaved well would be rewarded in the new country by being able to work occasionally on small lots of land set aside for them, which they would be granted at the expiration of their terms.[44]

The Fleet sailed from Teneriffe on Sunday, June 10, 1787 and then the weather became hot and close as they crossed the Tropic of Cancer. Shoals of fish swam by and at night, flying fish would land on the deck. Once in the distance, a sperm whale was sighted and another time they caught a shark and examined it.[45]

As they had been unable to obtain all the neccessary supplies at Teneriffe, Phillip had decided to call at Praya in the Cape de Verde Islands. However, when they arrived at the entrance on June 18, unfavourable winds and a strong current made the undertaking risky so it was decided to make for Rio De Janiero instead.[46]

The weather now became squally with heavy rains at night. Though they would catch rain water, because of the unexpected length of this passage, it was necessary to reduce the ration to three pints per day to each man. It was a thirsty time and their mouths grew sore, for the fresh meat from Teneriffe being gone, they were drawing on the casks of salt provisions.[47]

Now the Fleet had lost the North East Trade and were in the Doldrums, that area so detested by mariners because of the heat and unpredictable winds. As can be seen on the map, they were blown several miles eastwards of their course. At this time the marines were put to work repairing the old topsails, caulking the quarterdeck, scraping and painting the gunwhales and spinning yarn. The Lieutenant from the *Supply* came on board to inspect the ship for cleanliness, which was particularly important now that they were in the tropics. Gunpowder was exploded, windsails were rigged to try to get some air into the convicts' quarters and they were sometimes allowed on deck at night. It was hot and uncomfortable so that the convicts would count the bells that signalled the time and listen eagerly for the call of a rising wind. The tedium might have been relieved by second-hand reports of the ship's latitude for they were approaching the Equator.[48]

On July 7, they at last picked up the South East Trade and crossed the Equator on July 15 in longitude 26° 54′ W., the wind at 'East Sou' East', and the ship steering south for the bottom of the world with fine clear weather and light breezes. There were the usual festivities among the crew for those who were crossing for the first time, which the convicts would see from a distance and perhaps copy.[49]

The time at which they crossed the Equator, that is, the ship's latitude, was determined by each captain individually. But the longitude was calculated by Captain Hunter and Lieutenants Bradley and Dawes on the *Sirius* from lunar observations and with the aid of a time-piece made by Larcum Kendal, the most eminent English precision watchmaker of the eighteenth century and the man appointed for the task by the Board of Longitude. A signal would be made to the *Scarborough* and other vessels and they would sail under the stern of the *Sirius* where a blackboard, marked with large chalk characters would give the flagship's position at noon that day. These calculations were extraordinarily accurate all the way which was just as well, for their charts of the Atlantic had already proved unreliable. There was now, on July 28, a possibility that the island of Ascension might be sighted. It was not known whether the island really existed or not, but if it did, it was on the track of the Fleet, so lookouts were sent to the top of each mast.[50]

They failed to see Ascension but on Thursday, August 2, they sighted the coast of South America at Cape Frio and Phillip had a broad pennant raised to the masthead of *Sirius* to signify his presence to the Portugese preparatory to arrival. At the islands in the entrance to Rio de Janiero, the ships anchored once again and the convicts would experience the fascinating sight of the sailors crawling aloft in the rigging and out on the yards to furl the sails. On August 6, they entered Rio proper and the Commodore saluted the fort with thirteen guns.[51]

The month in Rio was spent in repairing sails and rigging, airing camping equipment and in taking new stores on board. Much had been learnt from the experience of Captain Cook and even now, after so long at sea, the convoy was remarkably free of disease and the convicts more healthy than when they had left England. Provisions here were cheap so that fresh meat, vegetables and fruit were served to everybody and the people on passing boats threw oranges to the convicts.[52]

During the month, the officers and crew enjoyed quite a social life on shore and when Matthew and the other transportees came on deck they would have seen a spectacle even more exotic than that of Teneriffe. Rio was a centre for the slave trade and negroes would come on board selling guavas, pineapples, coconuts and bananas, a sight which amazed our marine diarist, Private Easty, who wrote:

'... the neagoes men are slaves for the most part and they ware no aparell Ecept a Clout jest round ther Privits and negos weman ware A Short kind of a bed gownd wich jest Cover thier Brists and Shoulders and a Short Peticoat wich Come About half way down thier thies thay ware no kind of Shirts or Shifts So that thare Bellies is naked....'[53]

To the watchers on the ships, the population seemed to be constantly engaged in religious processions, and at the close of every day, lines of negroes knelt in the streets chanting their vespers. The Englishmen's own religious observances were not forgotten and here, on August 19, as in Table Bay later on, the Reverend Richard Johnson, Chaplain to the Fleet, came aboard the *Scarborough* and preached a sermon. Governor Phillip and Major Ross also came aboard again and spoke to everyone.[54]

On September 4, the Fleet sailed from Rio, which is located roughly on the Tropic of Capricorn. From now on they would be going south into a cooler climate, although it was Spring in the Southern Hemisphere at this time of the year. Heavy squalls, rain, thunder and lightning followed and it was very cold. During the tempest, says Easty, the *Scarborough* was 'nigh being fowl of the fishburn' and the rain was the heaviest he had ever seen in his life. The marines decided among themselves to punish any of their own number 'as was in Liqir', a reflection of the general awareness of danger.[55]

Although their next port of call was to be the Cape of Good Hope, steering south was found in the long run to be the wisest course. For they picked up the westerlies on September 24 at 32° S. and crossed from one continent to another, a distance upwards of 3,300 miles in the short space of five weeks and four days, anchoring in Table Bay on October 14, the birthday of their monarch, King George III.[56]

The Cape was at this time in possession of the Dutch, whom Easty thought to be harsh and bloodthirsty. Captain David Collins, another diarist, remarked on the fertility of the place but complained that it was very dry and that dust and grit permeated the flour, rice and sugar.

▲ 'Prespective [sic] view of the convict's [sic] at work on the Thames, drawn May 8, 1777 from the Butt at Woolwich.' *[see p20]*

▼ A typical prison hulk at anchor in an English Harbour *[see p22]*

E.W. Cooke

Huggins/Duncan

National Maritime Museum, Londo

▲ 'Reefing topsails' *[see p33]*

'Negro fandango scene, Campo St. Anna, Rio de Janeiro' *[see p32]* ▼

Augustus Earle

Rex Nan Kivell Collection — National Library of Austra

While at the Cape, a great number of livestock was taken aboard the ships, so that each one looked like 'Noah's Ark'. But this was their last chance to obtain such things as they were now saying good-bye to civilization.[57]

When they first put to sea on November 12, the winds were temporarily against them and then they became becalmed. At this time Phillip decided to split the Fleet, as the heavier, slow sailers had been seen to be delaying the faster ships. He would go ahead himself in the *Supply* taking with him the *Scarborough, Alexander* and *Friendship*, while Hunter in the *Sirius*, would bring on the others. On arrival of the faster ships at Botany Bay, the convicts could unload supplies and commence building in preparation for the arrival of the rest of the Fleet. As it turned out, the winds blew fair from now on and all the ships arrived within two days.[58]

On November 28, they encountered very rough seas and even lost sight of the *Supply* for a while. With decks awash, there were days when the convicts could not leave their quarters and most of them, being unaccustomed to the sea, must have been terrified. It is rather touching to read that, during such a time, Herbert Keeling, one of the convicts on the *Scarborough,* read a sermon to them. Once a great burst of wind carried away the foretopsail yard in the slings and all hands were called to hoist a new one. This was very dangerous work for the sailors, for if one missed his footing and fell into the sea, there would be little hope of seeing him in the troughs of the huge waves, let along picking him up.[59]

On December 6, the three merchantmen were shrouded in a thick fog and had to signal to each by firing their guns. December 21 was bitterly cold, with hail and snow and the convicts, with only their ordinary clothing and one blanket, must have been frozen. Christmas Day, 1787 saw the *Scarborough* at 42° 1' S., heading East Sou' East, in longitude 108° E., with the wind direction North by West, in fresh gales and hazy weather. As far as they could, the Captains tried to keep up the 'good old English custom of Christmas' and issued better fare than usual, but the weather was too rough to enjoy it. If Matthew were not too seasick or too cold to care, he might have reflected as December drew to a close that he had reached a half-way mark — three and a half years of his seven years' sentence was now past. New Year's Day, 1788 opened with a violent northerly gale though it moderated in the evening; and for the next few nights they saw phosphorescence on the water and in the sky, the beautiful Aurora Australis or Southern Lights. Their spirits rose and on the evening of the second, the convicts on the *Scarborough* made a play and sang many songs.[60]

The ships were now in the roaring forties, surging along in an almost constant Westerly, that breeze which would take Hunter in the *Sirius* next year, around the globe in record time on his mission to bring them food from the Cape. Later too, the tea, gold and wool clippers and the immigrant ships were to delight in racing the clock through these waters, assisted by the ever present westerlies.

But now the vanguard of the Fleet were expecting their first sight of New Holland. The weather settled a little on January 3 and they got the anchors over the bows, bent the cables and tried soundings for depth but found none. On the sixth at 10am., they made the easternmost point of South Cape and commenced to round the bottom of Van Diemen's Land, which at the time, was thought to be joined to the great continent of New Holland, seeing many birds, fishes and seals on their way.[61]

As they passed the east coast of what is now Tasmania, they had contrary winds for a time, then they headed out to sea for the final leg and a landfall at Bateman's Bay. Even now, they stood well out, for it was never advisable to take sailing ships too close to land. Only Cook had been here before and there was always the danger of getting under a leeward shore, losing the wind under a cliff and drifting helplessly on to the rocks.

On the nineteenth at eight in the morning, the vanguard of the First Fleet stood outside Botany Bay and could see several fires 'made by the Indians on Cape Banks and Point Solander'. Then at 9.30a.m., they sailed up the Bay and came to anchor about two miles inside near a handsome, sandy beach. The natives came down to the shore, held up their weapons menacingly and shouted to the watchers on the *Scarborough;* 'Warra, warra! Warra, warra!' Go away! Go away![62]

But in vain. Like their seafaring forefathers on that other island a thousand years before, the northerners had come to stay.

CHAPTER THREE

Sydney Cove

IT WAS THE following year and a fine Saturday morning in August
when Matthew walked down the hill to the shed on the water's edge
where the hoy was being built, smiling to himself all the while. When
he arrived, as he had expected, the others were all waiting to hear his
story. Even Mr Parker, the Master Carpenter, was willing to let work on
the boat wait for a time while the men listened at first hand to the tale
that was now all round the Cove. For Matthew had been a witness that
morning in the 'Case of Sarah Bellamy', as it was termed, in the hut on
the hill that served as a court house for the Bench of Magistrates in the
new settlement.

'Is it true that Sarah gave Captain Meredith a trouncing and that he
got a black eye out of it?' asked one of the convicts and they all began to
question him in the same way.

'Hold your peace for a while, lads,' said Parker, 'and let Matt tell us
what really happened.'

'Well,' said Matthew, seating himself on some timber, for the story
would take a while to tell, 'it seems that Captains Keltie and Meredith
made quite a night of it on Wednesday night, it being the Prince of
Wales' birthday and all. Meredith had invited Keltie to sleep ashore so
after the Governor's dinner, they went back to his place to continue the
celebrations.'

'As the evening went on,' continued Matthew, 'they grew more
and more convivial and Keltie fancied paying Sarah Bellamy a visit.
Meredith tried to dissuade him — by that time it was after midnight and
rather cold — but the more Keltie thought about it, the more he wanted
to go. It seems he'd been on good terms with Sally before and Faddy,
whose hut she keeps, said it was alright. He said he wanted to tell her
about the parrot he'd brought back from the Cape.'

'That's a good one, 'interjected Bill Jenkins, 'fancy trying to
sweeten her up with a parrot!'

'Well, off they went,' continued Matthew, 'arm in arm down over
the bridge and up to Sarah's front door — mind you, by this time it's
one o'clock in the morning. They knock on Sarah's door, but naturally,
she doesn't answer. So Meredith goes round the back to her bedroom
and raps on the window shutter. You know what those shutters are like,
rough-made as can be, and of course, it collapses. It knocks off His
Lordship's hat, which falls in with the shutters on Sarah's head, for
she's sleeping just under the window. Then Keltie gives Meredith a
'leg-up' outside and he leans in to get his hat. But he almost falls in on
Sarah, grabs her night-cap instead and pulls her hair. Then Sarah grabs
his hat and starts to yell murder....'

'And that's when you arrived?' asked one of the others who had heard part of the tale before.

'Well, I heard the noise and thought perhaps she was really being murdered,' said Matthew. 'Her little girl was screaming 'Thieves!' so I didn't know what was happening. When I got there, Sarah was in full cry: 'Murder!' she screams, waving the Captain's hat, with Meredith falling in the window and Keltie dancing around, coaxing her to be silent. 'You terrible Faggot!' Meredith roars, when he finally gets on his two feet, at the same time shaking his fist, 'I'll have my revenge on you' and then, seeing me standing there: 'Take this woman to the Guard House!'

'I didn't know what to do,' Matthew went on, 'It's not easy taking Sally where she doesn't want to go and I didn't think she was to blame anyhow. But the next thing, up comes the Watch, with Harris, puffed up like a bull-frog since the Governor gave him the job last week and wanting to know who's disturbing the peace. 'Open the door!' he bellows, knocking on it with his stick....'

'His 'staff of office' he calls it,' cut in Bill Jenkins again, puffing himself up in imitation of Harris, who was a convict like themselves, 'but go on, Matthew!'

So Matthew continued: 'Open the door!' Harris bellows, making more noise than everyone else put together, 'and prepare to go to the Guard House!' Well, Sarah opens the door at last and Harris tells her to get a tinder-box so that he can see what is going on. 'No,' says Sarah and this is a gem, 'The hour is too improper for a light.'

'Too improper', gasped Bill Jenkins, now convulsed with laughter, 'Sarah, of all people! Too improper!'

'Well, Harris was taking it all very seriously and agreed that it was an improper hour to be striking lights,' said Matthew, 'so we all stood there in the dark while he tried to quieten her down. I could tell that the Captains were as drunk as lords, though I didn't say so in Court. Meredith was starting to sober up a bit and he says to Harris: 'I suppose there'll be the Devil and all to pay about this in the morning?''

'Harris tried to smooth him over and to bustle them back off to the marine quarters when all of a sudden, two more of the Watch, Neale and Marshall turned up. 'Gawd save us!' bawled Harris, 'What are you two doing here? We'll 'ave the Guvnor himself 'ere next! You two is supposed ter be up at the Brick Kilns!' And then, remembering the dignity of his new position and sounding for all the world like one of the marine officers, 'Return to your posts immediately!'

'It must have been funny in Court,' said Parker, 'What did Collins have to say?'

'He could hardly keep a straight face and even old Hunter had a twinkle in his eye,' said Matthew. 'Well, I ask you, there's Sarah, all outraged virtue, and Keltie looking a proper fool and saying he found it difficult to remember what had happened, owing to having been 'in a fit of intoxication'.

'Aye,' added Brown, in broad dialect, 'Sal were a loively one on ship out, but she got better fish to froiy now.'

'Yes,' said Bill, 'she's got her eye on Jamie Bloodworth. For the Captain be only wanting her for one thing, parrot and all. And him and the others will all go home to England one day. Good Luck to Sarah is what I say, for she's a spirited girl.'

'And it's not often we get a chance to laugh so hearty in Sydney Cove,' said another, as they picked up their tools and returned to planking the boat.

* * *

THE COURT CASE was held on August 15, 1789, just nineteen months after that beautiful January morning on which the First Fleet had sailed into Botany Bay. In that time, a small English town had been reared in Sydney Cove, just a few miles to the north of the original landing place. Sarah's hut was but one of a group which were by now located on both sides of a spring known as the Tank Stream and no effort had been spared to superimpose upon the bushland a copy of that civilization which had its place twelve thousand miles away.[63]

Though the painting reproduced is of a later date, when the settlement had grown considerably, it gives an idea of how the Cove looked in 1791. Here, as we look at neat rows of cottages with thatched roofs, we can see to what extent the colonists were succeeding in giving the settlement at least the exterior character of an English village.

But closer examination would have shown that the thatching was of grass and the walls were of cabbage-tree palm or wattle and daub. No suitable slate had been found for tiles but shingles, made from the wood of the she-oak or casuarina were beginning to replace thatching. There was but one building of two storeys, the Governor's six roomed mansion, for no limestone had been found. Even houses of brick and stone had to be made with very thick walls for the only available mortar was clay, which limited the height of building to twelve feet. There were no conventional shutters on the windows, as can be seen in the illustration of Sarah's hut, but boards were nailed together to be put up at night and taken down in the day to allow for fresh air and light; and there was no glass in anyone's windows but those of the Governor. Most huts, like Sarah's were of two rooms and hers had a chimney and a hearth.[64]

There were vegetable patches here and there, attached to the houses and a few vines; but there were no flower gardens or hedges. No cattle, horses or sheep were to be seen near the Farm, they had either died on the voyage out or escaped into the bush, but pigs and chickens roamed at will through the settlement.[65] One looked in vain for a church steeple or an inn, two essentials about which village life at home revolved, but there were storehouses, a hospital, a barracks, a bakery and a smithy. And while in England a picturesque stone bridge would span the stream, here was a crossing of a few eucalyptus logs, hastily rolled together.[66] Two streets, four rows of huts and a burial ground — this is how a woman convict writing home described it. Four acres clinging to its fresh water supply and its two beloved ships moored in the cove, four acres of England surrounded by tall gums and dense scrub, well described by a later writer as a small 'limpet port' clinging to a continent.[67]

Modest though it was, this achievement had been the result of the efforts of everyone since the day the Fleet had sailed into the Cove on January 26, 1788. The decision to settle here had been made during the previous week, for Botany Bay, chosen for the site of a colony on the suggestion of Sir Joseph Banks, who had accompanied Captain Cook on his brief visit some eighteen years before, had been found unsuitable. Its fresh water was limited, its soil poor and its anchorage shallow and dangerously exposed to the south-easterly breeze. By sheer good luck, the next haven northward, Port Jackson, named but never entered by Cook, was found to be the finest and most beautiful harbour in the world, 'where a thousand ship of the line might ride at anchor in perfect security'. So Phillip decided to remove to the new anchorage and after a perilous exit through the heads of Botany Bay, the Fleet sailed up the coast and entered Port Jackson, coming to anchor in Sydney Cove at 7.30 p.m. in daylight. At sunset the Governor, who had arrived the day before, the principal officers and many private soldiers took part in a ceremony on shore. The Union Jack was raised on a flagstaff specially erected for the purpose, the marines fired volleys and toasts were drunk to the health of His Majesty and the Royal Family and to the success of the new colony.[68]

It is likely that Matthew took his first step on Australian soil the following day, Sunday, January 27, 1788, at two o'clock in the afternoon when, being a strong healthy young man of nineteen years, he would make one of a party of a hundred convicts from the *Scarborough* who were sent ashore to clear the ground for tents. Although the *Supply* had arrived on the Friday, the work of clearing had hardly begun and as Lieutenant Bradley said, they 'stepped ashore literally into a wood', their axe strokes the first sounds made by white men here since its creation. As many tents as possible were erected, the Governor having a large portable one made specially in England, but the first nights were very uncomfortable for those who had disembarked. Even the marine officers slept on the bare ground with just pouch for pillow and like everyone else, were preyed on by spiders, ants and other insects.[69]

Exactly a week later, on the following Sunday, February 3, Matthew and the rest of the convicts assembled under a large fig (?) tree to hear the Reverend Richard Johnson conduct the first church service in the colony. The text chosen, 'What shall we render unto the Lord for all his blessings to us?' reflected gratitude for what had seemed Providential treatment until this time. They had come thirteen thousand miles through uncharted waters with no major accident and very little loss of life.[70]

But when they had been ashore a week, the bulk of the population, as they enjoyed but a temporary respite from back-breaking work in muggy weather, might well have wondered whether the period of blessings had ended. Although the Saturday on which they had sailed in had been a fine, sunny day, every succeeding day of the week had been either cloudy or rainy. The wet weather was to persist over the first month and the newcomers were often surprised and alarmed at the violence of summer storms with their thunder, lightning and hail.

Such a storm occurred on the afternoon of the next Wednesday, February 6, when the women convicts were disembarked. During the voyage, segregation from the men had been fairly successful even on those ships which carried both sexes. And as most of the men convicts had previously been in gaols or prison hulks, for several years, the consequences of the landing can be imagined.

Although the supply of clothing ordered for them had had to be left behind in England, the women 'climbed into the longboats clean and neatly dressed, some even well dressed'. How they looked at the end of the day has not been recorded but one writer tells us that the men got at them as soon as they landed and it was beyond his ability to describe the scenes of debauchery that followed. To celebrate the departure of the women from the ships, the sailors were issued with spirits and their drunkenness added to the general confusion. It was at this time, before the women's tents had been properly erected that the violent thunderstorm had come on. Trees were struck by lightning, a man blinded, sheep killed and it was feared that the ships might move their moorings and the sailors be unable to cope with emergency.[71]

Governor Phillip wisely turned a blind eye to the behaviour that night, but now that everyone was ashore, ordered an assembly for the next day for the formal reading of his Commission and for an opportunity to address them.

Despite the effects of the previous night when even those who had not shared in the revelry can have had little sleep, it is likely that Matthew and the rest of the convicts would remember this ceremony for a long time for it was colourful and impressive. It began when the marines under arms and with flying colours, marched on to the site to the sound of drums and fifes and formed a circle around the whole of the seven hundred and fifty men and women convicts. The colours were lowered to Governor Phillip and he took off his hat. At this time he, Captain David Collins, the Judge Advocate, Major Robert Ross, the Lieutenant Governor and the Reverend Richard Johnson stood at a camp table whereon were two leather cases containing the Commission and Letters Patent.

The convicts were ordered to be seated and then Collins began to read the King's Instructions. It was the first time in history that the total population of a British dependency heard the Charter of its foundation and the Governor's inaugural address. The Instructions were simple and concise and would be easily understood by all. They told how the

Courts to judge offences, would be constituted, of the rules regarding trade, relations with the natives and how a colony was to be founded at Norfolk Island. Of most interest to the convicts, were details regarding the Governor's power to emancipate or pardon for good behaviour and industry and to grant land to expirees, confirming what Phillip had earlier told them.

After the formal reading, the Governor spoke to the marines and thanked them for their dedication to duty. Then he addressed the convicts in what has been variously described as a harangue and a very sensible speech, but which was very much to the point. He said that there was a great deal to be done and that they were going to do it. They would begin by building the officers' houses, store and other necessary buildings and finish by building their own huts. He was aware that many had been shirking work by loitering in the woods. He who did not work would not eat. He spoke of the previous night's immorality and urged marriage. All men guilty of promiscuous intercourse would be dealt with severely and the sentry would fire 'with a ball' at any man found in the women's camp after a certain hour in the evening. He said that he had come to the conclusion that some of the convicts were worthless and utterly incorrigible. However, others were not and it was to these he appealed, enjoining them to be honest and industrious. Good conduct would be rewarded and it was possible that some would later regard their day of transportation as the happiest day they had ever seen.[72]

The rest of the day was declared a holiday and the prisoners had leisure to think over what they had heard. There were probably many, and it seems likely that Matthew would be one of them, who had it within them to respond to Phillip's appeal and to nurture the hope that this new country did present the prospect of a fresh start. But it was not easy to preserve the dream over the months ahead, when they settled to what proved to be the grim business of building.

The store house went up first, for preservation of their rations was vital. Then a hospital was built, wherein the patients were dosed with wine and other medicines but had no blankets or sheets. The main ailments in the camp were dysentery and scurvy but venereal disease had also been brought out, despite all Phillip's efforts to avoid it. Strangely, the camp was free of the epidemic of small-pox which decimated the aborigines, the only fatality among the Europeans being that of a Red Indian sailor from the *Supply* who died well after the height of the epidemic. After completing the hospital, the convicts went on to building the barracks and other necessary buildings and the dwelling huts.[73]

The empty transports departed and Matthew must have watched the *Scarborough* sail out on its way to England via China with mixed thoughts, the only reminder of the ship being Hector, the Captain's Newfoundland dog, who now trotted at the heels of Zachariah Clark, the Assistant Commissary.[74]

The empty transports had gone but the expected new ones, laden with stores, had not come to take their place, so food had to be rationed and working hours shortened. Nevertheless, they kept on at a slower rate, struggling to cut timber with axes that became blunt on Australian hardwoods and often finding that the trees they had felled were rotten within. Little sawpits were dotted everywhere around the settlement.

One of the greatest disadvantages was the absence of skilled people for a third of the convicts came from London and were town dwellers. In most cases lack of training, unemployment, poor wages or just plain indigence had led them into crime and in other cases, they were bred to it. There were found to be only twelve carpenters among them and a mere handful of people who had had any agricultural experience.[75]

The establishment of the Farm on an adjoining cove had begun almost as soon as they arrived and many of the officers and later, the convicts also, had their own vegetable plots. But the work of clearing land was painfully slow and cultivation was difficult because the hoes and spades were blunted by the rocky soil. There were no beasts to pull ploughs, had there been ploughs and the convicts, new to the work, were inefficient or lazy — sometimes purposely losing their tools. Much of the wheat planted failed to germinate, the barley rotted in the ground and the weevil destroyed the seed; and what crops and vegetables were raised were frequently ruined by rats. By July, 1788, Phillip was writing in his despatches that it would be inadvisable to send any more convicts unless they were artificers and that fifty farmers and their families would do more in a year to render the colony independent of the mother country as to provisions than a thousand convicts.[76]

For those convicts who, like Matthew, were learning building and farming the hard way, it was an irksome existence once the novelty of their new surroundings had passed. His day would begin when the sounds of reveille floated across the Cove from the Marine camp. Quickly sluicing his face and hands with water, he would head for his gang and workplace. There would be a short pause for breakfast which was probably a hunk of bread or damper which he had made himself and then work would continue until one o'clock. He would then return to his hut to toast on a fork, a little salt pork, cured two years before, catching the drippings with a sop of bread; or he would boil his few ounces of salt beef and turnip in his small iron pot, perhaps thickening it with some flour. In the beginning, there had been a siesta for two hours in the middle of the day, the convicts having been drummed back to work at two o'clock to work until sunset. But now, with shortened rations, work finished at one o'clock and one had the afternoon to tend one's own garden. At night Matthew would perhaps have another morsel of damper and a drink of sweet tea, picked from a vine which grew wild in the bush. As there was no fruit, he would from time to time squeeze a few sarsaparilla or 'acid' berries and drink the juice to guard against scurvy.[77]

Thus five days of the week would pass with occasional incident and variety. Perhaps his way might take him past the Governor's House, (on the corner of present day Phillip and Bridge Streets), and he would

catch a glimpse of the aborigines, Bennelong and Colbee, who were fet-
tered in the front yard. Or someone would be injured and they would
take the patient on a makeshift stretcher up the hill to the hospital.
There he might perhaps wave to a friend among those being dosed with
a concoction of red-gum in spirit for their dysentery. Or he might see
the Reverend Richard Johnson moving among the patients giving comfort.[78]

Some mornings the convicts would be dejected because a mate had
died through malnutrition or disease; and other days there would be
high spirits because the fishing boats had come in with a great haul of
bream or whiting. Whatever had happened, whether Major Ross had
been bedevilling the Governor again, whether there had been a duel
among the officers, or if the Governor had decided to send the *Sirius* to
the Cape for food, they knew about it. For Sydney Cove was like a small
country town where everyone knew each other by sight if not by name
and news travelled fast.[79]

Saturday was set aside for collecting provisions and looking after
one's own hut and yard. Mending clothes was a constant job but they
were rarely washed because of the danger of them dropping to pieces.
Should this happen, there were few replacements and footwear had
become so scarce that some marines were doing duty in bare feet.[80]

Sunday meant muster and church parade and then, at last, leisure
for the rest of the day. So another week would pass in this strange place
where the seasons were reversed, where the trees shed bark instead of
leaves and where venomous snakes were likely to appear in one's path
at any moment. For the first time they realized what it meant to live
near waters that were shark-infested and to their amazement, saw that
the jaws of one monster which had been caught would comfortably
encircle the largest man on the *Sirius*. One day a shark chased a boat all
the way up the harbour and savaged the paddle and the rudder, which
terrified the fishermen. Fish they must, however, for the settlement
was dependent on this source of food.[81]

Fortunately, the aborigines whose welcome had been so unpromis-
ing were dangerous only when provoked or to stragglers in the bush.
Quite often, they were friendly, helped with the fishing and even
acquired the newcomers' songs. They could sometimes be heard singing to the tune of Marlbrook, ('For he's a jolly good fellow') as they
paddled around the harbour. But they declined to live in the settlement
as Phillip had wanted so that he reluctantly decided to capture a few to
let them know his plans. It was clear, as had been expected, that the
natives did not present the threat which the Maoris would have posed,
had settlement of New Zealand been attempted, for they were neither
so numerous nor so well organised. But then this land was less hospi-
table by far than the rich, volcanic earth of those other islands visited by
Cook.[82]

The inhospitality of the land and its isolation from the mother
country are the themes which dominate every account of this period.

Having found richer soil at the head of the harbour at a place which he called the Crescent, (later to be Rose Hill), the Governor decided at the end of September, 1788, to send a detachment of marines and seventy convicts there to establish a farm. But it would be months before this would produce food and as there was no way of telling when store-ships would arrive from England, Phillip decided at the same time to send the *Sirius* to the Cape of Good Hope for wheat, flour and other necessaries. However it would be mid 1789 before she could be expected back and in the meantime, morale began to decline. Only the Governor seemed at all optimistic about the future as their first year of occupation drew to an end.[83]

Any escape from such a wretched existence was welcomed but there was little diversion for the convicts. They seem to have played cards, for some were punished for gambling in the street and they also played a game called cross-sticks. Surprisingly, they produced a play among themselves and performed it before the Governor but such interesting events were rare and their day to day lives monotonous. The only reading matter would be the Bibles and improving tracts brought and hopefully distributed by the Reverend Richard Johnson — there was a choice between Stonehouse's 'Advice to a Penitent,' Woodward's 'Caution to Swearers' and 'Exhortations to Chastity', author not named. Government and General Orders, probably displayed in a prominent place, and signposts indicating the women's area and warning against trespass presented the only alternative literature to the few who could read. The exorbitant price of tobacco, through its scarcity, put it well outside the convicts' means and they were forbidden spirits.[84]

From time to time sailors smuggled liquor ashore and bartered it with the convicts for food and clothing or the convicts managed to procure drink in some other way, whereupon they seized the opportunity for temporary forgetfulness. On February 7, 1789, Matthew was charged with 'drunkenness and falsehood' and ordered twenty-five lashes. The entry has a tick beside it, which may indicate that he received the punishment. There are no details regarding the charge of 'falsehood' but it could refer to Matthew's efforts not to divulge the source of the liquor. The sentence of twenty-five lashes, later to be known as a 'Botany Bay dozen' was light compared with others ordered on the same day.[85]

Convicts were not alone in being flogged. It was standard punishment for sailors and marines at this time and was frequently ordered where theft or misappropriation of food occurred, because the colony's very survival depended on strict adherence to rations. By now the Governor had placed his own flour in the public store and everyone received the same amount of food.

Thefts of food were the most common offences at this time and reading over records of them in the early Bench Book, one is reminded of that chapter in *Alice in Wonderland* where a court was convened to decide 'Who stole the tarts?'. On June 2, 1788, there was a case where a pie was stolen from an oven, while a month or two earlier, a man's flour was stolen and made into a pudding. The victim was cunning enough to wait at the copper early on a Sunday morning until he saw someone boiling a particularly large pudding and that way, the culprit was caught.[86]

Justice was administered with impartiality and marines were hanged along with convicts when they were detected robbing the storehouse. Everyone was in the same plight during these months of hunger and hardship so that the colony seemed a gaol equally to the prisoners and their guards. Major Ross, the Lieutenant Governor, was once heard to say to a convict who came with the news that his time was up: 'Would to God that my time was expiring too!'[87]

On February 17, 1789, ten days after Matthew's misdemeanour and consequent brush with the law, the *Supply* left on her regular trip to Norfolk Island and during her absence, the Cove was empty for the first time. However, she arrived back safely in due course and then, on May 9, the *Sirius* returned from the Cape. Captain Hunter had decided to use the 'roaring forties' to travel via Cape Horn so that the *Sirius* had circumnavigated the globe in the record breaking time of one hundred and sixty-eight sea days. She had sprung a leak and met mountainous seas and icebergs on her route, so her survival was remarkable; but the flour she brought would last only four months at full ration.[88]

This was the position in August, 1789, when Matthew gave his evidence and why, as one of the characters in the story remarked, there were few occasions for mirth in Sydney Cove. It is now time to return to the actual record of the Court Case concerned, for the information it furnishes about Matthew and about life in the early days of the settlement. Let us begin with Matthew and with those details which tell us indirectly what he was doing and where he was living at this date.

In that section of the evidence where his testimony is recorded, Matthew is described as 'Mr Parker's servant'. There is fairly accurate information on who was in the colony during this period and the only person named Parker who was designated 'Mr' and who would have had a servant was Charles Parker, the Master Carpenter of the *Sirius,* one of the most valuable men in the colony. Until the departure of the *Sirius* to the Cape in the previous October, Parker and his crew had been continuously engaged in erecting storehouses and other buildings. Whether Matthew had been his servant at that time is unknown but a literate man such as he would have been useful for keeping inventories of tools and nails, which were as precious as gold, and also for keeping a record of the men working on the various jobs.[89]

The *Sirius* returned in May 1789, and the carpenter and crew, Captain Hunter tells us, were again employed upon the business of the settlement. Then, on June 19, they were ordered on board again to attend to repairs because the vessel was now quite unseaworthy. She was taken to a cove opposite on the north shore, (Mosman Bay), to be careened and repaired 'away from the women's interruption'. But it was discovered that the task would take months, because of the shortage of artisans and tools. It was November 7 before Hunter was able to bring her back into the Cove.[90]

Meanwhile, in May, 1789, another project which would soon require Charles Parker's attention had begun, the construction of the first boat of local timber ever built in New South Wales. Its frame had been put on the stocks and the job commenced by Mr Robinson Reid, the Carpenter of the *Supply* but when the vessel had to leave for Norfolk Island on July 6, the direction of the few people building the boat was left to Parker.[91]

This work was proceeding in a boat house which had been specially built for the purpose and is thought to have been located where the Customs House is today. For convenience, Parker was probably quartered nearby and it can readily be seen why he would need a servant. As well as building the hoy, he was probably called upon, at least for advice, in other building. It seems likely that when Matthew had finished personal chores for his master, he too would work on the boat. And from time to time, he would perhaps row Parker across to the *Sirius* to see how the work there was progressing.[92]

We know that Matthew, too, lived fairly close to the boathouse and somewhere between the Governor's house, on the corner of present day Phillip and Bridge Streets, and the Tank Stream, present day Pitt Street, the very heart of Sydney even in those days. For John Harris, the Night Watchman, testified that he had heard the 'cry of Murder' as he was returning from the Farm near the Governor's House. Captains Meredith and Keltie had had to come 'over the Bridge' to get to Sarah's, which puts Sarah's hut between the Governor's house and the Tank Stream. Matthew's hut must have been one of the closest to Sarah's, for he had been lying in bed when he heard the cries and was the first person on the scene.

Little is known about Parker, Matthew's master, but he seems to have had a quick temper and had once struck a seaman in an argument over some fish. Nor is there much known about the boat he was building as there is no positively identifiable sketch or painting of it. We do know that she was of barge or hoy type construction with one mast, perhaps a boom, and was rigged as a smack or sloop. She was almost certainly fastened with hardwood trennels, metal nails being used only in the most important parts. And she was of very heavy construction, being almost solid timber, her intended role being to transport stores up the river to the new settlement at Rose Hill. When launched on October 5, 1789, she was officially named the *Prince of Wales* and three hearty cheers were given as she went down the skids. But 'with an happiness that is sometimes visible in the allusions of the lower order of people', the convicts promptly christened her *The Rose Hill Packet*. Still later she became known as *The Lump* but was most useful over the months ahead.[93]

Not only is the Bellamy Case helpful for the information it gives about Matthew but for vivid glimpses into daily life which remind us that the First Fleeters were Eighteenth Century people. One thinks of Sarah's clothing, her night-cap or kerchief and her shift, the kind of clothes to be seen in a Nursery Rhyme book. This reminds us that the early transportees were not subjected to the indignity of distinctive clothing. As we saw, Matthew and others would have received clothes from the stock of the *Sirius*, but the newly convicted and the women came in what they stood up in and brought what wardrobe they possessed. Phillip was later to suggest that one distinctive stripe be woven into the convicts' slops but this was to prevent them from selling their issued clothing to marines and others for rations and liquor.[94]

The comic escapade involving Sarah and the Captains might well have come from the pages of Fielding's novel, *Tom Jones,* demonstrating as it does moral and social attitudes of Georgian society. Despite Phillip's efforts and the denunciation of the Reverend Richard Johnson, irregularities involving both officers and convicts continued. Most of the officers had a woman housekeeper and although Captain Keltie can be excused because he was 'in his cups', his assumption that Sarah was a chattel that went with the loan of Faddy's hut, reflected a general attitude. So too does his arrogance and that of the enraged Meredith when Sarah refused them entry.

The officers had the benefit of privacy for their dalliances but the convicts must be content with the bush. From time to time, straggling labourers would meet a couple of women who had gone into a quiet place over the hill to bathe and beg them to 'come into the woods'. The women sometimes refused or sometimes held out for a few pounds of flour or a shirt — and sometimes didn't.[95]

Keltie's amorous endeavours had occurred as a follow on of the celebrations for the Prince of Wales's birthday, which reminds us of yet another aspect of Eighteenth Century life. The First Fleeters had a love of ceremony and the outward signs of the system under which they lived, even though most were outcasts from it. Affection for the monarch and the whole Royal Family was common to all and the King's uncertain health was considered a matter of concern or rejoicing as the case might be. The birthdays of the Queen and the Prince of Wales were celebrated by bonfires, the flying of flags and the firing of canon, while on the King's birthday, the officers had a dinner and the convicts were issued a half-pint of spirits per man. The toast to which Bennelong drank that first draught, that was to have so pernicious effect on his own life and on that of his race was: 'The King!'[96]

The system was self-consciously Protestant, the Governor having taken an oath to abjure Transubstantiation and loyalty to any would-be catholic usurpers. The Irish were looked down upon as troublesome, superstitious and ignorant and a request for two priests to be sent with the Fleet had not been deigned acknowledgment. For Roman Catholicism was still 'popery' and was allied in Englishmen's thoughts with interference in England's domestic affairs by outside forces. Jacobean troubles were still fresh in men's minds and while the French were traditional enemies, all foreigners were regarded with suspicion.[97]

Ceremony extended to general greetings among acquaintance and to superiors, to private and public letters, petitions and memorials. Even punishment was formalized to demonstrate to the populace that law and order prevailed. On one occasion, two men and a boy found in the women's camp had their hands tied behind their backs and were drummed out of the camp to the tune of the Rogue's March, while another time, a woman transgressor had her head shaved and was made to wear a cap with the initials 'R.S.G.', Receiver of Stolen Goods. Drums signalled the time by day and at night, bells from the ships in the cove marked the hours — there was as yet no clock in the settlement.[98]

It was a time too when tidings were still spread by the call of a human voice. At night, the marine guard bawled an assurance of 'All's Well' over the sleeping cove, a sound which terrified the natives when they heard it for the first time. Then too, a 'cry of Murder' was always taken seriously and anyone who raised a false alarm was charged with disturbing the peace. 'Stop Thief!' set neighbours and passers-by running in pursuit, as many of those who found themselves in Sydney Cove could attest.

These were the ways of the old country, yet the society differed perforce from that at home and would change even more as time went by. It lacked the broad stratification of English society, for here there were but two classes, the gaolers and the gaoled and even these were becoming merged.

While the establishment of a Night Watch might be considered to be one more way in which English customs were being instituted, yet that Watch consisted entirely of convicts and had been formed at the suggestion of John Harris, a Jewish prisoner already mentioned. The principal purpose of the patrol was to prevent the theft of food from either the stores or gardens, an object in which everyone, bond or free had an interest. In the beginning, members of the Watch had the power to detain anyone, even their marine gaolers, who was found out of bounds after the drum-beat of tattoo. However, as Major Ross considered this an insult to the Corps, the Governor was reluctantly forced to except marines from the rule. Their inclusion in the first place demonstrates that in Phillip's mind, the need to preserve the food stock superseded the need for subordination of the classes.[99]

In a society of a thousand and thirty people, there was a chance to be known and recognized, to achieve a sense of identity which had been impossible at home. Here a man's place depended far more on his capabilities and on his response to the challenge of the environment than on his crime.

Thus Sarah would come before the Bench to complain of her treatment by Meredith and Keltie with the knowledge that she is known and that, though her reputation is not without blemish, she will be given a fair hearing. One of the earliest cases on record concerns two other convicts, Henry and Susannah Kable, who were awarded damages against a ship's captain for withholding their property.[100]

Sarah testified that she had appealed to Meredith on the grounds that he was a 'gentleman' and she but 'a poor prisoner', thus indicating the social gap that separated them. Yet her insistence on her right to select her favourites reflects the realization of her value as a woman in a society where men outnumbered women by five to one. This advantage was to help many of the early convict women to break the class barrier and take a step up in society in those cases where they held out for marriage.

The incident, as we saw, took place in August, 1789, and over the next few months the food situation continued to worsen. Every week, someone was sent over to Botany Bay, in case a ship had arrived there and was unaware that they had moved to Port Jackson. Soon the ration had to be cut again so that conditions were like those of a besieged town. As one young man was to write of this two and a half years when the First Fleeters were the sole white occupants of the continent: 'In all the Crusoe-like adventures I ever read or heard of, I do not recollect anything like it'. It was one of history's unique experiences and years later, those who had been there in the beginning would look at each other and at old landmarks with remembrance.

When by the end of February, 1790 no storeships had arrived, the Governor decided to send the *Sirius* a second time to the Cape for stores. On her way she was to call at Norfolk Island where a good harvest was expected and leave a group of people from Sydney in order to relieve the strain on the base food supply. In doing this, she was blown on to the reef and wrecked. Fortunately, there was no loss of life for Captain Keltie, the Ship's Master, rowed through dangerous surf to take a line ashore.[101]

But the situation of the colony now became desperate. A close consultation took place in the Governor's house and it was resolved to send the *Supply* to Batavia as a last resort. Though she could carry only a small quantity of stores, her captain, Lieutenant Henry Lidgebird Ball, was directed to hire another vessel for this purpose. When the *Supply* sailed on April 17, 1790, Captain Tench wrote that anxious eyes followed her all the way out of the Heads for 'in her all their hopes lay'. She could not hope to return in less than six months so the ration had to be reduced to 2lbs. flour, 2lbs. salt pork, 1 pint of pease and 1lb. rice per person per week. During this time one of the surgeons wrote that he, himself, had eaten dog and that 'happy was the man who could kill a rat or crow'.

They now felt more isolated than ever and morale became very low. Only Phillip was still hopeful and wrote, 'We shall not starve though seven eighths of the colony deserve nothing better....' A lookout had been placed at South Head and a flagstaff erected there to signal the arrival of a ship, but another month went by and there was none.

At last on June 3, 1790, there was a joyful cry: 'The flag's up!' Peo-

'Brickfield Hill and village on the high road to Parramatta' *[see p38]*

Walling/Daves

'Sydney Cove, 1794' *[see p37]*

'A Partial View in New South Wales' Sydney Cove circa 1795 *[see p37]*

ple rushed from their huts, the officers wrung each other by the hand and women kissed their children, eyes and hearts overflowing. Despite the wild weather, everyone ran down to the shore and perhaps Matthew stood there in the rain with the rest, waiting for the ship to come into sight. Captain Tench and some of the others were putting out in a boat to meet the vessel and calling: 'Pull away my lads! Hurrah for a bellyful and news from our friends!' Food would be uppermost in Matthew's mind for it would be unlikely that he would receive a letter. What else could the arrival of this new ship or fleet of ships mean to him?[102]

Composite diagram showing by firm lines the map of Sydney Cove surveyed by Captain Hunter about 1st March, 1788, illustrated in the Journal of Lieut. William Bradley and by broken lines existing Streets of the City of Sydney.

Scale 4 chains to an inch.

HUNTER ST

GOUGH ST

PITT ST

ST

Southsorth's Observatory

Female Convict Tents

Male Convicts Tents

Judge

L. Governor Garden

Cooking place

Marine Encampment

PHILIP ST

BRIDGE ST

Gov.
Store

Company

Governor

Provost

Guard

Blacksmith

Parade

Guard

Store

Store

GEORGE ST

GEORGE ST

HARRINGTON ST

Men convict Tents

Women Convict Tents

Wharf

ALFRED ST

ST

EXPRESS WAY

Scarborough

Friendship

MACQUARIE ST

Fishburn

Prince of Wales

Bakehouse

Oven

Guard

ARGYLE ST

Lady Penrhyn

Golden Grove

Borrowdale

Alexander

Hospital Garden

Wells

GLOUCE ST

Charlotte

OVERSEAS TERMINAL

WEST QUAY

Supply

MAGNETIC

OPERA HOUSE

Observatory

Sirius

SCALE OF FATHOMS
50   100   150   200

Courtesy of Mr. J.H. Luscombe, Town Clerk, City of Sydney.

Two Elizabeths

OLD NELLY was dying. She had been ailing and weak when they left Portsmouth but the continual tossing of the ship in the last few days had hastened her end. With wizened face and motionless limbs, her body already had the look of a corpse to those around her. Bound by no ties of affection to their companion, they merely watched and waited because there was nothing else to do.

One only, a girl, sat by the woman and tried to soothe her by bathing her face with a torn piece of cloth, moistening it from time to time in a pannikin of dirty water.

'It can't be long, Lizzie, ' said the sick woman. 'I know that. You've been good to me, that you have, an' I'm grateful. But it can't be long, thank God!'

'Don't talk so,' said the girl, 'The storm will be over in a day or two and then you'll mend.'

'No, lovey, I'll be feeding the fishes directly,' sighed the other with acceptance and closed her eyes again.

At this, one vicious crone began to chuckle and winked to her companions. 'Ye'll be feeding us afore ye feed the fishes, old girl,' she said.

But the young woman was instantly upon her. 'Shut your mouth, old beldame,' she said, 'and let her die in peace. Get back to your berths, all of you!'

Then, when the others had temporarily retreated to the shadows of the cabin as a result of this warning, the woman took the girl, Elizabeth's hand and pulled her close.

'Lizzie,' she whispered urgently, 'don't let me lie here when I'm stiff and stinking, call the Guard and let them know!'

'I will,' said Elizabeth, wondering how this could be done. It would certainly cause a brawl in the cabin, for the others would want to conceal the death to draw the old woman's rations. She could only hope that the surgeon, whose visits were erratic, might come in the late afternoon, having previously expressed his opinion that Nelly could not survive the journey.

As it chanced this was the case. Two hours later, the key rattled in the door and the surgeon, accompanied by a soldier, stepped into the half light of the cabin.

'God, what a stench!' he said as he did, 'Why have these buckets not been removed?'

'Begging your pardon, sir,' said Elizabeth, who was closest, 'but the guard will let us take them up but once a day. And if they're left stand in the passage, it worries the gentleman yonder,' nodding her head towards the passage outside.

'Blast Mr Macarthur!' said the surgeon, 'Get them out now!'

So Elizabeth lifted a stinking pail in each hand and moved towards the doorway, staggering with their weight and the motion of the ship. As she stepped into the passageway, she could see Macarthur himself at the door of his cabin. He was conversing with a soldier and she could tell by his tone that he was once again complaining. At his shoulder, could be seen the worried face of his wife, Elizabeth, who held her sickly baby to her breast. And it occurred to the girl that this gentle-woman, for all that she had a nurse to help her, was not without troubles. It could not be easy being married to man like Lieutenant Macarthur, whom nobody seemed to like.

When she returned from emptying the buckets, the surgeon had come out of the convict women's quarters and was giving the guard an order. 'That woman will be dead by morning,' he said. 'Get her some fresh water and as soon as she dies, let me know. And you,' he said to Elizabeth, 'get your things and come with me. We're in need of a servant up yonder and you look cleaner than the rest.'

As Elizabeth obeyed and began putting her few things in a bundle, she thought over what this change in her fortunes might mean. She was under no illusions as to what her role among the officers would ultimately be; but as if to put her thoughts into words, the crone, Lydia, who had sidled up and now stood watching, said: 'Going up top, are ya, Love?.... Up top with Kitty, eh?' And then in a different tone: 'Alf ya luck — Gawd, if I was only a few years younger....'

Elizabeth ignored her, staying only to let Nelly know she was leaving. But the eyes were closed and there was no response to her words. Even now the woman's face was acquiring a dignity it had never had in life. Lines on the forehead and a scar above the eye, once received in a beating from a man, were smooth and barely noticeable. It was so with mouth and eyes, and with the pinched cheeks that told of meals foregone in exchange for gin and foregetfulness.

Once out of the cabin, Elizabeth would tell the surgeon that Nelly was dead. But she could sympathise with those left behind who would thus be deprived of extra rations. 'You'll likely have more victuals in here tomorrow,' she said, as they watched her go and the guard made fast the door. She would see what she could do for them....

* * *

THUS AN impression of life on the *Neptune,* the worst ship in the worst Fleet of convict transports that ever came to New South Wales. Thus also, a fleeting glimpse of Elizabeth Rimes and Elizabeth Macarthur, two women from two worlds who, for a few brief months, were passengers on the same ship, separated, it may have been, by only a thin partition.

The *Neptune* was not the first of the new vessels to arrive in the Cove nor the one whose arrival was so eagerly anticipated by the crowd we left standing on the shore. The approaching ship proved to be the *Lady Juliana,* which had been ten months in coming, but whose convicts had been well treated and arrived healthy. Although the quantity of supplies carried on her was not great, the Governor decided to increase the flour ration which was a great relief to everyone.

The thought that the settlement was once more in touch with the world meant as much as the improvement in diet. 'With amazement', the First Fleeters heard of the French Revolution, which had taken place the previous July and of King George III's illness and recovery. News also came that the Second Fleet of ships carrying a thousand more convicts and a corps of foot soldiers to replace the marine garrison were following. And at last there was a partial explanation for the non-arrival of storeships. The settlers heard that the *Guardian,* which should have arrived in January, 1790, had hit an iceberg near the Cape of Good Hope, had been forced to jettison most of her stores and had ultimately been wrecked on the African coast. On June 20, however, the *Justinian* arrived, laden with stores, which thus compensated in some measure for the loss of the *Guardian.*[103]

The jubilation caused by the arrival of these first ships faded on June 26 when the three transport vessels of the Second Fleet, the *Scarborough, Surprize* and *Neptune* staggered into the Cove with their cargoes of dead and dying convicts, to be but a burden on the newly arrived stores. But disappointment changed to horror and sympathy when the boats started to come ashore. Some of the convicts died as soon as they reached the fresh air, while still others were carted ashore over the sailors' shoulders 'like goods', more dead than alive. Corpses had been thrown overboard all the way down the harbour and floated ashore for days after the arrival of the ships. Convicts and officers alike were shocked and disgusted at the condition of the new arrivals and the Governor was overheard to say that the Captains had virtually murdered many of the convicts. The Reverend Richard Johnson went on board the *Scarborough* and the *Surprize* but even he could not stomach a visit to the *Neptune,* by comparison with which the slave trade was said to be merciful. Conditions described in the story are factual. Dead bodies were concealed as long as possible so that additional rations could be drawn; and convicts were seen to remove the quids of tobacco out of dead men's mouths for the little solace it might afford them, the living. The irons used on the *Neptune* had formerly been used for slaves, so that the men convicts could hardly move and they were frequently up to their waists in water.[104]

The contrast between conditions in the First and Second Fleets hardly needs emphasising but the importance that attached to supervision in the two undertakings can most clearly be demonstrated in the case of the *Scarborough,* a vessel which made the voyage on both occasions. It will be remembered that when the *Scarborough* had sailed in the First Fleet, she had carried two hundred and eight male convicts of whom Matthew Everingham had been one. Before leaving Portsmouth, Captain Phillip had complained that his vessels, as a whole, were over-crowded. But because he had insisted on clean living conditions, good food and regular exercise on deck for the convicts and had made sure that regular inspections had taken place throughout the voyage, few people died on the passage of the First Fleet; and there were actually no deaths at all on the *Scarborough*. In the Second Fleet, the *Scarborough* carried two hundred and sixty-one male convicts, over a quarter as many again. Of these, seventy-three died on the voyage while ninety-six were landed sick, lean and emaciated. Even allowing for the possibility that the health of the men embarked might not have been as good as that of the prisoners in the First Fleet, the death rate is appalling. Not only was the ship overcrowded but after another threatened mutiny the captain, Marshall once again, kept the prisoners closely confined, which was the cause of many deaths. Ironically, Hector, Marshall's Newfoundland dog, was so overjoyed to see the *Scarborough* back in the Cove and to think that his master had returned that he swam out to the vessel to greet him.[105]

The one supervising officer in the Second Fleet had been Lieutenant John Shapcote on the *Neptune*, who had died at the Cape but the task of supervising all the ships had been an impossible one. The real blame lay with the British Government, which had arranged to pay the contractors on the number of convicts taken on board in England, rather than on those landed safely, as had been the case with the First Fleet. Thus the contractors had no interest in whether their charges arrived dead or alive and in fact, the dead were more profitable. On the *Neptune*, whose captain was Donald Traill, the convicts were treated with savage brutality and deliberately starved by the ship's master, Nicholas Anstis, who had been chief mate on the *Lady Penrhyn* in the First Fleet. Out of five hundred and eleven prisoners embarked, one hundred and fifty-eight died. Reports were sent to England and charges made but Traill escaped justice, probably because a full enquiry into the Second Fleet would have brought discredit on the whole transportation system.[106]

Among those who arrived alive on the *Neptune* was the convict girl, Elizabeth Rimes (Rymes), heroine of the story; and it is likely that, as with Molly Morgan and Catherine Crowley — the Kitty mentioned in the tale — her survival might have been due to the protection of one of the officers of the Corps. Molly Morgan, a ripe beauty who capitalized on her charms many times during her exciting history, is said to have emerged blooming from an upper deck when the ship arrived, while Catherine Crowley had already accepted the protection of Dr D'arcy Wentworth and was pregnant with the child, William Charles Wentworth, the future explorer and politician, before the vessel arrived in Sydney. Dr Wentworth, incidentally, had been charged on three counts of felonious assault, threatening people on the king's highway and theft. A lesser person would have hanged for these offences, but the wealthy and powerful Fitzwilliam family, to whom he was related, arranged for the charges to be quashed on the condition that he became surgeon to the New South Wales Corps. All three of these young women, Elizabeth Rimes, Molly Morgan and Catherine Crowley would become matriarchs of Australian families but this was in the future.[107]

For the present, Elizabeth Rimes, the one whose history we are following, would have been sent up the river to Rose Hill soon after her arrival, there to work with other convict women at making slops (clothing), with the newly arrived cloth, or perhaps at keeping a hut for ten men prisoners. She would live in the single women's huts, which were located in what is now Church Street (Parramatta), and which was the only cross street on a road which led from the hill to the river. At about this time, most of the convicts were transferred from Sydney to Rose Hill, as the land here was found to be much better for farming. Sometime during the next eight months, Elizabeth met Matthew Everingham and they were married on March 13, 1791, three months before the expiry date of Matthew's sentence. In the next chapter we shall see what happened to the young couple after their marriage but before we do so, and because Elizabeth is as important to our story as Matthew, let us go back and look at her background to see how she came to be aboard the hell ship, *Neptune*.[108]

In trying to trace Elizabeth's parentage, there were similar difficulties to those encountered with Matthew, because the exact date and place of her birth were unknown; and in her case, the task was complicated by the fact that she was illiterate and possibly not able to spell her own surname.

Regarding an approximate date for Elizabeth's birth we have two sources, the 1828 Census, in which her age is recorded as fifty-four and her age at death, given by others, in the record of her burial, that is, sixty-eight in December, 1841. Both of these dates indicate that Elizabeth was born in 1774 but they are both open to question because by the time of the 1828 Census, Matthew Everingham had been dead for eleven years and Elizabeth had remarried a man several years her junior. It would have been understandable if she had falsified her age on this occasion and at the time of her death, her husband and family would record what they had been told by her. She may not have known the exact date of her own birth, a fact that was allowed for in investigations made in London.[109]

Because Elizabeth was tried at the Old Bailey, London, and in the absence of any evidence to the contrary, the search was confined to that city. Here upon request a Guildhall librarian searched Boyd's marriage Index 1751-1775, which is an index to the marriage registers of many, but by no means all, of the parishes of the Church of England in London. In the register of St. George, Hanover Square, there is a marriage entry for April 22, 1764 between a John Rimes and Ann Buffin but unfortunately no births are registered for this couple in the following years when it might be supposed that our Elizabeth Rimes was born.[110]

As Elizabeth was apprehended in Spitalfields and because people in the Eighteenth Century generally did not move far from their birthplaces during their lifetimes, a search of the register of Christ Church, Spitalfields was made but was equally unproductive. Also, as there are family legends that Elizabeth was of dark colouring or a Jewess and as there was and is a large Jewish settlement in Spitalfields, recourse was made to Jewish genealogical records in London but the name, spelt either way, is completely absent from these.[111]

We are therefore in the same position with Elizabeth as with Matthew, ignorant of the exact date and place of her birth and of the names of her parents. And as with Matthew, any assumptions regarding her background must be based on the evidence revealed in her trial, and on the general information now available as a result of research into the backgrounds of the convict settlers of Australia.[112]

Elizabeth was tried at the Old Bailey in the Session which commenced October 28, 1789, having committed her crime on September 11, six weeks earlier. If we accept 1774 as her date of birth, she must have been fifteen or sixteen at the time but as we have already seen, she could have been a little older. She was already co-habiting with a man, Moore and there seems to have been a mutual affection between the two.

Now it would be pleasant to suppose that Elizabeth may have been a poor innocent country girl who had somehow been driven to dishonour in the heartless metropolis, and to commit a single crime through desperation. One might even see her and Moore as two lovers fleeing away from parental disapproval, determined never to be parted no matter what the cost. But it is much more likely that she was born in the area in which she resided when arrested, that she had taken up with Moore, who does not seem to have been a bad sort, as a temporary protector, that she had been accustomed since childhood to living on her wits to survive and was now living on her physical charms as well.

There were literally thousands of young women in Spitalfields and all over the East End of London living this hand to mouth existence and thousands of men also, to whom petty crime was a way of life. It was they who formed a large proportion of the earliest settlers of Australia and among whom many of our ancestors must be numbered. If we were to invent excuses for Elizabeth, we would need to do likewise for Thomas Chaseling, Michael Napthali, Charles Butler and many others who people this story who, all but one, were to lead meaningful lives in the colony and to die respected by their peers and betters. To whitewash their backgrounds is to miss the great theme of early Australian history, a new life in a new land. Let us therefore have a closer look at this part of London from which so many of the early transportees came.[113]

Addresses of defendants if they had any, are not given in the trials of people with whom we are dealing in this book but it will be noticed that Elizabeth and Moore were staying at an inn, No. 5 Rose Lane, Spitalfields. There is very little left of Rose Lane today, for, like many of the streets running parallel to it, it was levelled when Commercial

Road was built in 1845. What little remains is close to Stepney railway station. Spitalfields took its name from the shortening of St. Mary's Hospital Fields and had developed after the Great Fire. Streets and streets of its slums were devastated by bombs during World War II because of their proximity to the docks and have now been replaced with modern buildings of flats.

At the time when Elizabeth lived there, the district was positively dangerous for respectable people and it was not the place where good country folk would choose to stay. It was full of cheap lodging houses, thieves' dens and rookeries, where burglars, pickpockets, vagabonds, beggars and prostitutes congregated, although, as Dr. Lloyd Robson points out, there existed respectable dwellings side by side with the most unsavoury. What Richard and Mary Williams's inn was like, where Elizabeth and Moore had stayed for more than three weeks, we do not know. But the inns which were especially characteristic of Spitalfields were known as 'flash houses' or 'Hell Houses'. All of these had a back door so that a quick escape from the law could be effected and some had a half door opening inward at the front, so that thieves could quickly throw in their bundles when on the run.[114]

It was in such a place, the *Jolly Weavers,* that Michael Napthali was apprehended. He was a Jew of twenty-seven who committed a theft at Trigg Wharf, tried to fence the goods at Artillery Passage near Bishopsgate and then at Raven Row, Spitalfields, to Jews in each case. Hatred of the police was general and when Napthali was found at the skittle ground behind the inn, twenty 'common thieves' rushed the constable and rescued their 'pal'. In Wentworth Street, Spitalfields, stood the inn which was the setting out point for the highwayman, Dick Turpin. A century after Elizabeth Rimes had resided in the area, Duval Street, almost the extension of Artillery Passage, mentioned above, was the scene of the last murder of Jack the Ripper, whose specialty was prostitutes. On the lighter side, one notices Middlesex Street on the map, famous as 'Petticoat Lane', where it was possible to be robbed of your watch at one end and to buy it back from one of the street stalls at the other.[115]

A little north of Spitalfields is Shoreditch, where, near St Lukes, Old Street, Thomas Chaseling was caught stealing two hundred and thirty handkerchiefs. If Chaseling had not been caught, he would probably have taken his haul to the Jews in Field Lane, Saffron Hill; for Fagin's den in *Oliver Twist,* festooned as it was with 'wipes', was no figment of Dickens's imagination. In 1819, it was estimated that there were six thousand boys of the Artful Dodger type in London and eight thousand criminals under seventeen years of age. Chaseling was nineteen. Whole families in this notorious district were bred to petty crime while children were cast out into the streets or ran away to be picked up by men of Fagin's type. Thus many did not know who their parents were and from earliest childhood had woken each morning not knowing where the food for that day was coming from nor where they would sleep that night.

Others areas which furnished large numbers of their populace for Botany Bay were St Giles's, Seven Dials, Drury Lane, Marylebone, Clerkenwell, Saffron Hill, Chick lane, Bethnal Green, Whitechapel, Ratcliffe Highway, Kent Street, the area at the back of the mint in the Borough, Poplar and Stepney; and it will be seen that Spitalfields is in the very heart of these.[116]

William Hogarth's eighteenth century drawing of Gin Lane can be identified by its church steeple as being near St George's, Bloomsbury, close to Seven Dials. it demonstrates how, underemployed, demoralized and lacking in hope, many people in the depressed areas turned to drunkenness and prostitution and finished up like old Nelly in the introductory story. Hogarth gave his pawnbrokers names like Gripe and Pinch, to emphasise a point. The name of the pawnbroker in Elizabeth's story is not given, but ironically, the woman who worked in the shop and who identified both Elizabeth and Moore, was Jolly.

Mary Jolly knew both the prisoners very well by seeing them at her master's shop and Elizabeth had eleven 'duplicates' in her possession when apprehended, which would indicate that they had probably pawned everything they had. Poor and illiterate, with seemingly no occupation or training, Elizabeth might well have become a prostitute had she not been transported. It is interesting that here, once again, is an instance where the sentence of transportation was passed for a comparatively small theft, value seven shillings — Elizabeth received a year for every shillingworth stolen. There is no evidence of a previous offence but she might have thieved a hundred times without having been caught.

From the evidence, it is clear that Elizabeth was a girl of some spirit and used to taking the initiative. It was she who went along to engage the room at the inn, she who stole the sheet and blanket to pay the rent, she alone who was found guilty and transported. In so many ways, she resembles the Nancy of Dickens's *Oliver Twist* although seemingly her paramour, unlike Bill Sikes, had not given up the struggle to find honest employment.

Elizabeth would wear the same kind of clothes as Nancy and speak the same cockney speech. For Spitalfields was not far from the church of St Mary-le-Bow, within earshot of whose chimes, the *Bow Bells,* the true Cockney dwells. Cockney speech or 'St Giles Greek' has flavoured Australian speech and in addition, the early London transportees spoke a 'flash' or 'kiddy' language, which in some cases in colonial courts necessitated the services of an interpreter. Since a sense of humour is characteristic of the cockney, Elizabeth probably had this too. Like Nancy, Elizabeth would be capable of tenderness and we know that she had loyalty, resourcefulness, resilience and was prepared to take her punishment when the time came. 'You need not turn down the bed,' she told Mrs. Williams, the innkeeper's wife, resignedly when the latter came with the constable, 'there is a blanket and a sheet missing.'[117]

So she was sent on board the transport, *Neptune,* moored in the

Thames; and her youth and tough background probably helped her to survive the months the vessel spent there in one of the coldest winters England had ever experienced and to endure the frightful voyage to New South Wales.

The title of our chapter celebrates the coincidence of our Elizabeth and that more famous Elizabeth, wife of John Macarthur, having been co-passengers on the *Neptune* and there is more purpose in this than to evoke sympathy for Elizabeth Rimes. As our story unfolds, we will see that these women were each to be faithful and loving wives to men whose paths and interests were diametrically opposed. Macarthur's role was to have vital repercussions on the lives of the Everinghams and their class, the small emancipist settlers, so it will be of considerable interest to the reader to follow his history from the beginning, or at least from the time when he and his little family came aboard the *Neptune* on November 13, 1789.

John Macarthur was coming to New South Wales as a subaltern with the newly recruited New South Wales Corps or 'Botany Bay Rangers', who were to replace the Marines as a law keeping force, an irony in itself, as many of the Corps were deserters or malefactors who had been given the choice of prison or Botany Bay and a red coat. Being of small means and having lived for years on half pay, Macarthur had transferred to this corps because of the opportunities colonial service presented for promotion and pecuniary gain. Such a decision showed commendable courage and an awareness of the responsibility he now had for his young wife Elizabeth, a Devonshire woman of noble birth, and for their infant child, Edward. For the rest of his sane life, his character within his own family circle would prove to be the very antithesis of that old Scots saying, 'a causey saint and a house de'il'. Family and servants were to have a high regard for him but to outsiders his arrogance was insupportable and he seemed to bring the worst out in everyone with whom he came in contact — even Governor Phillip.[118]

The commander of the new regiment was Major Francis Grose, who did not actually arrive in the colony until 1792, while Macarthur's senior captain was Nicholas Nepean. To accommodate Nepean and Macarthur on the voyage, the great cabin of the Indiaman had been partitioned so that they should each have a side; but Nepean found Macarthur so quarrelsome and difficult that he moved his quarters during the first few weeks on board. The vacant space had therefore to be filled with women convicts, of whom we have imagined Elizabeth Rimes, our heroine to be one.

Certainly Elizabeth would have known John Macarthur by sight for he became well known to everyone in a very short space of time. When the ship reached Plymouth, by mistake for Portsmouth, Macarthur complained to Nepean that his wife could not continue in this cabin because of the stench of the sanitary buckets of the convict women, which stood just outside the door, and because the language and behaviour of some of the women could be heard through the bulkhead.

This resulted in a pistol duel between Macarthur and the ship's captain, who was later replaced by a worse commander in the person of Donald Traill. The ship then sailed back to Portsmouth and finally left England on January 17, 1790.

Relations were so bad between Macarthur, Nepean and Traill that Nepean finally agreed to allow the Macarthurs to be transferred in mid ocean to the *Scarborough* before they reached the Cape, which was much more comfortable, but greater troubles lay ahead of them. Macarthur himself, the nurse and the baby all became ill during the remainder of the voyage while Elizabeth Macarthur gave birth to a premature baby girl who lived only an hour. Meanwhile, below decks on the *Scarborough*, *Surprize* and back on the *Neptune* more convict men died daily while who knows how many convict women underwent a similar experience to Mrs Macarthur and themselves did not survive.[119]

Elizabeth Macarthur was to forget quickly the hardships of the trip in the novelty of Sydney Cove and the popularity she enjoyed as the first educated young woman to arrive here. Surgeon George Worgan taught her to play his piano, the only one in the colony, Lieutenant Dawes instructed her in astronomy, while pleasant days were spent picnicking on grassy headlands in the harbour.

Macarthur's career, however, did not advance very far in these early months, for no news of promotion arrived and the officers were given little encouragement to cultivate the land. In June of 1791, they were transferred to the new barracks at Rose Hill but were glad to get back to Sydney, unaware that their fortunes would later be centred in the Parramatta region. The Macarthurs were at this time losing hope about their future in the colony and seemed to feel that their stay would be a temporary one only.[120]

By contrast, there would be high hopes in a small hut on one of the new settlements two miles north east of the Rose Hill outpost. Matthew Everingham's seven years' term had expired in the month in which Macarthur had come to Parramatta and he and Elizabeth had been settled on fifty acres of land at The Ponds on July 18, 1791.

Many other convicts whose time had expired were also given an opportunity to settle on the new areas laid out by Phillip but few chose to do so. They were told that they had the alternatives of returning home by working their passages on ships, but would be given no help in this by the Government — or that they could work for the Government or for the officers or settlers for wages. Most wished to return home and it is significant that Matthew did not, but saw his future in the new land. There was evidently nothing in England to draw him back.

There had been a severe drought during the preceding summer of 1790-1791 and food had to be rationed again in April, so that many of the convicts were emaciated. Still, these few settlers were prepared to take a chance on the land. They were encouraged by the example of James Ruse who, having been settled on a plot at Rose Hill by Phillip in November, 1789, had gathered his first harvest and announced to the

Governor in January, 1791, that he could now live 'off the stores'. Ruse, incidentally, had married Elizabeth Perry (or Parry,) who was given a pardon. She had arrived on the *Lady Juliana*.[121]

Elizabeth Everingham had become pregnant immediately after her marriage but like Elizabeth Ruse, would have continued to help her husband with cultivation and probably in building the hut. Their efforts were unskilled by comparison with those of Ruse who had been bred a farmer, but still they would be optimistic about the future and excited by the thought of having their first child. And that is where we are going to leave them for the present.

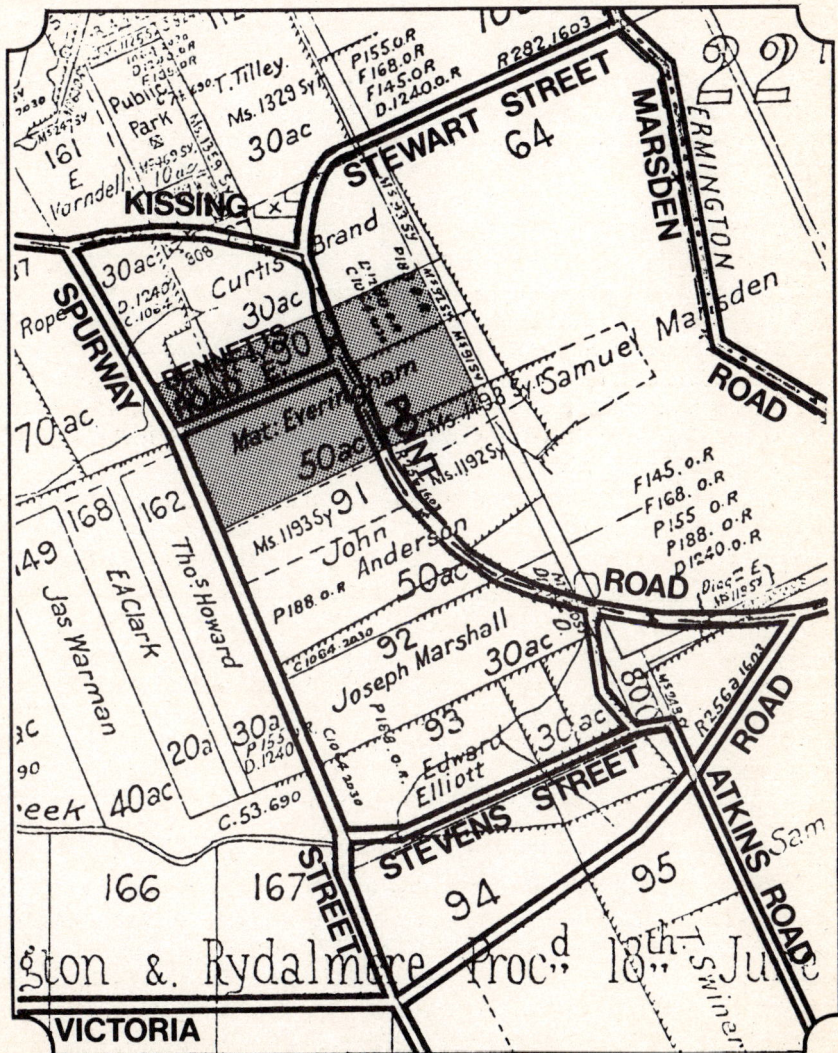

PLAN

of part of the County of Cumberland

showing position of

OLD GRANTS AT AND NEAR TOWN OF PARRAMATTA,

Referred to in Gov. Phillip's Despatch to Secretary of State of 5th Nov. 1791.

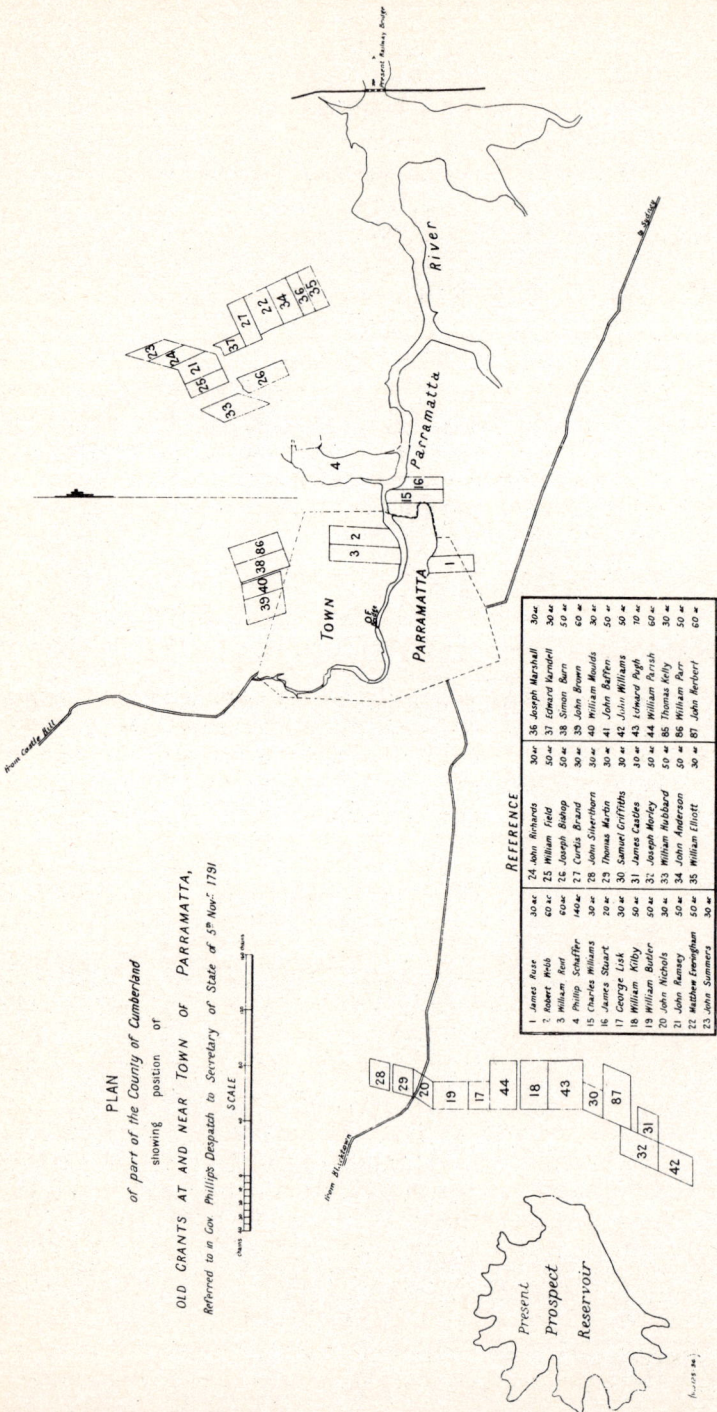

SCALE

River Parramatta

Parramatta River

TOWN

PARRAMATTA

From Castle Hill

From Blacktown

River

Present Prospect Reservoir

REFERENCE

No.	Name	Area	No.	Name	Area	No.	Name	Area
1	James Ruse	30 ac	24	John Richards	30 ac	36	Joseph Marshall	30 ac
2	Robert Webb	60 ac	25	William Field	50 ac	37	Edward Varndell	30 ac
3	William Reid	60 ac	26	Joseph Bishop	50 ac	38	Simon Burn	50 ac
4	Philip Schaffer	140 ac	27	Curtis Brand	30 ac	39	John Brown	60 ac
15	Charles Williams	30 ac	28	John Silverthorn	30 ac	40	William Moulds	30 ac
16	James Stuart	20 ac	29	Thomas Martin	30 ac	41	John Batten	50 ac
17	George Lisk	30 ac	30	Samuel Griffiths	30 ac	42	John Williams	50 ac
18	William Kilby	50 ac	31	James Castles	30 ac	43	Leonard Pugh	10 ac
19	William Butler	50 ac	32	Joseph Morley	50 ac	44	William Parish	60 ac
20	John Nichols	30 ac	33	William Hubbard	30 ac	85	Thomas Kelly	50 ac
21	John Ramsey	30 ac	34	John Anderson	50 ac	86	William Parr	50 ac
22	Matthew Everingham	50 ac	35	William Elliott	30 ac	87	John Herbert	60 ac
23	John Summers	30 ac						

CHAPTER FIVE

Ponds

THE BABY had been buried in the large paddock which was now the graveyard, Matthew, Elizabeth and the Reverend Mr. Johnson its only mourners.

Johnson was a good man, within the limits of his own imagination. He remembered the mite he had baptized only three weeks before and after pronouncing the formal words of comfort, had done his best to console the parents, albeit with platitudes.

Then the couple had made their way back from Parramatta along a bush track to the silent hut where the fretful crying of the sick child was no more. Beside the cradle that Matthew had made from bush timber, Elizabeth sat hunched, her arms crossed before her, sobbing.

'Betsey, love.... I'm going to take a turn about outside.... I'll not be long....'

He walked down to the corner where his own fifty acres met those of Anderson, leaned on the rough fence they had started and not finished and looked to the valley where the river lay. Overhead the sky was as blue as the ocean, so different from his memories of that other misty river he had once known so well. No wonder the Governor held on, he thought, for he was beguiled by these surroundings. How long would it take Phillip to realize that this country was not meant for the white man to farm, that the blue skies bore only a false promise? That for farming you needed grey skies and rain, My God, how you needed rain....

In his helplessness he kicked the bottom rail of the fence, turned and walked slowly back to the hut. As he closed the wooden door softly behind him, he could see that she was still sobbing.

'Liz,' he said, 'it might be for the best that this has happened. Look at this place – it's a wilderness! What did the poor child have coming to her but heat and no victuals like the rest of us? Nothing but rotten, weevily flour for months and it can only get worse....'

'We would have done,' she said, 'we would have done....'

'Aye, done,' he said, 'but how? Cursed flies crawling over the poor babe, no matter what we did and never knowing when we went out into the maize field whether a snake would crawl in, as it did with Evans' child. It's no place for children, Elizabeth, no place!'

There was no reply, as he had known there would not be and he was talking as much to console himself as her.

'And there'll be other babies, Liz, there'll be others.'

Still she wept, rocking now in pain and anguish, as wet patches began to form on the rag of her bodice from her swelling breasts, milk for the child whose need was not.

'My baby,' she whimpered, 'my baby....'

* * *

THE CHILD thus mourned was Mary Everingham, born six months after Matthew and Elizabeth had settled at The Ponds. 'There will be other babies,' Matthew had said and there were, five in the next ten years. The last chapter closed in the middle of the year 1791, when the couple were twenty-two and eighteen years old respectively. By the time the present chapter concludes and they are about to move to the Hawkesbury, they will be in their early thirties, ripened and no doubt toughened by their experiences at The Ponds.

The period of time we are now going to cover is a long one compared with that dealt with in the preceding chapters. The reason for this compression will be apparent when we see that this was a period of 'standing still' for the small expiree settlers, if indeed they did not fall backwards. The story is one of frustration and despair, of perseverance in the face of overwhelming difficulties, with the happiness of family life perhaps the one compensation.

As we have seen, few ex-convicts wanted to become farmers but of those who did, Governor Phillip carefully selected those who were most likely to succeed. Some were given probationary periods on the land but others were judged by their work at the Government Farm at Rose Hill. It is likely that Matthew was one of those who had worked on the farm, for we know that he was at Parramatta at the time of his marriage, a good four months before taking possession of his grant in July, 1791. He was going to need every bit of grit he could summon to stay on that land for twelve years. [122]

After Governor Phillip, in poor health and dispirited from his efforts in establishing the settlement, sailed for England in December, 1792, a new era began for the colony. In the period between his departure and the arrival of a new Governor, Major Grose of the New South Wales Corps, the Lieutenant Governor, was left in charge. Within a month, the whole system of Government was changed and power fell into the hands of the Corps and ultimately, John Macarthur. What has been called 'the experiment in national communism' was over and a government controlled economy gave way to monopoly and unscrupulous exploitation. [123]

It had always been the intention of Phillip and the Home Government he represented that the officers of the Corps, marines and free settlers should be granted land in excess of that granted to expired convicts. Phillip greatly favoured and in fact, begged the Government to send free farmer settlers who were to be given large grants, the idea being that they would set an example for the expirees who had land and that they could employ other expirees. Had Arthur Phillip remained or

Trial of Elizabeth Rymes — entry in Old Bailey Sessions Papers. [see p55]

...sey are could take any notice of it, only the clerk, to give it me to pay; and several times owe hundred pounds and one hundred and twenty pounds, therefore I appeal to your my lord, and the gentlemen of the jury, I hope it will never be thought that I made any ill use of what is here pretended; I desire to God that I know no more of what is there before you, than any one here present; had I had any dishonest intention I might have done it to hundreds of pounds; neither Mr. or Mrs. Atkinson can say, I either bought or sold this property.

Mr. *Sheridan.* Mr. Woodfall, until that day, you had no reason to suspect the character of this man?—Till the fact came out, I should as soon have suspected the nearest relation: it is most true, he was at times intrusted with large sums of money; he is the last man I should have suspected: I had not the least idea, till it came out: I take it for granted, that I may have given the clerks surplus money.

GUILTY.

Transported for seven years.

Tried by the London Jury before Mr. Justice HEATH.

763. JOHN MOORE and ELIZABETH RYMES were indicted for stealing, on the 11th of September last, one woollen blanket, value 3s. and one linen sheet, value 4s. the property of Richard Williams, in a lodging room.

(*The witnesses examined separate.*)

MARY WILLIAMS *sworn.*
I am wife of Richard Williams; I let a ready furnished lodging to this woman prisoner; a room on the first floor: Moore was not with her; he came the same night; he paid three shillings a week; they were there rather better than three weeks; I took them to be man and wife; but ...ing their room, was stripped: I made a great outcry, and sent for an officer: I missed a bed-gown, a sheet, and a blanket; the duplicates were found in the woman's pocket; I saw them taken out by the officer.

MARY JOLLY *sworn.*
I know both the prisoner very well, by seeing them at our shop; I obtained ... a sheet were pledged at our house; I did not take them in, I do not know who brought them.

JOHN FLINGHAM *sworn.*
I am a carpenter; on the 12th of September, and the prisoners, by information ... took the prisoners the 12th of September, at ... No. 5, Rose lane, Spital-fields: I searched her, and found ... even duplicates on her; and two of which led to the discovery, one of a blanket and the other on a sheet.

THOMAS HUCKWELL *sworn.*
I am a constable: on the 12th of September, I took the woman, and found on her these duplicates.

(*Produced.*)

Mrs. *Jolly.* These are our duplicates, my master's name is printed upon them.

JOHN LODWICK *sworn.*
I went with the constable to find out the prisoners: the woman was at home; ... said to Mrs. Williams, you need not turn down the bed, there is a blanket and a sheet missing, she said they were pawned; and I saw eleven duplicates taken out of her pocket.

PRISONER RYMES's DEFENCE.
I proposed to get the things out: I did not mean to let the things lay in.

PRISONER MOORE's DEFENCE.
I went out about eleven in the forenoon, with intent to get some work; I had been out of work for a long time, I went and got a job; and with the money, I had intention and pay the rent, which was not due for fifteen hours.

How came she to pass as your wife?— She is not so by law, Sir, but we cohabit together.

JOHN MOORE, NOT GUILTY.
ELIZABETH RYMES, GUILTY.

Transported for seven years.

Tried by the London Jury before Mr. Justice HEATH.

764. ROBERT SHARP was indicted for stealing, on the 16th of October, one woollen cloth great coat, value 5s. seven yards and a quarter of white callico, value 12s. 6d. the property of William Romney.

WILLIAM ROMNEY *sworn.*
I am officer at the Bell-inn; I lost my great coat and some callico; I saw the prisoner in the morning in the yard; I saw him unlock the door, and bring the things out.

PRISONER's DEFENCE.
I went up the yard, in order to get some work.

GUILTY.

Imprisoned two years.

Tried by the London Jury before Mr. Justice HEATH.

765. MARY STULTZ was indicted for stealing, on the 29th of September last, a flannel petticoat, value 1s. and a linen shirt, value 1s. the property of William Foreman.

LYDIA FOREMAN *sworn.*
I am wife of William Foreman; we are lodgers; I knew nothing of the prisoner; in Catherine-wheel-alley, Bell-lane, No. 2; I missed my child from the door, and the things from off the child; he is five years old; he was taken from the door; it was about five in the evening; he had on a shirt and a flannel petticoat; I saw my child again in about two hours; it was stripped; I never saw the things again: I saw the prisoner at a publick house, and the child on her knee; the things were gone then: the prisoner said she was taking care of my child; the child never goes from its own door; nor hardly down stairs; the child said, in the hearing of the prisoner, that she fold his things at an old iron shop, but he could not tell where; I have tried but could not find the place; I was so frightened: I do not know whether the child was crying or not, he said, in her presence, that she took him from the door and pulled his clothes off, and wanted to drop him, but he cried and would not be dropped; he said, she took him into a necessary, to strip him, and wanted to drop him in an alley, the publick-house was the Duke's Head, in Wingfield-street.

WILLIAM FOREMAN *sworn.*
The prisoner said at the watch-house, in my hearing, that she found the child in Castle-street, Spital-fields: the next morning, before the Justice, she said she found it in Bell lane, Spital-fields: I saw the child brought home; his petticoat and shirt were missing.

JOHN KEY.

Court. Have you ever taken an oath my little boy?—No, my lord.
Do you know the nature of an oath, and what will become of you, if you tell a story?—Yes, Sir; I shall go into brimstone and fire.
Have you been taught your catechism? —Yes.
Do you know you will also be punished in this world?—Yes.   B

JOHN

William Hogarth   British Museum

'Beer Street'. A companion piece to 'Gin Lane', this drawing was intended to show prosperity and the advantages of drinking beer rather than gin. Note door of N. Pinch, the pawn broker at right. *[see p58]*

Motif from the *Sydney Gazette and NSW Advertiser* 1803-1804 *[see p65]*

Philip Gidley King followed him as Governor, as Phillip had recommended, the history of New South Wales would have been different. It is likely that a tighter control would have been maintained and a paternalistic eye kept on small expiree settlers such as Matthew.[124]

The reverse side of the Great Seal of the Colony, which arrived in October 1791 and which was later adapted as the emblem of *The Sydney Gazette*, depicted a scene which clearly demonstrated the Home Government's wishes for the Colony's future. It showed convicts arriving at Botany Bay and being received by Industry, who freed them from their fetters and pointed towards the land. Nearby, a town rose on the summit of a hill with a fort for protection, the motto for the whole being *Thus we hope to prosper*. How far the guardians of the fort exceeded their role and what hope the released convicts had of prospering from now on constituted the melancholy story of the next few years.[125]

For the first time a distinction was made in rations issued to the military and the convicts. Military rule replaced the civil magistracy and in the area in which we are now most interested, Rose Hill or Parramatta, John Macarthur ruled unchallenged.[126] The corps officers were given large grants of land and convicts to work it. They were given the exclusive right to buy the cargoes of ships which now began to visit Sydney Cove and they resold the goods to the settlers and others at profits of up to two hundred per cent.

Most importantly, in disregard of definite instructions from London to the contrary, Grose allowed spirits to be imported by the Military and sold at enormous profit, thus inaugurating a system known as the 'rum traffic' which exploited the weakness of convicts and expirees. Men who had barely had a drink for years would gladly slave in the fields all day in order to procure a few hours oblivion at the end and many settlers sold their land or incurred debts to satisfy a mania for liquor. Thus the area under cultivation doubled in no time and made the efforts on the Government Farm at Toongabbie seem ridiculous. But the land thus cultivated was in the hands — as had never been intended — of a very few.[127]

When Grose resigned in 1794 because of indisposition due to old wounds, Colonel William Paterson became Administrator, but the situation remained the same. Captain John Hunter finally arrived as Governor in 1795 but though, as we have seen, he was a man of courage and integrity, the task of restoring Governmental control was beyond him. Even King, when at last appointed Governor in 1800 after Hunter's recall, was unable to turn back the clock a decade to the time of Phillip's departure. It was in King's term as Governor that Matthew moved to the Hawkesbury.[128]

While Matthew and Elizabeth and their young family lived at The Ponds, the character of the colony altered in many other ways. The population increased, agriculture and other industries such as whaling and sealing began and trade with the outside world commenced. As a result of exploration, new land was opened and settlement expanded to the Hawkesbury and Nepean districts.

This expansion began in the final year of Phillip's term. Rose Hill or Parramatta we saw as an outpost in 1789 and we noticed the beginning of agriculture with James Ruse's experimental farm during 1790. In 1791 Phillip laid out areas of settlement at Prospect Hill, The Northern Boundary, The Ponds and The Field of Mars so that the population was now dispersed. (See map.) No longer were the inhabitants part of the close knit community based in Sydney Cove, though for many years afterwards, that settlement was still described as 'The Camp'.[129]

The population grew naturally by births but was greatly increased by the continuing arrival of convict transports. After the arrival of the Third Fleet between August and October, 1791, the population was over four thousand, compared with the one thousand people who had been there 'in the Beginning'. After this the Fleets are not named and no longer does everybody know everybody else and Governor and spiritual pastor alike find it more difficult to supervise their charges. 'When numbers were small' wrote the Reverend Richard Johnson, regretting the loss of personal contact with his flock, 'I could speak to all and converse privately....[130]

Some of the expired convicts and the marines go home and there is a realization of the uniqueness of those early days and already, a feeling of nostalgia. Thus the old marine diarist, John Easty, refers sadly to the sailing of the *Sirius* people:

'.... thar was two partys of men Saparated which had Spent 4 years together in the greatest Love and frindship as Ever men did in such a distant part of the globe.'[131]

So Matthew and Elizabeth face their first grief in a quiet place. They are on their own, away from the bustle of life in London, the crowding of the convict ship or even the relative 'busyness' of the Cove or Rose Hill where most of the population was now located. Their nearest neighbours are Curtis Brand on one side and John Anderson on the other as can be seen by the map; and though it is likely that one of the older wives would have come over to help Elizabeth in childbirth, there was dense bush between the huts.

Today, as one drives along Kissing Point Road, Dundas, it is hard to imagine the area as a frontier region. The general name for the place was 'The Ponds at Rydalmere' and it was described as being two miles to the north east of Parramatta. As can be seen by a comparison of a Parish Map with a section of Gregory's Street Directory, the grant is bisected by Kissing Point Road. Present day Spurway Road appears to have formed the western boundary and Delaware Street, the eastern limit, while Bennett's Road and Bartlett Street would be the northern and southern boundaries respectively. In 1978, this is red brick suburbia, the residents, in the main, unaware of the antiquity of the grants of which their portions are subdivisions and of the history of the area.

It is possible to stand on the hill, on what must have been

the 'Everingham Farm' and to look down to the Parramatta River, as Matthew must have done, without too many high rise buildings obscuring the view. One must imagine land covered in trees and cleared only in the small patches around the settlers' huts. The main connection with Sydney was by water. There was only a bush track on the other side of the river and roughly in line with the present Parramatta Road, to link Rose Hill to Sydney Cove. For their own trips to Parramatta, Matthew and Elizabeth would have walked the track which is the present Kissing Point Road. This road, even as late as the Meadows Brownrigg map of 1850, terminated in the Middle of Curtis Brand's property. A trip to town must have been exhausting in summer, so that, in the first years, they would go only to collect stores or on such occasions as the baptism and burial of their baby, Mary.[132]

As time went by and access was safer and easier, they would go more often to take their wheat and maize to the store and to sell their vegetables at the market. Parramatta, Australia's first country town, was the first town that the older children of the family knew. As we mentioned it only briefly now is an opportune time to look at what it was like during this period. It will be remembered that Elizabeth lived there for a good twelve months in its earliest days and we suspect that Matthew was also at Parramatta for about a year prior to taking up his land.

The main street, George Street, had originally been planned by Phillip as a magnificent thoroughfare, two hundred feet in breadth and rivalling Pall Mall. It stretched, as it still does, for a mile from the Governor's House on a rise straight down to the river and landing stage. Only one cross street had been laid out before Phillip's departure and this was the present Church Street, of interest because it was here, in one of nine huts built for unmarried women and for good convict families, that Elizabeth would have lived from June 1790 to March 1791, prior to her marriage. The other main buildings were the barracks and storehouse, close to each other and within one hundred and fifty yards of the wharf and a hospital. Thus Parramatta in 1791, looked much like the illustration.[133]

It will be noted that in 1791, there was no church. It has been said that the first services were conducted by the Reverend Richard Johnson in the shade of a tree near the river and later the hut of James Bloodworth, the carpenter, was used. By the time Matthew and Elizabeth were married and Mary Everingham baptized, it is likely that a barn was used but its exact location is unknown.[134]

The entry in the Marriage Register of St John's records that the witnesses to the Everingham marriage were Thomas Barnsley and Peter Stewart. These two men had no particular connection with Matthew and Elizabeth but would be known to them by sight. Barnsley seems to have taken the position of Chaplain's Clerk to the Reverend Richard Johnson after the death of Samuel Barnes and there is evidence of his witnessing weddings from December 1790 onwards and then all through 1791 in company with Richard John Robinson. As Robinson was certainly employed at the public barn and indeed, later pardoned for his efficiency as its keeper, it seems likely that it was here that the marriages were being performed. The other witness to the Everingham marriage and to that of William Butler and Jane Forbes on the same day, was Peter Stewart, a Sergeant of Marines who had a hut at Parramatta. He was probably selected by Johnson as a responsible and literate person who happened to be present at church at the time. For weddings usually took place on a Sunday at Rose Hill after the church service and March 13, 1791 was a Sunday.[135]

Letters to friends in England written by the Reverend Richard Johnson give us a glimpse of life at Parramatta in 1791 and also an insight into the character of this humble man of God. At first, he wrote, he used to go up to Rose Hill, a fourteen miles' journey, by boat, which sometimes took six hours, perform his public duty and return to Sydney Cove the same day. However, after a while, he found it too much and so obtained a room which he described as 'a miserable one but a spiritual Bethel'; and he would sleep there Saturday and Sunday nights and return on the Monday morning. He also wrote that during this time, he would visit the convicts in their huts and this gave him more pleasure than preaching. Thus he and Matthew and Elizabeth would be well known to one another before they moved to The Ponds.

In March 1792, Johnson wrote that the foundations of a church at Parramatta had been laid in the previous spring (1791), but that before it was finished, it had been turned into a gaol or lock-up and then another granary; and he was now turned out again because the granary was full.[136]

The site of this second granary is also unknown but it was here that the Everinghams' baby, Mary would have been baptized on Monday, January 2, 1792. Three weeks later, on Tuesday, January 24, she was buried. No cause of death is recorded but in that month, Collins mentions in his diary that several people at Parramatta had been struck suddenly by an illness, which killed them within twenty-four hours.[137] Thirty-three died that month.[138]

The cemetery in which it is thought Mary is buried is the oldest extant in Australia. It is located in O'Connell Street, and its high brick walls give it an old world character which matches the antiquity of its headstones. In 1792 it had only a wooden fence, as it had originally been intended as an enclosure for cattle. Mary Everingham's name is not listed in the transcription of the monuments in St John's cemetery prepared by Vernon Goodin, for the Society of Australian Genealogists. The grave may have been marked only by a wooden cross, for the parents were poor. A convict named Valentine Godsby was buried on the same day but the site of his grave is also unlisted. However, the grave of Henry Edward Dodd, Governor Phillip's servant, who had been in charge of the convicts on farming duty at Rose Hill and who died on January 29, 1791, is in Section Four in the South West corner of the cemetery; perhaps this is the oldest part of the cemetery and where the infant Mary is buried.[139]

The Register of the Parish of St John, Parramatta, predates the erection of a church. It was not until August, 1796, that a church, formed out of the materials of two old huts, was opened by the Reverend Samuel Marsden and even this was only a temporary building. Thus the Everinghams' second and third children, Sarah Elizabeth and Matthew James born in 1793 and 1795 respectively, would, like Mary, have been baptized in the granary. William, born 1797, and George, born 1799, would have been baptized in the new temporary church. There is a slight possibility that Ann (later Chaseling), born 1802, may have been baptized in the present St John's, on the corner of Church Street and Macquarie Street, which at the time did not have its distinctive towers. She is registered in St John's but it is uncertain whether she was born at The Ponds or at the Hawkesbury. Sarah, the eldest surviving child was baptized by the Reverend Richard Johnson, Australia's first clergyman but the other four children also recorded in St John's Register were baptized during the term of the Reverend Samuel Marsden, who arrived in the colony in March, 1794 as assistant chaplain and assumed responsibility for this parish almost immediately.[140]

The first temporary church of St John, where William and George were baptized and which was 'church' to the family for six years, was located on the south eastern corner of the intersection of George and Marsden Streets. Today the site is occupied by the Woolpack Hotel, a fact which would highly displease Johnson and Marsden, appalled as they were by the 'vice and depravity' which obtained more than ever after Phillip's departure.

The licence for the first hotel, *The Mason's Arms,* was granted to James Larra, an ex-convict and French Jew, about the same time as Marsden's church opened, 1796. Little more than a wattle and daub hut at first, it stood opposite the church on the north east corner of the same intersection, where the courthouse stands today. Matthew, who, as events have shown, was not averse to 'a drop' would doubtless have quenched his thirst at *The Mason's Arms* when he came to town.[141]

During the twelve years when Matthew and his family lived at The Ponds, Parramatta, as the transit centre for the Toongabbie, Camden and Hawkesbury districts, grew from a village into a town. But now we must return to The Ponds for a more detailed picture of this new life that Matthew and Elizabeth had begun, on the soil.

In granting land, Phillip had been instructed to leave, between every two blocks granted, an area equal to the larger grant, which was to remain Crown land. He soon realized that this arrangement was impracticable and decided to vary it, because the intervening blocks were covered by tall trees and dense bush which isolated each settler. Though a guard of a corporal and two soldiers had been stationed in the middle of each settlement, this was found ineffectual against the sudden attacks of the hostile Parramatta natives and the swift depredations of runaway convicts. Thus it was necessary to place the settlers on adjoining blocks and to issue them with muskets. This also facilitated the work of the settlers in clearing the land because the help of neighbours was needed to move the larger trees.[142]

In December, 1791, when Matthew had been at The Ponds five months, Captain Watkin Tench was sent to inspect the new settlements and it is to him that we are indebted for a vivid description of the progress made to this time. Tench begins his account by stating the terms under which the land was held, and then goes on to describe the practical assistance given to the farmers. He begins:

'.... The estates shall be fully ceded for ever to all who shall continue to cultivate for five years, or more... they shall be free of all taxes for the first ten years; but after that period to pay an annual quit-rent of one shilling. The penalty on non-performance of any of these articles is forfeiture of the estate, and all labour which may have been bestowed upon it. These people are to receive provisions, (the same quantity as the working convicts) clothes, and medicinal assistance, for eighteen months from the day on which they settled. To clear and cultivate the land, a hatchet, a tomahawk, two hoes, a spade and a shovel are given to each person, whether man or woman; and a certain number of cross-cut saws among the whole. To stock their farms, two sow pigs were promised to each settler; but they almost all say they have not yet received any, of which they complain loudly. They all received grain to sow and plant for the first year. They settled here in July and August last. Most of them were obliged to build their own houses; and wretched hovels three-fourths of them are. Should any of them fall sick, the rest are bound to assist the sick person two days in a month, provided the sickness lasts not longer than two months; four days labour in each year, from every person being all that he is entitled to....[143]

Tench goes on to say that the outlook of the settlers varied a great deal. Some were determined to persevere, provided encouragement was given but others were despondent and predicted they would starve unless the period of aid was extended to three years.

It is clear from his account that he walked from farm to farm and spoke with each person individually, many of whom he mentions by name. He appears to have asked each man what his trade or calling had been prior to conviction and he noted this in a column of his report to the Governor. Tench's account is *the only place* where Matthew is described as an 'attorney's clerk'. In the official Government account of the settlers sent home by Phillip, Matthew's calling is not mentioned, nor does it appear in any other document so far discovered.

The passage in which Tench mentions Matthew Everingham specifically has created much conjecture in the minds of descendants and others, and runs:

'The attorney's clerk I also thought out of his province: I dare believe that he finds cultivating his own land, not half so easy a task, as he formerly found that stringing together volumes of tautology to encumber, or convey away that of his neighbour.[144]

In Tench's day the phrase 'tautology of lawyers' was frequently used derogatively to express the distrust which the legal profession had engendered. In other words, when Tench thought of attorneys or their clerks, he thought of people like Dodson and Fogg in *Pickwick Papers.*[145]

In describing himself as a former 'attorney's clerk', Matthew would be putting the best face on his past, unaware that the mention of a legal calling conjured up an unfavourable impression in Tench's mind. Quite obviously, Tench could not have known, and Matthew was not going to tell him, that he, Matthew, had spent three years as a convict before the departure of the First Fleet and had last been in a legal office at the age of fourteen, when he would certainly not have been handling property conveyances.

What Tench's remarks do reveal is that Matthew was finding farming hard work; for here it was necessary to 'exert more than ordinary activity' to raise crops. At this time Elizabeth was within a few weeks of bearing her first child, so the full labour would no doubt have fallen upon him alone. Tench also remarks that the settlers were having a great deal of trouble with a destructive grub which ate the young maize plants so that the farmers had been obliged to plant twice or three times on the same land. In addition, the weather had been very dry, as Matthew lamented in the story.[146]

Nevertheless, Tench records that Matthew had two acres under cultivation, which was better than the average. In Governor Phillip's despatch of November 5, 1791, which would have been taken as at the end of October, he had one acre, two roods in cultivation, so he had cleared two roods or half an acre in the intervening month.[147]

Tench, though a keen and intelligent observer, was not a farmer. On February 24, 1792, three months later, David Burton, a gardener, was sent to examine agriculture at Parramatta and it was his opinion that all the settlers at The Ponds, with the exception of Kelly, Marshall and Elliott would succeed very well.[148]

Throughout 1792, things went fairly well for the first grantees. A few grew tired of farming, sold their livestock and wanted to give up their land but most persevered. Owing to the ignorance and mismanagement of the authorities in England, the colony again became short of food; rations had to be reduced and there was a dreadful sicklist. This was to be the pattern over what came to be known as 'the hungry years'. Just when enough food had been produced to cater for the existing population, a new influx of convicts, sent without adequate provisions or clothing would arrive to swell the numbers of hungry mouths.[149]

Yet the settlers were better off than others because they could grow and exchange pumpkins, melons and vegetables and keep a few chickens. Thus a newly arrived convict was to write home: 'Will Butler, who is a settler here, has forty acres and his wife twenty and is very well to do — he made me a present of three chickens'. And Richard Atkins, the magistrate at Parramatta, visiting The Ponds in May 1792, was to remark that the people here were comfortably lodged and had plenty of vegetables and that they were, in every particular, much better situated than they could possibly be in England. Due to their own efforts, their ground was flourishing, yet they had started off with only a spade, a saw and a hoe. In June, he was to write that there were three hundred acres of wheat around Parramatta but that it was a precarious crop compared with the Indian corn which never failed, given proper attention. In hard times, both here at The Ponds and later at the Hawkesbury, the Indian corn or maize was to be their staple food as they ground it and ate it like porridge.[150]

In October of the same year, 1792, Matthew had seven and a half acres under cultivation in all, consisting of five and a half acres of maize, three quarters of an acre of wheat and a quarter acre of barley. No acreage of vines or garden is given so he probably had only a small patch near the house; but he had obviously been busy during the intervening months and by this time, may have been aided by the labour of an assigned convict.[151]

In winter, it was bitterly cold out here compared with Sydney, ice forming on the surface of the 'Ponds' on occasions and the summer was appallingly hot. On December 5, 1792, the thermometer reached 114°F at Parramatta and at times fires raged through the 'woods', burning the trees to the tops and destroying every blade of grass. These vicissitudes, together with natives, snakes, plagues of grubs and marauding convicts were to be the norm over the next ten years at The Ponds but would have been bearable had sympathetic treatment from Government quarters continued.[152]

Before the end of Phillip's period as Governor, in December, 1792 there is one event to record of great interest to Everingham descendants. That is, the arrival in October, 1791, of the transport, *Royal Admiral,* for she bore with her two men who were to be co-ancestors with Matthew and Elizabeth of many Australians. The first was Thomas Chaseling, already mentioned in the last chapter and the second was a lesser known Irish Catholic, (Patrick) James Dunne, who had presumably come to England seeking work like many of his countrymen, and not finding it, had broken into a house and as a result, been transported. Both men, like Matthew, had already served part of their sentences on the hulks at Woolwich, Dunne on the *Censor* and Chaseling (or Chaseland) on the *Stanislaus.*[153]

Three of Chaseling's children were to marry three of Matthew's and there were numerous other connections by marriage in later generations. James Dunne's Napthali grandchildren were to contract at least three times with the Everinghams, thus mixing Dunne and Chaseling descendants as well. And not only were Chaseling and Dunne to be close neighbours of the Everinghams at the Hawkesbury but Dunne was first juror on the list of those empanelled at the inquest into Matthew's death.[154]

The *Royal Admiral* prisoners were sent directly to Parramatta and it is thought that Chaseling went to Toongabbie, where it is said that he later became a guard. (Another notable passenger was Mary Haydock, later Reibey who with typical spirit, later called her hotel in what is now Reibey Lane, Circular Quay, after the ship.)[155]

On the *Royal Admiral* also came clothing supplies so that Matthew, along with the other men, would have received two frocks, two pairs of trousers, one pair of yarn stockings, one hat, one pair of shoes, one pound of soap, three needles, four ounces of thread and a comb. Elizabeth received one cloth petticoat, one coarse shift, one pair of shoes, one pair of stockings, one pound of soap, four ounces of thread, two ounces pins, six needles, one thimble and one pair of scissors. The comb alone would be prized as gold, for the settlement had been desperate for them until now.[156]

Unfortunately, the frocks and trousers were of coarse and unsubstantial osnaburg (linen) and scarcely lasted three weeks. When clothes wore out it was not uncommon to see gangs of naked labourers in the field, 'working unconcerned'. Adults and children must have grown accustomed to scanty clothing and become hardy as a result. The first generation of native born children were noticeably fine specimens, despite their mixed backgrounds.[157]

From the little light that such records throw on clothing, it is thought that a farmer such as Matthew would have looked something like the illustration as he went about his work. The list also demonstrates the meagre possessions and simple life style of a small settler. At most, they would receive an iron kettle and perhaps a pot when they started off and the rest of their bowls were fashioned from 'greenwood' as Mary's cot in the story.[158]

The cottage itself would have had but two rooms, one in which Matthew and Elizabeth would sleep and the other a kitchen/living room where the convict servant assigned to each settler about 1792, would have slept. The addition of a chimney which Phillip ordered for each settler in 1791 would have been a welcome one.[159]

It will be noticed in the illustration of Parramatta that there are no tanks near the huts. Each settler would have had one or two casks issued from the store and would have drawn and carried water from the creek at the property near where Delaware Street is today. This creek linked the 'Ponds' and was the headwaters of the Subiaco arm.

The settlers' lives were lived close to the soil — nearly everything they had, they had made themselves or with the help of the little community around them. Life had a biblical quality and they understood the terms and allegory of what could have been their only book far better than we do now. Matthew hand-cast his seed like the Sower in the parable. Like Christ, as prophesied on the Day of Judgement, he threshed his crop with a fan, gathering the wheat for the 'garner' or granary and throwing away the chaff. The Wise and Foolish Virgins they understood, for there was always a shortage of oil for lighting; and when the butter from the *Royal Admiral* was found to be rancid, they put wicks in it and used it for tallow.[160]

It was necessary to see that the hut was locked when unattended, for runaway convicts, particularly the Irish, were a constant threat. In the middle of our period, (1795), the hut of Thomas Tilley, on the property next door but one to Matthew, was broken into from the side by one James Barry, who was caught and received the appalling punishment of a thousand lashes as a deterrent to others.[161]

Jobs mentioned in a list of wages were 'falling forest timber', 'falling timber in brush ground', 'chipping in wheat', 'hilling', 'reaping wheat', 'pulling and husking Indian corn', 'sawing planks', 'ditching' and 'carrying wheat'. They tilled the land themselves, in the absence of horses and oxen, their livestock being confined to the swine and chickens issued in 1792 just before the Governor's departure.[162]

We now come to the end of Phillip's term of government, December 1792. During the next five years, from 1793 to 1798, conditions deteriorated for Matthew and the other emancipist settlers. But before we pass on to the final years of the story of Matthew as a farmer at The Ponds, a few important family events should be mentioned.

In 1793, the first of the free settlers requested by Phillip arrived aboard the transport *Bellona*. Among their number was Thomas Rose, the first free settler to be granted land in Australia at what was appropriately called Liberty Plains but is now known as Concord. Rose was later to move to the Hawkesbury River and two of his grandchildren and Matthew's would later marry.[163]

On June 9 of the same year, 1793 Matthew and Elizabeth again had a daughter , Sarah Elizabeth Everingham, baptized on June 30. This time, the baby not only survived her first few months in the coldest winter the colony had yet experienced but in maturity became the matriarch of the extensive Woodbury family. The names of the first two Everingham children may have been those of Elizabeth's and Matthew's mothers respectively. This was a common practice and often provides a clue to the genealogist.[164]

Three months later in September, 1793, there arrived after a riotous voyage from Cork, the *Sugar Cane* transport, the third ship to come from Ireland, with a complement of one hundred and ten male and fifty women prisoners. Among the latter was Catherine Barry, later to be the wife of James Dunne, mentioned previously.[165]

On May 23, 1795, a baby brother for Sarah was born and was baptized on July 8, six and half weeks later, Matthew James. The concerns of harvest time and the fact that the natives were accordingly troublesome may have accounted for the delay.[166]

In February of the following year, 1796, the fourth Irish transport, the *Marquis of Cornwallis,* arrived from Cork with a load of 'Defenders' or Irish patriots and rebels. This ship, also, had experienced an attempted mutiny, the women's contribution on this occasion having been the pulverisation of glass to be mixed with the flour from which the seamen made their puddings. Such occurrences as this reflect the background from which the Irish came. Starved — literally living on potatoes and water — downtrodden by their English overlords, they were in many cases reduced to crime to survive. Since the early Irish convict records were destroyed in the troubles of 1920 when Dublin

Castle was blown up, details of their trials, if any, will never be known. Nor can it be determined to what extent their crimes, when noted on the ship's indent, were acts of rebellion disguised as trumped up charges of larceny.[167]

'What an importation!' lamented Collins. Yet one of these women, Margaret McMahon (or McMaude) was to marry Thomas Chaseling and so become ancestress to a third of the Everingham family. Her daughter, Ann Chaseling, was to marry Matthew James Everingham, the younger, whose birth has just been mentioned. About a third of the total number of convicts who came to Australia were Irish and many married their own countrymen and women in the colony, thus preserving their own faith and national traditions. The fact that many of them spoke only Gaelic and could barely understand or be understood by the English helped to keep them together. In the case of Margaret McMahon and Catherine Barry, because they changed their names and officially, their faith, probably few of their descendants realise that they carry a few drops of that rebellious Irish blood in their veins.

On August 8 of the following year, 1797, the second Everingham son, William, was born and baptized on September 3. He was to marry Jane Chaseling, the second daughter of Margaret McMahon.

This brings us to the year 1798, an opportune time to take another look at Matthew Everingham's farming endeavours, for the colony was now ten years old. By now, Hunter had been Governor for three years and his efforts to reassert the authority of the Crown and to implement those policies that had been intended for the penal colony were having little success. On the one hand, the Secretary of State was complaining of the enormous expense to the British Government of maintaining convicts whose free labour had been given profusely to the military settlers and on the other, Hunter himself was convinced that the prosperity of the colony depended on the efforts of these settlers. His orders for the return of some of the convicts for government works had been ignored, so that he had been forced to commandeer one or two for a few days' labour each week on the roads.[168]

Thus we find that, in the *Government and General Orders* of January, 1797, all officers with farms were required to furnish two men for three eight hour days each week, while every settler had to furnish his own labour or that of one man for the same time for the construction of a road twenty feet wide from Parramatta to the Hawkesbury. The people from the Ponds were to begin repairs from their own neighbourhood and continue them for two thirds of the way to Parramatta; this would have been along the course of Kissing Point Road towards Victoria Road. As a concession, they were allowed to suspend roadmaking while their grounds were being prepared for the ensuing season.[169]

Distressed by injustices such as this, for they could ill afford the loss of a man's labour, by the high price of labour and necessities and by the fact that the more opulent settlers had preference at the stores when wheat was brought, some of the oldest settlers had become bankrupt.

Those remaining voiced their complaints to the Governor when he visited the Parramatta settlement in January, 1798. He then ordered a general muster on February 14 and assembled the settlers the following morning to discuss their 'heavy grievances'. At this meeting he appointed two men, the Reverend Samuel Marsden and Dr Thomas Arndell to visit the different districts and to take down complaints in writing.[170] Here are a few extracts of what the settlers at The Field of Mars, which included The Ponds, had to say:

'We, the settlers of ye above district,.... beg leave to approach y'r Excellency,.... as y'r immediate interposition will save us from gliding down that precipice on which we have so long stood. We will therefore point out to y'r Excellency ye source of our misfortunes.... also the method by which they can be effectually abolished. We will begin by observing ye exorbitant prices that are charged for every article that a settler has occasion to use.

Tobacco. — This is an article that is more in use in this colony than even in Virginia, where it grows; ye consumption in one yr. amounts to some thousand of pounds. A wholesaler purchases it at from 8d. to 1s. yet, shameful to be told, he never retails it at less than 5s. per pound, and still there is abundance in the colony.

Sugar,.... purchased from captains of ships at 7d. to 13d.... before such captains a fortnight's sail from Port Jackson ye very same sugar 2/6 to 3/— per pound, and now five shillings.

Tea,.... not less essential than the former article .... bought from five shillings to twenty shillings.... fifteen shillings to twenty shillings as soon as it's landed, and at this period can't be had for less than forty shilling per pound .... Soap.... Clothing .... Spirits, generally purchased at from five to ten shillings per gallon is now vended at fifteen shillings per bottle.

Heaven has now sent y'r Excellency as the angel of our deliverance; you will abolish ye evils of which we complain... To you all the avenues of our hearts are opened....

Suffer us, therefore, to say that as the colony is now infested with dealers, pedlars, and extortioners, it is absolutely necessary to extirpate them.... they are the engines of our destruction... They are snares for settlers.... But by what means has a publican in his power to give credit? It's well known there is not one amongst them brought a penny into the colony and in the course of two or three years they can mount a saddle-horse, ride out to a farm and reckon three or four hundred of goats which they call their property. The sober and honest settler, who ought to be considered as the chief support of the colony is by such means often in want of the common necessaries of life while an illiterate grog-shop-keeper is rolling in every luxury that the colony can afford.... permit us to become the purchasers of a proportionable part of a ship's cargo. We will place in the hands of an agent what little payments remain from our ruined property.... your Excellency can run no risk in advancing.... what may be deemed deficient; our grain we will make forthcoming to you as your security.... if.... you'll afford us some house room for the cargo,.... y'r Excellency (will) be furnished with an inventory or invoice of the cargo and price.... you will establish as fixt price by which it is to be retailed by settlers and dealers (if any there be)....[171]

The petition has been quoted at length for its impact survives the clerical ring of Marsden and clearly demonstrates the resentment felt by the settlers. Almost certainly, it was signed by Matthew, he and others calling upon Hunter to be the father-like figure that Phillip had been.

Arndell and Marsden informed Hunter that only four of the original settlers at The Ponds were still there. One of the four, grimly clinging to his patch, was Matthew. The enquiry came to nothing for by now the 'dealers, pedlars and extortioners' were in an unassailable position. And at the head of the monopolists was John Macarthur.

Now let us consider the change that had taken place in the fortunes of the two Elizabeths, Elizabeth Everingham and Elizabeth Macarthur since 1791. The disillusionment at the lack of encouragement given to military settlement and a tendency to regard their sojourn in New Holland as a temporary episode were now things of the past for the Macarthurs. Seven years had rendered them lands and wealth; and Parramatta had become 'home' to Elizabeth Macarthur, her only regret the fact that her children must be sent back to England to be educated. Their farm had grown to between four and five hundred acres and forty servants took care of it and its beautiful orchard and gardens. One hundred and twenty acres were under wheat while there were fifty head of cattle, a dozen horses and a thousand head of sheep; and Macarthur had the only oxen-drawn plough in the colony. A second house in Sydney completed the picture of life as led by the new landed gentry and Elizabeth was duly grateful for the bountiful way in which 'Providence' had dealt with them.[172]

Providence had evidently forgotten the toilers on the hills on the other side of the river. In 1800, therefore, they decided not only to write to the Governor, whom they deemed disinterested or ineffectual or both, but to petition the Duke of Portland himself, repeating their complaints. Matthew signed this petition as a deputy for the settlers at The Field of Mars. They maintained that the high price of labour together with the fixed price of wheat was making it unprofitable to farm. If something were not done, they claimed, they would be reduced to going on to Government stores for subsistence.[173]

Matthew's position deteriorated with the birth of another child, George, on December 9, 1799, (baptized February 16, 1800). Thus the muster taken in July of 1800 shows Everingham with six hogs, four goats, six acres of wheat, five acres of maize and a wife and four children on Government stores.[174]

At last, in September of the new century, the Home government recalled Hunter and replaced him with Philip Gidley King, who set about clearing up the mess as best he could. By now, however, it had become apparent that the land at The Ponds was 'proving to be a very steril spot', to use Matthew's own words. It was worked out with repeated croppings and good for nothing but grazing, though the 1802 Muster shows that Matthew was persisting with it and now had seventeen acres under cultivation, thirteen in wheat and maize, fourteen hogs and now only two people of the stores.[175]

Despite its tendency to flooding, the Hawkesbury River district was proving to be the richest so far discovered and the best place for farming. So 'His Excellency, Governor King, removed [Matthew] to the District of Portland Head at the Hawkesbury', sometime after April, 1802.

Though an entry in a later family Bible is reported to date the move February 1802, it would not appear to have been earlier than April. At that time, the Irish population of the colony having grown to the proportion of a quarter and numbering many who had taken part in the 1798 rebellion in Ireland, those stirrings which finally resulted in the Battle of Vinegar Hill, prompted King to order a Register of Arms. On April 10, 1802, Matthew is recorded under the heading, 'Field of Mars or Northern Boundary District' as having one gun and one pistol.[176]

Matthew seems to have sold the Ponds property to Andrew Hume, the father of the celebrated explorer Hamilton Hume. In 1804, it was auctioned as part of William Cox's estate and was bought by John Savage. Later it is said to have been owned by Samuel Marsden, who used it to graze sheep; and later still, ironically but not unexpectedly, it appears to have been owned by Hannibal Macarthur nephew of John.[177]

As the nineteenth century advanced, roads were made, and eventually, the farm at The Ponds became subdivided into building blocks. The bush is gone and only the creek remains, where children play as the Everingham children must have done. There is no tangible sign of the past nor of the tribulations of the early settlers. Only the Parish Map records the name of the man and his family who were now setting out, once more full of hope, on the road to the 'Oxboro'.

A seed-sower of the 1800 era. *[see p73]*

Leaning About Australia   Paul Hamlyn Pty Ltd.

CHAPTER SIX

Hawkesbury Saga

ALTHOUGH THE sun shone, a chill wind blew on the cheeks of the harvesters as they worked, pulling the cobs from the cornstalks and tossing them into the baskets, then moving the baskets along the row and beginning again. From time to time, Matthew would break into some 'Old Country' song and Elizabeth would join in; or Larry, the assigned convict, would whistle an Irish jig to give rhythm to their task.

After a time, when their work brought them close to the house, Matthew and Elizabeth stopped for a while to straighten their backs and to chat, while looking down the hillside to the river. It was then that William, a seven-years-old, came to the door of the dwelling and called to them from within: 'Mother, Annie won't go to sleep.... and I've been holding her eyes shut for ever so long.'

'Let the child get up then, Liz,' advised Matthew, 'and she'll sleep all the more soundly tonight.'

'Alright,' said Elizabeth, 'she may get up and play with you, but stay close to the house and don't go down to the water.'

The river was a constant worry to Hawkesbury mothers until the children reached the age when they could swim, and even after — for the channel was deep, the current strong and there were often snags. And the children were naturally drawn to it, so great was the fun of hurling in stones and sticks and of watching leaves and pieces of bark go floating off round the bend on their way downstream to the great sea beyond.

So the parents stood and watched as all the young ones, William, George, a plump four-years-old, and little Ann, full of the new joy of walking at eighteen months, trotted out the door and round to the side of the house to play near the woodheap.

'Come on, then,' said Matthew to the rest of his helpers, 'we'd better get on with it. We must get all this maize into the outhouse safe and sound before nightfall.'

'Just a minute!' said Elizabeth, clutching his arm, 'I think I saw something move on the hill.'

Matthew looked in the direction to which she pointed, where huge sandstone boulders marked the limits of his arable land and where the grey eucalypts, soughing with the westerly wind, moved to and fro; but he could see or hear nothing, 'You've got 'native fever', lass,' he said, 'there's nothing there.'

'Matt, fetch the musket, 'Elizabeth persisted, 'it won't do any harm to have it close by. You know how they threatened Will Addy when he was netting ducks in the swamp yesterday se' enight.' So Matthew brought out the old Brown Bess, stood it near a stump and her fears were assuaged.

While this was happening, young Matthew and Sarah, in the middle of the field, had taken advantage of their parents' preoccupation to stop their gathering and pelt each other with some of the poorer husks which had come to be called 'Hawkesbury Ducks'.

'Well, my boy,' said Matthew sternly to his son, 'if cobbing corn doesn't suit your fancy, you might prefer an hour or so with your letters now the house is quiet.'

'No father, I'm sorry,' said the boy, contritely — anything was better than that; and his sister, Sarah, snickered smugly and exchanged a smile with Larry, the convict servant. She need not worry about learning but Matthew senior was determined that his sons should write and count, for they would be farmers and landholders themselves one day; and so poor young Matt spent hours with his slate, trying to meet his father's exacting standards.

'Then stop this sport and do some work,' said Matthew and the little group moved on among the tall brown cornstalks.

So it was that young Matthew, who was now working quickly, was first to reach the far end and to turn in order to go back along the next row. Glancing up as he did so, it was he who saw the first dark figure appear from the boulders.

'Look out, Father! Blacks!' he screamed.

Rushing to the stump for the gun, Matthew called to the children to run for their lives, but it was too late for himself and the other adults. As he turned, a shaft went into his side and he fell. Before Elizabeth or Larry could get to him, a rain of spears came down on them and Elizabeth felt the sharp pain of a wound in the arm. Downed and expecting any moment to be finished off with clubs, the three lay motionless, feigning death.

This ruse, which was their only hope, succeeded, for once the natives were satisfied that they had immobilized the adults, they moved on to the storehouse and the cabin. Then, with the corn screening them, the three sat up to see what should follow.

For a time, the blacks were fully occupied in filling their nets with corn that had been gathered on the previous days, which gave Matthew and Elizabeth some hope that the babies may have fled into the brush in time. Now the savages entered the hut and soon Elizabeth saw one emerge, stuffing a handful of damper into his mouth.

Soon, with bags of sugar and flour over their shoulders and their nets full of cobs, the natives seemed to be on the point of departure, merely looking about to retrieve those spears which had missed their mark. Then, however, one muttered something to the others, put down his load for a moment and went back into the house. Presently, the three white people, again lying motionless, heard the crackling of fire and though their hearts sank, they dared not move.

As the smoke began to billow into the sky and the trio apprehended that the natives had finally gone, they raised themselves and gazed with

Facsimile of an entry in the Register of Marriages of the Church of St. John Parramatta.
[see p67]

'A View of the Governor's House at Rose Hill in the Township of Parramatta' *[see p67]*

'A View of the Banks of the River Hawkesbury in N.S.W.'

horror on the burning outhouse and cabin. Larry uttered a moan as he pulled a splinter out of his thigh but, as soon as he was able and could see Elizabeth tending Matthew, limped towards the house to see what could be done to save it. If all this went up in smoke, Everingham might be unable to keep him and he might be sent to some other master.

Meanwhile, Elizabeth tried to free the spear from Matthew's side while he, crying with pain and anger, gazed at the burning buildings. 'The bougres!' he swore unconsciously. 'The dirty bougres!' as he watched the work of many months disappearing before him.

By now Elizabeth had got the barb out but the wound was bleeding and needed staunching. As she tore a wide strip off her petticoat, the action awakened the memory of once having done the same thing for old Nelly on the *Neptune*. That, too, had been a time of despair, as had been the time when her first baby had died. Then as young Matthew and Sarah came up the hill from the water, bringing the little ones and she realized that all her family were safe, Elizabeth reasoned that she had much for which to be thankful. Houses could be rebuilt and land replanted. It now appeared that Matthew and Sarah had found the children playing near the river in disobedience of Elizabeth's commands, so they had put them all in the boat and headed up river until they had seen the natives retreat.

The shed and house had been burnt to the ground, though Larry had managed to drag a few things away in time. Elizabeth wondered how she was going to feed two men and five children now that her bread and flour were gone and how they would stay warm sleeping out overnight. George began to whimper and Sarah picked him up.

'Sssh!' said Matthew, 'what's that noise?' 'It's alright, Father,' said young Matthew, 'It's Mr Cavanough and Mr Stubbs and Mr Davison, I think.'

'Holla!' then came a call, 'Matt.... Matt Everingham, are ye there?' and Owen Cavanough's large, friendly face could be recognized as he came up the track, followed by the sandy-haired Will Stubbs and Jim Davison.

'Aye, we're all here, thank God, but there's not much left,' said Matthew.

'My God, there's not, is there?' said Owen Cavanough, when they arrived, his voice a mixture of sympathy and horror. 'We were coming to warn you and Addy that they were on the rampage again, for John Howe had a visit and they fetched him a spear too.'

'Well, Will Addy will have seen this from his place but he dursn't move in case it's his turn next,' said Matthew. 'We had no chance. The devils came up over the top of the hill and rushed us from the rocks.'

Then they all stood silent for a while, regarding the smoking ashes. 'Good God!' repeated Jim Davison, shaking his head, unable to think of anything more adequate to say.

'Well, it's put me back ten years,' said Matthew, clearing his throat.

'I thought I'd finished with all this. We always had them around at harvest time in the early days back at the Ponds, but I didn't bargain for it again.'

'Never mind, man,' said Owen, coming over to the boulder upon which Matthew was leaning and putting his arm round his neighbour's shoulder. 'You can all bed down with us and Will here until we get you a proper roof for your heads again. Come on now, you children, we've got a couple of boats down below.'

'Something will have to be done,' said Jimmy Davison, ignoring this and reluctant to leave the scene until they had thought their way out of the problem. 'For a start, we've all decided to ask the Governor for permission to fire on the natives on sight. And it might help to get the redcoats out from Green Hills to teach them a lesson.'

'Redcoats are a waste of time,' said Matthew. 'The natives can smell them ten miles off and dodge them silly in the bush. What we need is neighbours, people around us as we had at the Ponds, so that one can help the other.'

'Well, the ground's measured up for them,' said Jimmy, 'but they're all sitting back and letting us clear the way first, it seems.'

'You get nothing in this country without work, hardship and danger,' said Matthew. 'I've had enough of being up here with just a handful of us against a tribe. And as soon as I'm well enough to get over the Cattai, I'm going to tell Tom Arndell as much.'

'Well, in the meantime,' said Owen, 'put your arms round our shoulders, Matt and let us get you to our place, first. We'd best get Arndell to have a look at this wound anyway, so you can tell him then.'

So they helped him down the track and into one of the boats. Then Jim Davison headed off downstream to Addy's to let him know that the Everinghams were safe and to stay the night there in case there was more trouble.

By this time the baby Ann had fallen asleep in Sarah's arms and the others were quiet but young Matthew, seated alongside his sisters in Owen Cavanough's rowboat, was deep in thought. Just before fleeing the attack, he had recognized one black as the father of Damulwaree, who had taught him to swim and to paddle a canoe last year when the natives had been friendly. Damulwaree would eat his, Matthew's, bread tonight. But he knew from the men's conversation that the natives would not have the advantage for long. Soon the white men would organise themselves in ways unknown to the natives. And despite everything, it saddened him to think of the bloodshed that would ensue and of the inevitability of its outcome.

* * *

THE SPEARING of Matthew, Elizabeth and their servant and the firing of their house and barn occurred on Tuesday, May 29 or Wednesday May 30 of 1804. For a report of it appeared in the *Sydney Gazette* of Sunday, June 3, 1804, stating that the news of the attacks was received by Governor King on the preceding Thursday evening.[178]

As the reader may be curious as to how the background to these stories is built up when often the initial source of information bears little detail, the following may be of interest. The weather was able to be checked in the *Sydney Gazette* and found to be 'fair' for May 29 and May 30, with the winds from the west and south west and the temperature varying from 53° to 66°F on those days. It is known that it was harvest time for maize, that the natives used blankets and nets in such raids, that the Troopers were sent immediately the Governor heard of the attacks and that Matthew did have an assigned Irish convict at the time, Lawrence (or Larry) Byrnes.[179]

That Matthew had a musket (and a pistol) and that it had probably been issued in Phillip's time, we saw in the last chapter. This was almost certainly a 'Brown Bess', the general name given to four models of a flintlock musket because of its walnut stock.

It was the weapon that had been used on both sides in the American Revolutionary War. And the Marine and Militia Pattern, with a shortened barrel of 42″ was most likely the arm of the Royal Marines who came with the First Fleet. Later the Short Land Pattern was used by regiments serving in the colony.

The effective range of the musket was eighty yards and it was, of course, muzzle loading, the method being as follows.

The settler had a powder horn which could be strung around his neck and attached to this, on a short cord, was the tip of another horn. Using this as a measure, he dropped a quantity of powder down the bore of the gun, then rammed wadding or tow down tight onto it with the gun's new-type steel ramrod. Then he wrapped a ball in a bit of cloth and pushed this firmly down on top.

With his firing pan filled with powder and his gun in the safety position on half cock — this is how he kept it while walking through the bush hunting, or how Matthew would have had it near the stump — he was ready to fire his one charge at a moment's notice.

Obviously, the reloading of the musket, (or a pistol), took time. A soldier, using time-saving cartridges, was expected to be able to deliver one shot every fifteen seconds in concerted fire. Firing at will, he could probably manage six loads a minute.

In emergencies, he or the settler used a quicker way. In the settler's case, this was to use his palm as a rough measure and then throw the powder and the ball down the barrel. Then he rammed the butt on the ground to seat the ball on the powder. The touch-hole being wide enough on a worn 'Bess', some of the powder would be jarred into the firing pan which would save cleaning and refilling it. Then if he had a nice sharp flint, his gun would fire. He could continue this for a short time only, due to fouling from the black powder and it was very bad for the gun.

Even this method took time so that the gun was of limited protection to the isolated settler in a surprise attack and against numbers, even if he got the chance to use it. On the Hawkesbury, particularly below Sackville, because of the distance between each area of alluvial flat and the fact that sometimes one grant absorbed the entire area, the settlers were particularly isolated.

So, in the same issue of the *Sydney Gazette* that recorded Matthew's experience, General Orders were issued that every person who had lands measured below Cathai Creek [sic] was to reside on them immediately for the protection of the settlers from the ravages of the natives. The magistrate at the Hawkesbury, Dr Thomas Arndell, was to report the names of absentees after the ensuing week. The newspaper stated that 'neighbouring' settlers came to the succour of the victims. James Davison, Owen Cavanough and William Stubbs were selected as Good Samaritans just for the story.[180]

There is only one place on Matthew's property where his dwelling could have been located and rough stone ruins of a house which could have been the foundations of the original hut still remain. Backing on to this are the 'tremendous rocks' which Matthew later described when he applied for a new grant of land. These would seem to have afforded the cover which the natives needed to effect their surprise attack. Sackville Reach or Portland Head, as it was then called, is still relatively sparsely settled. Unlike The Ponds, Progress seems to have passed it by. One cold May day, when a small interested group visited the site, the same vigorous south-westerly wind that so successfully disguised the approach of the predators, blew through the tall gums on the hillside. We could see and feel it all.[181]

In the story, the rescuers arrive and the children escape by boat, for every settler who could afford to buy or who could build one, had a boat for transporting stores from Green Hills, (Windsor), and for communication with his neighbours. Since we suspect Matthew to have helped in the building of Australia's first boat and his sons were later boat-builders, it is highly probable that he had a boat of his own construction. These were river people and just about every event in their lives involved the noise of clanking rowlocks or the sight of a small gaff-rigged sailer coming up or down the Reaches.

On April 5, 1804, seven weeks before the time of our story, Governor King had ordered all boats on the Hawkesbury to be registered by Andrew Thompson. the Head Constable. The settlers were 'not to suffer their boats to be rowing about after dark' and they were to secure them with a chain and lock, taking the oars to their houses. They were also to report or detain all suspicious boats. These instructions were to prevent escaping convicts from stealing the craft, as had happened more than once before. The Irish prisoners who had staged the uprising at Toongabbee on March 4, had been on their way to the Hawkesbury when they were overtaken and defeated at 'Vinegar Hill', present day Rouse Hill.[182]

The newspaper, *The Sydney Gazette and New South Wales Advertiser,* in which all such orders appeared, was now a fact of life for eager readers in the 'interior'. Published by an emancipist, George Howe, the first issue had appeared a year earlier on March 5, 1803. Though primarily the means by which the Government made known such promulgations, it also contained items of overseas news, such as the Battle of Trafalgar, weather and crop news, private advertisements and letters from colonists. At the Hawkesbury, it was distributed by Andrew Thompson and when the June 3 issue came down the river, the Everingham children must have been rather excited to see the account of their great adventure in print and the copy would long be preserved.[183]

Matthew and Elizabeth appear, as the historian A.J. Gray has written in the *Australian Dictionary of Biography,* to have been 'well established' at Portland Head when the attack took place, (May 1804), and had moved there from The Ponds sometime after April, 1802. The land grant is dated April 28, 1803, but it is possible either that Matthew was living on the land before it was officially granted or that he did not take it up until later in that year. The fact that the child, Ann's baptism on August 28, 1803, appears in the Register of St John's Parramatta, does not necessarily mean that she was baptized at the church and the family still living at Parramatta. All baptisms at the Hawkesbury were registered in St John's register by the Reverend Samuel Marsden until the Parish of St Matthew, Windsor, was inaugurated and its register commenced in 1810. We know that 'Everingham's Farm' at The Ponds was already part of William Cox's Estate when it was advertized to be auctioned on April 1, 1804, indicating that Matthew had vacated it some months previously, so that it would seem that the move to the Hawkesbury took place sometime during 1803.[184]

Although boats were constantly sailing up to the Hawkesbury from Sydney, it is most likely that the family travelled by road to Green Hills from The Ponds, perhaps hiring a cart for their few possessions. Matthew and the convict servant would have gone ahead, probably living in a tent until they had erected a dwelling for the family. The walk from Parramatta to the Hawkesbury took eight hours, so Elizabeth and the children would break their journey, either camping on the roadside or staying in someone's hut.[185]

The family at the date of the story, May, 1804, numbered seven. Matthew, described as an 'industrious' settler in the Governor's Return of Land granted from 1800 to 1803, would have been thirty-five years old and Elizabeth about thirty-one. The five children ranged in age from Sarah, eleven years, Matthew James, nine years, William, seven years, George, four and a half years, down to the baby, Ann, now eighteen months old. A new baby arrived every two years but by now the older ones would help with the farming. Each one would have his or her chores such as chopping wood, carrying water from the river, laying the fire and cleaning the fireplace, washing and mending. Like country children in big families ever since, as soon as they were free, they would probably head for the bush or the river, lest by lingering about the house, they would be given another job to do. Up river at present day Wilberforce, two brothers, the sons of John Howorth, were minding their father's flock one day in October, 1804, when a fatal accident occurred. The elder boy, John aged 11 years, had put his arm into a hollow log, in which holes had been cut for the purpose of searching for the 'bandy coot', when he was bitten by a black snake and died within twelve hours. From now on, at least the Everingham children would not need to be cautioned about the natives, signs of whose former habitation on their own property and nearby were obvious from caves in which were, (and still are), the drawings of hands.[186]

The attack on Matthew Everingham and John Howe came after a period of friendly relations with the natives following conflict at the time of settlement around Green Hills in the nineties. The forays occurred as a direct result of new settlement in the Portland Head area whereby the natives were once again driven from the river banks where their food was procured.

In June, 1804, the month following the attack on Matthew, William Knight, who had also recently been robbed, prepared a fraudulent memorial asking permission for the settlers to shoot the natives who were frequenting their grounds at sight, because the latter had threatened to fire the settlers' wheat when it ripened. As a result, Governor King sent for three natives to discuss the problem. They told him that they did not like being driven from the river banks and that many of the settlers were angered at their presence and did frequently fire on them. They said that if they could have the lower part of the river they would not trouble the white man again; and King assured them that there would be no more settlement in this region.

It is clear from the dates of the land grants, however, that much of the good riverland between Portland Head and present day Wiseman's Ferry had already been granted and the grantees were at this very moment, being ordered to reside thereon. Also, in September, the Governor directed that the *Ann*, pinnace, should trace the Hawkesbury from Portland Head to Mullet (Dangar) Island, to estimate the area of cultivable land. This she did for twenty-five miles, with no doubt, the natives watching her all the way.[187]

It was therefore not surprising that the following year, a native by the name of 'Branch Jack' led his fellows in a series of raids on the settlers in his own neighbourhood of 'the Branch' or the present day Colo River. On April 10, 1805, he went to the farm of John Llewellyn, one of the military settlers, whose grant was later Matthew Chaseling's *Australian Farm* in the Leet's Vale area. When Llewellyn invited the native to share dinner in a field with him and his labouring servant, Branch Jack seized the settler's musket and powder horn, made off with a loud yell and returned with twenty of his companions. Both Llewellyn and his servant were speared and attacked with tomahawks, Llewellyn fatally. The servant's body was hurled down to the river bank, where he lay for two days before being picked up by a passing boat. The same day, Thynne Adlam's farmhouse, on the next promontory upstream at Upper Half Moon Reach, was set fire to, the owner hacked to pieces and his scattered limbs found in the ashes.[188]

Following this, armed boats were sent out from Green Hills in a vain effort to catch the culprits and then Major George Johnston of the New South Wales Corps was sent to enquire into the extent of damage to the various settlers' properties.[189]

A month later in May, 1805, back in the Portland Head area, the natives surrounded William Stubbs's house while he was absent. His wife, Sarah, ran towards the river to jump in but one of the natives assured her she would not be harmed, they merely gutted the house of its entire contents. Stubbs (and others?) later chased them into the 'Mountains' but failed to catch them. It was the fourth time in a year they had been attacked and plundered. That night, Sarah Stubbs set off for Parramatta to replace their immediate needs and during her absence, her husband was the next day drowned by being 'entangled in the reeds' after falling out of a boat, the calamity being witnessed by his eight years old son, William. (The baby daughter of this family, Keturah was one day to marry George Everingham).[190]

A week later, on May 31, 1805, while Henry Lamb, whose farm was just around the bend from Matthew's, was away from home, the natives began kindling their fires on a nearby ridge in a seemingly peaceful manner. Then they suddenly commenced an assault on the house, hurling firebrands by means of the 'mantang' or 'fishgig'. Seeing smoke come out of the house, Mrs Lamb rushed into the blaze to rescue her sleeping child. The Lambs lost their house, barns, barley stack and cask of meat. Once again, the natives eluded pursuit in 'the Mountains' by a feint and struck off for the head of the Nepean. The same month, William Knight at Boston's Reach, (whose farm would later belong to Matthew the Younger), was once again plundered, this time of his musket, bedding, wearing apparel, tea and sugar to the value of £100.[191]

After the Lambs were burnt out, Abraham Youler, two properties up river, took the family in. Then on June 22, he too was attacked and his barn and stacks burnt down. The Lambs were now taken in by Thomas Chaseland, (Chaseling) and Margaret McMahon next door. All this while, a little thirteen years old native girl had been a member of the Lambs' household. She had been rescued 'in the woods' as a baby from her dead mother's breast and was a 'stranger to the dialects and manners of her own kind'. It was now discovered that she had become friendly with a young local native, that she had instigated the firing of Lambs' and Youlers', being detected in the act of putting a firebrand to Chaseling's house.

Following this, nine natives were apprehended, taken to Parramatta and two freed on the promise of them helping to search for the notorious 'Mosquito' and Branch Jack. The natives on the road from the Hawkesbury expressed a desire to 'Come In' to meet the Governor at Parramatta and were ordered not to be molested, after which it was announced that a reconciliation had taken place.[192]

But the Branch natives seem to have eschewed this arrangement. Seeing was believing. As the settlers took up their land and an increasing number of boats passed up and down, whether with grain to Sydney or on sealing voyages, it was clear that even the lower part of the river would be lost to them and they grew desperate. In early September, 1805, the *Hawkesbury* lay off Mangrove Point, (seemingly the entrance to Mangrove Creek), which is downstream from present day Wiseman's Ferry. Sleeping down below with Pendegrass, the captain, and the crew was a 'salt boiler' in the employ of Andrew Thompson. This man had set out for Thompson's salt pans at Mullet (Dangar) Island, but being menaced by the natives, had accepted an offer to go in the *Hawkesbury*. As he and the others slept, Branch Jack, Woglomigh and a party of natives paddled out to make a surprise attack. The natives were beaten off and Branch Jack swam for the bank. As he rose to breathe he was fired at three times and died on the bank before his father and the rest of the tribe.[193]

Though the Branch natives were at first blamed for the murder of William Yardley, who lived at the junction of Sussex and Cambridge Reaches, for his 'activity' had been a constant curb to their excesses, it later seemed that his wife, Mary and a convict servant, Henry Murray, had been responsible for his grisly end. John Campbell, his neighbour on the south side, had pulled Yardley's body out of the burning house and suspicious of foul play during the Coroner's Inquest, had alerted Dr Arndell and chief constable Andrew Thompson, who now took the wife into custody. The interred remains were taken up and the removal of a head bandage revealed an aperture in the skull into which cloths had been stuffed, which went to prove that a white woman could behave as barbarously to her spouse as any black savage to an enemy.[194]

Nevertheless, it will be seen from all this that Matthew and the other settlers were living their lives in constant danger of being murdered and their property destroyed by the natives, at least throughout 1804 and 1805. There was also the danger of escaped convicts, sometimes desperate men, referred to as 'bush-rangers' for the first time in 1805. Some settlers harboured them and in January, 1806, one, Russell, was found to be doing household work in the house of John Campbell at the Branch, the suspicious neighbour referred to above. He incurred the twofold penalty for employing a person without seeing his pass and employing a convict absconding from public labour, for which he was fined £20 'to the Orphans', that is, to the benefit of the orphan home established by Mrs King.[195]

Despite the dangers and great efforts needed to establish and re-establish farms, agriculture at the Hawkesbury promised to be more successful than at The Ponds, for the rich soil yielded much wheat and maize. Under Governor King, (1800 to 1806), the settlers were receiving fairer treatment and the monopolies of the officers and others had begun to crumble. New people were moving in and a community at Portland Head was taking shape. Families, necessarily interdependent, were forming associations that would last the best part of two centuries to the present day. Let us take a closer look, then at Matthew's small menage at Portland Head or Sackville Reach, as it was referred to for the first time in 1805, and at his neighbours in the district.

The original Hawkesbury Everingham property, (Portion 107, Parish of Wilberforce, County of Cook), today belongs to Sackville Ski Gardens and is located on the Tizzana Road just before one comes to the Sackville ferry. A small palm tree grows near the stone foundations where sandstone boulders edge the hills to the back. The house which the family would re-construct after the attack was a simple wooden edifice, probably slab built, with a shingled roof and it may have had a verandah in front. There were outhouses and an orchard. Scarcely would the house be rebuilt before Elizabeth would find herself pregnant with a new baby daughter, named for herself, Elizabeth, who was born on June 10, 1805. Perhaps because the birth took place at the height of the native attacks at Sackville, the baptism was not performed until the child was eighteen months old on December 7, 1806, when it was recorded in the register of St John's, Parramatta.[196]

The accompanying map shows Matthew's neighbours at this time. The dates of the grants do not necessarily signify the date of occupation but it is reasonable to assume that most of these people were here by the end of 1804 in response to the Governor's orders to reside and certainly, they were all in occupation by the time of the Muster of August, 1806. Incidentally, Matthew's land had been surveyed by Charles Grimes on April 27, 1803 and inside the front cover of his Field Book, Grimes noted that he also had to survey lands for 'A. Yoular, Tho. Chestland, James Dunn, Hy. Lamb, Cheshire, Wm. Hubbard, Wm. Addy and Yeoman', which he seems to have done at the same time.[197]

As the book progresses, the reason for the present in-depth study of the settlers and the location of their lands will be appreciated for certain people and properties will be mentioned time and again. Most of the following information has come from the *T.D. Mutch Indexes* to early land grants, to the 1802, 1806 and 1820 Musters, and to Births, Deaths and Marriages, from Goodin's *Index to the 1814 Muster,* from the 1828 Census, the *Registers of Assignment* and from various issues of the *Sydney Gazette,* all in the Mitchell Library, Sydney. In cases where the name is a common one, it has been difficult to be precise about the settlers.

So new was settlement north of Portland Head, where Matthew lived, that farms were described by the name of the Reach on which they lay, by the description, 'near the Branch' or quite often merely as 'Down the River'. The ultimate Portion numbers used on Lands

Department Parish maps are supplied for the reader's convenience.

Furthest down the river, as we have seen to their cost, were John Llewellyn, (Portion 2, Parish of Hawkesbury, County of Hunter), and Thynne, ('Feen') Adlam, (Portion 6, Ph. Hawkesbury), on Lower and Upper Half Moon Reaches respectively, both former members of the New South Wales Corps. After their deaths, Llewellyn's farm passed into the hands of his sister-in-law, Mary, widow of Joseph Llewellyn, then to her son, John Bray and then to his son, Joshua Bray. Adlam's property went to John Pender, then to James McGlade and the Reverend Samuel Marsden.

Furthest out on the other bank of the river, that is, on the southern side of Liverpool Reach, were Richard Reynolds, (Portion 60, Ph. Cornelia), who called his property *Flat Rock* and who would seem to have come on the *Atlantic* in 1791 and Michael Duggan, (Portion 59, Ph. Cornelia), who also described his farm as being at the Flat Rock. The remarkable natural formation is actually opposite both properties, is a favourite fishing spot and gave its name to the Reach for many years.

On the northern side of the entrance to the Branch or Colo River were Thomas Jones, (Portion 18, Ph. Hawkesbury, Co. Hunter), on what would later be known as Paradise Point and William Macdonald, (Portion 19, Ph. Hawkesbury), both of whom are thought to have been privates in the Corps. Jones was possibly ex the *Scarborough* of the Second Fleet, 1790, while Macdonald would seem to have been Dublin tried and transported in the first Irish ship, the *Queen* in 1791.

On the first promontory of the Branch was Peter Hibbs, (Portion 48, Ph. Meehan, Co. Cook), a former sailor from the *Sirius* of the First Fleet, who had been a settler at Norfolk Island. There is a legend and it is quite feasible, that Hibbs had first seen this land as a member of Governor Phillip's exploratory party in July, 1789. It has also been written that Hibbs was settled at the mouth of Mangrove Creek by 1806 but this is untrue. On the next promontory in the Branch, Hibbs's son, George, had been granted one hundred acres, (Portion 21, Ph. Hawkesbury), while on Peter Hibbs's eastern boundary, right at the mouth of the Colo, was James Sherwin, (Portion 49, Ph. Meehan), referred to many years later as 'Sergeant Sherwain' and therefore also thought to have been in the Corps.[198]

Opposite Sherwin, on the other side of the river where the Lower Portland ferry is today, was John Brown, (Portion 58, Ph. Cornelia, Co. Cumberland), who had come free as a marine on the *Scarborough* in the First Fleet and married his wife, Judith, sometime after 1808, when she arrived as a convict in the *Speke*.

Below Brown, on a promontory to become known as Maun's Point, where the Lower Portland Methodist Church stands today, were Joseph Maund, (Portion 57, Ph. Cornelia), an expiree from the *Matilda* in the Third Fleet and John Cross, (Portion 56, Ph. Cornelia), transported in the *Alexander* of the First Fleet, who had also been in the Corps. On the same side of the river, where *Dargle* Ski Gardens is now located, was

Bartholomew (or George) Morley, (Portion 54, Ph. Cornelia), who would seem to have come free on the *H.M.S. Glatton* in 1803.

Opposite Morley was William Yardley, (Portion 42, Ph. Meehan), transported in the *Surprize* of the Second Fleet, 1790, who was murdered, after which thirty acres of his land were sold to Thomas Jones. Next to him was John Campbell, (Portion 43, Ph. Meehan), who may have come in the First Fleet and been in the corps. On Campbell's southern boundary was Richard Evans, (Portion 44, Ph. Meehan), a discharged corporal from the Corps.

On the other side of 'Boston Reach', now Cumberland Reach, was William Knight, (Portion 53, Ph. Cornelia), ex the *Surprize* of the Second Fleet and William Smith, (Portion 52, Ph. Cornelia), who may have been ex the *Scarborough* of the First Fleet.

Crossing the river again, on the west bank of Kent Reach were Philip Roberts, (Portion 45, Ph. Meehan), Samuel Little and James Bradley on Portions 46 and 47. Roberts had been transported in the *Pitt* (1792), had married Sarah Geddings, (*Mary Ann,* 1791) and had also been a private in the Corps. He later became District Constable for the area and lived to the age of ninety-four, dying in 1849. Sarah Roberts lived until 1845 and both are buried at St John's, Wilberforce. Samuel Little had also been a private in the Corps and when he died about 1811, Roberts seems to have been his executor. Bradley, an expiree, may have been the person of that name to have come in the *Scarborough* of the First Fleet.

On the promontory formed by Kent and Sackville Reaches and at once opposite these three and Addy, Hubbard and Everingham on the other side, was John Yeomans, (Portion 51, Ph. Cornelia), who was about thirty-seven years old in 1804 and had been transported by the *Britannia* in 1791. On July 1, 1805, he set out from his farm with two others and sailed a small open boat containing twelve bushels of wheat to Sydney in the short space of two days, returning the same way.[199]

Opposite Yeomans on the creek that bears his name was William Addy, (Portion 104, Ph. Wilberforce, Co. Cook), a character used in the story because we are certain that he was there at that date. In the issue of the *Sydney Gazette* which related Matthew's misfortune, Addy was mentioned as the owner of a remarkable Mountain parrot which he had taught to talk. He had been transported in the *Royal Admiral* in 1792, had been a private in the Corps and would become District Constable at Portland Head about 1810, but died and was buried, aged forty, on January 22, 1812. In the meantime, in 1807, he had married Elizabeth Crouch, ex the *Earl Cornwallis,* 1801, who stayed in the district and was the ancestress of the Tuckerman family.[200]

Between Addy and Matthew Everingham was William Hubbard, (Portion 106, Ph. Wilberforce), whose history had paralleled Matthew's in many ways. Tried at Surrey, Hubbard had been convicted for seven years and transported in the *Scarborough* in the First Fleet. He had probably worked at the Government Farm at Parramatta under

Henry Edward Dodd and had married Mary Goulding, (Second Fleet?) on December 19, 1790. He had been settled on land at The Ponds on the same day as Everingham in July 1791. During the short time he had been in Sydney Cove, he had been one of the original members of the Night Watch, established August 7, 1789 and later became a private in the Corps.

Everingham's land was bounded on the north east by a block of 115 acres, which, according to *T.D. Mutch's* cards relevant to these grants, was the first block granted at Portland Head, apparently to John Palmer. It was exchanged with him for land at the Limestone Plains and in Governor Hunter's Return of September 5, 1795, appears as granted jointly to three privates of the New South Wales Corps, Thomas Cheshire, (65 acres), John Pollard, (25 acres), and William Hambleton, (25 acres). Cheshire, (ex the *Neptune,* Second Fleet?), married Ann Teasdel, (*Lady Juliana,* 1790?) on October 6, 1790. Hambleton, also known as Hamilton, would seem to have married Margaret Marshall on December 20, 1795. The joint block was known as *Cheshire's* and is numbered C/1, C/2 and C/3 on the Wilberforce Parish map.

Opposite the three soldiers, on the other side of Portland Reach, were Henry Lamb, James Dunne, Thomas Chaseling and Abraham Yoular, (Portions 47, 48, 49 and 55, Ph. Cornelia). Lamb was transported by the *Albermarle* in the Third Fleet, 1791, became a private in the Corps and was a (Windsor?) constable in 1814. Dunne and Chaseling have already been introduced but it is interesting that Chaseling was to be appointed 'Constable for the Castlereagh District from Little Catteye Creek [sic] to the lowermost settlers on both sides of the Hawkesbury River' on July 6, 1806, just after the 1806 flood.

In this same year, Yoular's farmhouse was robbed of a palampore, (a kind of chintz bed cover made in India), a pair of duck sheets, a pair of calico sheets, 3 blankets, a linen shirt, a muslinet waistcoat, a muslin half handkerchief, a pillow case, a piece of nankeen and a scarlet cloth waistcoat pattern, indicating a degree of comfort in his home which was probably common to the other settlers at Portland Head. Yoular died about 1809 and his son, Alex., sold his farm to John Howe.[201]

This brings us to the *Coromandel* people, stout-hearted free settlers from the English-Scottish border, who had migrated as a group and arrived in New South Wales on June 13, 1802. On the way down towards Green Hills, back again on Matthew's side of the river were Andrew Johnston, James Mein, John H. Johnstone and John Turnbull, (Portions 125, 119, 118 and 488, Ph. Wilberforce).

Turnbull's house still stands, though in a derelict condition, but from there one looks down and across river to William Stubbs's property. He had also been an immigrant on the *Coromandel* and after his drowning, the property stayed in his family, farmed first by his wife and later by their eldest son, William.

Crossing the river again and adjacent to John Turnbull were the properties of John Howe, (Portion 101, Ph. Wilberforce), who was speared at the same time as Matthew, James Davison, (Portion 102, Ph. Wilberforce), both of these from the *Coromandel* and Owen Cavanough, a First Fleet sailor from the *Sirius*. (Portion 103). Cavanough, like Peter Hibbs, had been granted land at Norfolk Island after the wreck of the *Sirius* but had returned to the mainland in 1798 and seems to have been first renting land from John Boston at what is now Pitt Town. Margaret Dowling, (or Darnell), an expiree who had been transported in the *Prince of Wales* in the First Fleet was his life's partner and Cavanough, being a seaman, supported her and his children by running his boat to Sydney with Hawkesbury grain. The vessel was of a fair size and well found, for a party of escaping convicts boarded her one night in 1798 off Mullet Island and carried her and a smaller boat out to sea. The party numbered seven and once outside, they transferred to the smaller boat for fear that if Cavanough's vessel ran aground, they would not be able to launch her again. What happened to the boat is not recorded but Cavanough was granted land at the same time as the *Coromandel* people and was later to give the land on which they built the Ebenezer stone church, designed by Andrew Johnston. In the early days, a temporary slab hut, thatched with grass, formed the meeting place for the pious group, while the first regular Sunday services were held across the river at the homestead of Dr Thomas Arndell.[202]

Dr Arndell lived just down river from another *Coromandel* settler, George Hall, and had earlier assisted the Reverend Samuel Marsden with the enquiry into the grievances of The Ponds settlers. Present day Cattai Creek is named after his six hundred acres grant, 'Caddie', whence he had come from Parramatta and where he was to live until his death in 1821.[203]

This by no means covers the settlers in the Ebenezer, Wilberforce, Pitt Town area, the history of whom has been written elsewhere, but these people and a few others whose lands are shown on the map are those who most concern us. What we are doing now is setting the scene for the rest of the chapter and indeed, for the rest of the book. As well, before moving on to 1806, when a great rising of the river was to set in train circumstances and events which were to drastically influence the settlers' lives and the history of the colony as a whole, it is necessary to travel up river even further, to the village of Green Hills, to complete our background.

When Matthew and his servant arrived at the South Creek of the Hawkesbury for the first time on their way to take up the new land grant at Sackville, (1803), they would have hailed the ferryman to take them over the water to the Green Hills at a cost of fourpence each. This ferry or floating bridge had been the idea of Andrew Thompson, chief constable at Green Hills and reflected the enterprising character of the emancipist Scot, who had come to the settlement six years before in 1796, at the age of twenty-three.

As a result of his own efforts and the encouragement of Governors Hunter and King, Thompson had become very prosperous. King had by now appointed him assessor of the grain grown in the district, in order that the small farmers could be sure of getting their wheat accepted at the Government Granary, where formerly there had been a monopoly. Thompson was to become spokesman and leader for men such as Matthew Everingham of the small emancipist settler class and plays an important part in the story of Matthew, later on.

Before reaching the ferry crossing at South Creek, the Parramatta-Hawkesbury road wound through Thompson's property, the famous West Hill Farm, which ran from the present McGrath's Hill to the river. Here Matthew would have seen a mansion known as 'The Red House' from the fiery colour of its locally made bricks. Little did he imagine, as he walked through what were the colony's finest wheat fields, that he and his family would one day live at the West Hill farm. At this time his knowledge of the Hawkesbury would be limited to the reports he had heard in Parramatta, perhaps from James Ruse or Charles Williams, who had given up their Parramatta farms to try this new district and had been given the first grants here in 1794. He would have heard of the disastrous 1799 floods when the river had risen fifty feet in a few hours and the Government storehouse, kept by one William Baker, had been swept away. But he would know that, despite the flood danger, nearly a thousand people were now in the Hawkesbury district, which had become the food bowl of the colony.[204]

As he gained the top of the hill on the other side of the South Creek ferry, Matthew would stop to refresh himself at Thompson's store and perhaps stay overnight before going on to Portland Head by boat along the river. In half an hour, he could have walked around Green Hills, which at this time consisted merely of a small cluster of buildings. 'Government House' was a weatherboard, shingled cottage next door to Thompson's place, which stood on an acre of ground. This Crown Land had been leased to Thompson by Governmor Hunter in 1799 in order that he could establish a store to supply reasonably priced goods to the settlers who, like Matthew, had been the victims of the officers' trading monopoly. Next door again was a cluster of huts which formed the barracks for a detachment of the New South Wales Corps and nearby was the Government Granary. Thompson's store was sited on the eastern side of the square that now bears his name and faced the main Hawkesbury River. In what is now Thompson's square was a bell which called the convicts from their huts to work on the Government farm at Cornwallis and ominously, a whipping post and stocks.[205]

Down at the wharf on the Hawkesbury proper, Thompson's first ship, the *Hope,* might well have been moored. The river was navigable for large ships for at least sixty years after this time. Thompson built two other sloops at Windsor after the *Hope* was wrecked in May, 1803, the *Nancy* and the *Hawkesbury* and these and the *Speedwell,* (at first owned by Captain Grono), were often to be seen passing Matthew's property at Portland Head, as were the sealers of Henry Kable and Jonathan Griffiths, (*Scarborough* 1790), and of course the Government vessels.

This was the Green Hills of 1803. In 1804, after Matthew and Elizabeth were settled at Portland Head, Governor King ordered a brick building to be erected as a church and school and this was later used as a courthouse as well.

The Everingham children would have been brought to town only occasionally, as when perhaps they were inoculated against Small Pox sometime in 1804 by the Governor's orders; but it is unlikely that they would have attended the Green Hills school at this time. As the story shows, and we know from her marriage record, Sarah the eldest daughter was unable to write, for in the years when she might have learnt, she lived too far away from a school. Somehow, Matthew James II, William, George and Ann all became literate and one assumes that Matthew, senior taught the boys and that perhaps Ann might have attended school at Ebenezer. Although the Ebenezer chapel-school could not have been used until after 1809 (when Ann would have been seven years old), it seems likely that the children of the district were receiving instruction, perhaps in the temporary meeting house there. The neighbouring *Coromandel* folk regarded education as the way to grace and the group responsible for the building of Ebenezer in 1809 designated themselves 'The Portland Head Society for the Promoting of Christian Knowledge and Education of Youth'. But this was in the future and much was to happen between 1804 and the erection of the stone chapel-school.[206]

The 1805 harvest was a good one and by January, 1806, prospects were bright for Matthew and the other Hawkesbury farmers. Then in March, 1806, as was to be the case so often in the future, the river suddenly rose and thirty-six thousand acres of farmland were flooded to a depth of eighteen feet, the recorded high water mark being forty-five feet. At this time of the year a good deal of the wheat had already been harvested and sent to Sydney but there was still much lying in stacks, while the maize was just ready to harvest.

To read the hastily written letters to Governor King from Dr Arndell and the Reverend Samuel Marsden, by now also a landholder in the district, is to recapture the urgency of these days. On March 9, Arndell wrote that he had loaded the *Hawkesbury* with barley but the current stopped the boat getting in to collect the wheat that had been thrashed. On March 22, the flood reached a dangerous height and all the settlers were repairing to the high grounds as fast as they could be brought off. On Sunday morning, March 23, at six o'clock, the flood was now ten feet higher than ever known and, wrote Arndell: '...the whole exhibits a scene of horror and misery not to be described.'[207]

Over two hundred wheat stacks were swept away in one day together with stock of all descriptions. One man, Thomas Leeson, his family and eleven others, took refuge on a barley mow which was then carried off seven miles down river to be caught by a rowboat and brought in to John Howorth's. People clinging to rooftops and trees were rescued by Andrew Thompson and others.

'Sir,' wrote Marsden to King on March 28, to give the Governor an up to the minute account of what was happening, 'We have just returned from examining the lower part of the river from Green Hills to Addy's.... Everingham, Howe, Johnson, Main (Mein), and Hall have a great part of their wheat saved. Bradley, (K)Night and others down there have lost their all.'[208]

Though his wheat had been saved, Matthew's maize would have been buried in mud but he was better off than most for, when the Muster was taken in August, 1806, none of his family or servants were yet victualled by the Government store. This Muster showed that he had replanted eleven acres in wheat, six in maize, one in barley and had half-an-acre each of potatoes and orchard. He had eight male and ten female hogs, which he must have managed to get to higher ground before the inundation; but he had only three bushels of maize in hand.

The details of the Muster demonstrate Matthew's prosperity even allowing for the flood. One entry shows that he had one convict servant, whom he victualled himself and that he employed a free man. A separate account of males at this muster lists three people working for Matthew in all. One was James Thomas, the free man or expiree, who was in fact a First Fleeter from the *Alexander*. The second was Lawrence Byrne, aged about thirty-seven, an Irishman transported from Cork on the *Atlas* in 1802, the 'Larry' of the story. The third, curiously enough, was a lifer from London, transported on the *Fortune* and newly arrived on July 12, 1806, named John Rimes. It would seem that the muster details regarding Matthew were taken just prior to the assignment of John Rimes to him.[209]

Rimes had appeared at the Old Bailey for Larceny but found 'Not Guilty' two years before his final conviction. One wonders whether it was coincidence that he was indented servant to Matthew and Elizabeth, (nee Rimes), and that the last Everingham son was named 'John'. Rimes disappears from the records after this, is not in the 1814 muster or the 1828 Census, nor any of the Mutch Indexes to Births, Deaths and Marriages.

On the same ship, the *Fortune,* that brought Rimes to the colony, came a young brewer from Bristol named Richard Woodbury, who, by the time of the August muster, was working at the Government Farm at Castle Hill. He would later come to Green Hills and marry Matthew's eldest daughter, Sarah.[210]

About this time also, there occurred an event that was to concern Richard, the brewer, in a few years time. To try and wean the settlers from spirits to beer, Governor King had established a brewery. This failed and was closed but in the meantime, another set of brewing utensils arrived in April, 1806. King sold these to Andrew Thompson, in gratitude for his rescue work in the flood and leased him another acre of elevated Crown Land on the peninsula near South Creek, (from which the water for the beer was to be drawn), in order to establish a brewery at Green Hills. The Governor fixed the price of 'good beer' at one shill-

Joseph Lycett

Rex Nan Kivell Collection — National Library of Australia

'View of Windsor, upon the River Hawkesbury, New South Wales' [see p112]

Joseph Lycett

Rex Nan Kivell Collection – National Library of Au'

'View of Wilberforce on the banks of the River Hawkesbury c.1820' [see p118]

ing per gallon and 'small beer' at sixpence; and the licence to sell went with the brewery, the beer being sold at Thompson's store, which became more than ever the centre of activity at Green Hills.[211]

August 1806 also saw the arrival of a new Governor, Captain William Bligh, to replace King, whose health had deteriorated during his six years term. His appointment was the result of a suggestion made by Sir Joseph Banks and proved to be the second by that knight to change the course of the Australian continent's history. Banks had been asked if he knew a resourceful, independent thinking man of integrity who was a firm disciplinarian, the need being for someone who could control the rum traffic in the colony and keep order. Bligh had a hot temper an ill-guarded tongue, but he was also known to be courageous and hardworking. Upon his arrival, he was greeted with three addresses of welcome, from the military, the civil officers and from John Macarthur, who claimed to represent the free settlers.[212]

Macarthur had not long returned from England, where he had been sent to be court martialled, thus making King's term of office relatively free of interference from the 'perturbator' who had bedevilled Hunter. Macarthur had shrewdly used the visit home to resign his commission in the New South Wales Corps and to show samples of his fine wool to Lord Camden. Camden was able to see that Macarthur's efforts might result in an expensive colony becoming a lucrative one so that, when Macarthur returned to New South Wales, he had the promise of a grant of ten thousand acres of the best land in the Colony, on the Nepean. Since increasing the Macarthur fortune through wool production was Macarthur's prime concern, he was naturally reluctant to sell wethers for the meat that was now, since the flood, sorely needed to feed the colony.[213]

The settlers, who now sent two Addresses of their own to Bligh, claimed that Macarthur had withheld the wethers in order to force the price up. The Hawkesbury settlers added that their first knowledge of Macarthur's Address of Welcome had occurred when they had read it in the *Sydney Gazette*. They considered the act of John Macarthur in signing for them as the Free Inhabitants of the Colony an invasion of their rights and privileges as British Subjects. Had a Public meeting been held, they would by no means have authorised Macarthur as their spokesman. Among the two hundred and forty-four names on the Hawkesbury Address of Welcome of 1806, are Owen Cavanough, John Howe, Sarah Stubbs, James Dunne, John Cobcroft, Henry Lamb, Michael Nowland and James Davison.[214]

Bligh had already heard a great deal about Macarthur from Sir Joseph Banks and from Governor King, his predecessor and was, in any case, convinced that the immediate future of the colony at least, rested with the agriculturists rather than the pastoralists. While he was never under any illusions as to the vices of many of the expirees, Bligh was destined to be the champion of the industrious small emancipist and free settlers who put their signatures and crosses to this and future petitions.[215]

Since the flood, they had replanted as much wheat and maize as was possible, accepting philosophically the possibility of another flood in the knowledge that, in normal times, the yield was good from the low lying riverland. Prices had risen dramatically since the flood, however, wheat fetching two guineas per bushel and maize, two pounds, so that those settlers who had lost their all were in a bad way. The farmers thus complained of the high prices and lack of stability generally, asking for a better price for their wheat in normal times than the former Governor had offered and for certain other reforms.[216]

Bligh now directed the Reverend Samuel Marsden and Dr Thomas Arndell to form a committee of ten of the most respectable of the Hawkesbury settlers to receive information for a relief plan. Already he had offered the services of the Government mill free to private individuals, provided every eleventh bushel of corn were sent to the needy at the Hawkesbury. He also appealed for contributions but met no response; but from the mill scheme, he was able to send twelve hundredweight of seed maize up river in October and by November, 1806, 323 farmers had received from eight to sixty-four pounds apiece, while meat was being distributed for the most needy, to be paid for at a shilling a pound from the next harvest.[217]

Anxious that the settlers would not lose heart and knowing that the colony was dependent on their future efforts for food, Bligh called for tenders of wheat in mid-November and agreed to accept as little as five bushels in order that the greatest number would benefit. He fixed the price at an all time high of 14/9 per bushel at the Hawkesbury store, reduced the price of labour to widen the settlers' profit margin and guaranteed that those who supplied wheat this time would get ten shillings per bushel for wheat and six shillings for maize at the next harvest.[218]

To determine whether it would still be necessary to import wheat, Bligh approached the settlers for a guarantee of supply. While the settlers feared importation for it lowered their price and made farming unprofitable, Bligh, for his part, had to know how much wheat he could count on to feed the colony. For this purpose, Andrew Thompson organized a meeting at his house on January 27, 1807, at which those who attended promised a specified number of bushels and drew up a further Address to Governor Bligh, thanking him for his efforts and wisdom in the 'dreadful Crisis of General Calamity' in which he had found the colony. The address continued:

'And we... while enjoying our Native Laws and Liberty and living under a just and Benign Government... will be ready at all times, at the risque of our Lives and Property, lawfully to support the same.... We have subscribed all the Grain we can possibly spare from our own support to be carried to the Public Stores at your stipulated price, rejecting far greater prices in money which we could receive from the present Market Sale; and we hope the quantity subscribed... will furnish Your Excellency with means for the present Year's support without reverting to the ruinous necessity of Importation.... these fertile Settlements has ever furnished a Superabundance of Food.... evident from the low prices it sold at, and the great Surplus... annually spoiled, wasted and wilfully destroyed.... We will as readily supply.... at your fixed price next season.... praying for your Prosperity and a long continuance of your just and Benign Government.'[219]

To those readers whose impressions of 'Bounty Bligh', the tyrant, have come from earlier schoolbooks of Australian history, other literature and more importantly, the cinema, this instance of Bligh's popularity will be surprising. The petition was signed by one hundred and fifty-six persons, including Thomas Arndell, Andrew Thompson, Matthew Everingham, Owen Cavanough, William Addy, William Hubbard, James Mein, John Cobcroft, Michael Nowland, William Singleton, David Dunstan, John Yeomans, George Loder, Jack Cornwall and John Grono. But as Dr Brian Fletcher has remarked, in their adulation of Bligh, the settlers were really only 'warming up' at this stage.

On February 25, 1807, less than a month later, they sent another Address to Bligh, reaffirming their loyalty to him. Once again, an uprising among the Irish convicts was feared and Bligh had called for those who possessed arms and gunpowder to register with the authorities and for volunteers to suppress any trouble. This was signed by five hundred and forty-six settlers who had enrolled their names.

'for the Defence of the Country.... but sincerely hoping that your Excellency... by judging from the real and presumptive proofs exhibited in this Country now and for many years past by those disaffected People, of their relentless and incorrigible spirit of Rebellion, Murder, and Atrocity, keeping liege subjects in constant alarm, that you will be graciously pleased to dispose of the Ringleaders and Principals, so as to prevent future Concpiracy among them....'[220]

Matthew Everingham, Thomas Chaseling and even the Catholic (Irishman) James Dunne signed this petition as did most of the signatories of the January Address and also such people as Thomas Rose, John Howe, George Hall, Andrew Johnston, John Turnbull, James Johnstone, James Davison, Henry Lamb and Thomas Gosport. What is important here is the feeling of self-confidence shown by Matthew and other members of his class, who have by now lived down their past, whose signatures are mixed indiscriminately with freemen of undoubted respectability and who now have a stake in the defence of 'their' country.

By this time Bligh was known personally to many of the Hawkesbury settlers. He had purchased property at what was later to be Pitt Town and set up a Model Farm, in order to demonstrate agricultural methods to the farmers. Bligh himself profited by the farm and this was to be a weapon for his enemies later on; but Andrew Thompson, appointed manager, did not and was scrupulously honest in its management.

Whether Matthew and the others knew of Bligh's cupidity in regard to the farm is unknown and, in any case, irrelevant. By the middle of

1807, food prices had begun to return to normal and the future 'had never looked rosier' for the Hawkesbury settlers. They were right behind Bligh and led by Thompson, prepared yet another Address, this time signed by eight hundred and thirty-three people, including Matthew Everingham and Thomas Chaseling. In this they thanked the Governor for the 'present plenteous and flourishing state of the country' and also asked for consideration of Freedom of Trade with other countries and Trial by Jury.[221]

In the meantime, the Governor had become unpopular among the opportunistic dealers in the colony, although certainly one, Robert Campbell, the Scots merchant and trader, supported him. On February 14, of 1807, Bligh had taken the decisive step of prohibiting the barter of rum; for King's efforts to curb the rum traffic had been ineffectual. Many labourers still insisted on being paid wages in rum and the settlers had been obliged to pay enormous prices to buy it for this purpose. Forbidding the use of rum as a currency thus served the threefold purpose of restricting the unfair profit of dealers, keeping the improvident settlers away from temptation and most importantly, helping to keep the price of labour down.

The result was a consolidation of the military trading interest behind John Macarthur, who by now, having lost a court case to Andrew Thompson, was Bligh's sworn enemy. Thus one confrontation followed another between the rich and powerful party which stood for uncontrolled private enterprise and a governor who was determined to be 'master of his ship'.

Unaware that matters were so swiftly moving towards a climax, the Portland Head farmers went about their tasks, absorbed in their farms and their families. Another son, James was born to the Everinghams in 1807. No record of James's birth or baptism is extant, but the 1828 Census, for which James would most likely have supplied the information himself, lists his age as twenty-one.

The church at Green Hills had not yet a permanent incumbent but the Reverend Samuel Marsden was already seeing to that in England, whither, anticipating trouble, he had made his timely departure on furlough soon after Governor Bligh's arrival. He bore in his luggage two items which exemplify the duality of his nature, one being a dossier on the females of the colony, listing their immorality and its tangible proof, (legitimate and illegitimate offspring all itemised) and the other being a sampling of his fine wools, which he duly had made into a suit to wear before H.M. The King.[222]

The relationship between Marsden and people such as Matthew and the others, who signed a well-wishing address on his departure, will ever be a matter of conjecture, aware as the settlers were of his severity as a magistrate, (he was known as 'the flogging parson'), and of his prejudice against responsible offices being granted to emancipists. On at least two occasions, as we have seen, he had shown a true concern for the industrious among their number. The settlers' Address, now preserved in Marsden's Papers with so many other interesting items, is a veritable catalogue of the signatures and crosses of many of our forefathers.[223]

As Marsden had shrewdly foreseen, long ere his return from England, tremendous events were to rock the little colony to its foundations and to dash the optimistic expectations that the Hawkesbury settlers had come to enjoy during the Bligh era.

A soldier of the New South Wales Corps, shouldering a *Brown Bess* musket. *[see p83]*

Monty Wedd

COLO RIVER

FLATROCK or LIVERPOOL REACH

RIVER

R. Reynolds

M. Duggan

T. Adlam

UPPER HALF MOON REACH

LOWER HALF MOON REACH

John Lewellyn

Geo. Hibbs

Peter Hibbs

Wm. McDonald

T. Jones

John Brown

James Sherwin

GLOUCESTER REACH

J. Mound

John Cross

SUSSEX REACH

Wm. Yardley

Geo. Morley

SAWYER or CAMBRIDGE REACH

J. Campbell

Richard Evans

BOSTONS or CUMBERLAND REACH

Wm. Smith

Wm. Knight

Philip Roberts

Cheshire, Hamberton and Pollard

Henry Lamb

J. Dunne

T. Chaseling

Samuel Little

KENT REACH

Jas. Bradley

John Yeomans

SACKVILLE REACH

M.J. Everingham

Wm. Hubbard

Wm. Addy

PORTLAND

PORTLAND HEAD ROCK

A. Yoular

PORTLAND REACH

A. Johnston

James Mein

James Johnston

LOWER CRESCENT REACH

UPPER CRESCENT REACH

Wm. Stubbs

John Turnbull

John Howe

James Davison

O. Cavanough

Geo. Hall

SWALLOW ROCK REACH

HAWKESBURY

Little Cattai Creek

T. Arndell

D. Dunstan

Cattai Creek

CLARENCE REACH

T. Rose

J. Howorth

YORK REACH

CANNING REACH

N

0   1   2 Miles

CHAPTER SEVEN

Rum Rebellion

I<small>T WAS A</small> summer evening in January, 1808 and Matthew was seated on the verandah which now shaded the entrance to his house, smoking and reading aloud from an old Gazette to Elizabeth, who was busy in the kitchen, just inside the door.

'It's so hot tonight, my love, ' he said, 'why don't you come out for a while and take a breath of fresh air?'

'No,' said Elizabeth, 'I'd rather get supper over. Besides, the mosquitoes will be around soon and you'll be coming in yourself.'

'True enough,' said Matthew, as he smacked one of the large insects which had just alighted on his arm, 'we shall need the nets tonight.'

It was a scene so commonplace in its domesticity that the couple were later to marvel that it could prelude an evening of tension and drama. But so it happened, for as Matthew stepped down onto the path to empty his pipe, the nearest rosebushes moved and Will Addy appeared out of the gloom, puffing with haste.

'What is it, man?' asked Matthew, 'You're all out of breath!'

'Mischief, Matt,' replied the other. 'Where are the young folk? Best they be out of the way while I tell you the news.'

'Come on in, then,' said Matthew, 'They're all out the back somewhere at play.'

When they were seated round the scrubbed wooden table, Addy began his tale. 'Brennan will be here any minute, Matt, with that bloody bit o' paper!' he said.

'The Petition?' asked Matthew.

'Aye, the petition, ' said Addy, 'and there's no way out of it this time — they're making sure of that. They're taking the convicts from any man that refuses to sign. And they mean it, Matt.'

'Well, that settles it then,' said Matthew, 'I can't do without my men so I shall have to go quietly and sign.'

'But Matthew,' said Elizabeth, 'you said yourself that the Petition was treasonable and seditious — against both Governor Bligh and the King!'

'Mrs Everingham,' said Addy, patiently, 'I've just come from Cavanough's and he and George Hall have both put their names to it.'

'Owen?' queried Matthew in amazement.

'Aye, Owen — and quite a few of the *Coromandel* folk and even Tom Arndell. They mean business this time, Matt and they're determined to get solid men's signatures, not just the riff-raff. Laurie May has signed, Thomas Pitt, Dunstan, even John Cobcroft and Tom

Dargin. They're working their way down the river and drunk as lords, too, with the wine Hobby's been plying them with, but still getting names for all that.'

'And likely to shoot anyone that balks them, I'll warrant,' said Matthew. 'Well, ye'd best get on home then, Will — and thanks for the warning. What about the others further down? We'd better let them know.'

'I'll send my boy down to Maun's and then they can pass it on to the others at the Branch,' said Addy.

'Good man,' said Matthew, 'and thanks again.' After he had gone, Elizabeth called the children indoors while Matthew closed the front door and barred it, though it made the room unpleasantly close. The youngsters washed themselves in an iron dish near the back door and then sat at the table, but remained silent, sensing that something was wrong. Elizabeth laid out the salt meat and bread but Matthew, unable to eat, lit another pipe and smoked, the light of the oil lamp accentuating his grave expression. 'To think,' he said and cleared his throat, 'Twenty years almost to the day since we landed here.... and that it should come to this!'

'It would never have happened had Governor Phillip been here,' said Elizabeth, furiously cutting bread.

'Not even Phillip could do anything, were he to return now, lass,' said Matthew. 'Bloody Jack Bodice had a strangling grip on the place before Bligh ever got here. He has the money and he has the power.'

At the mention of John Macarthur, Elizabeth's mind went back to the *Neptune* and the first glimpse she had had of that arrogant face in the passageway. Though having arrived penniless, Macarthur's ambition had carried him to the point where he was now virtually ruling the colony and seemingly, there was no one who could control him. 'If only Governor Bligh had been able to get up here to the Hawkesbury that night the Corps marched,' she thought aloud.

'Aye, we all vowed to help him last year when the 'Paddys' were playing up,' said Matthew. 'But they were too quick for him and caught him unawares. Certainly if he could have got to the 'Oxborough,' we'd 'a given the Corps a run, rough farmers though they think us.'

Matthew's voice was warm when he spoke of Bligh for the Hawkesbury settlers were behind the Governor to a man. Although they suspected that he had been feathering his own nest and had made money out of his 'Model' farm, it concerned them little. He had treated the small settlers better than any Governor since Phillip and was just the kind of man for whom they had waited all these years. For Bligh was a plain seaman who had first gone aboard a King's ship as cabin boy at seven years. With all his oaths and noise, at least you knew where you stood with him, Matthew reflected, and he had very little time for the fancy airs of the officers. In fact he had said that he much preferred to sit down with a Hawkesbury man; and it was not unusual for the settlers to see him step ashore at their landings.

Elizabeth, too, was now thinking of Bligh and of the time last year when she had looked out the window to see Matthew walking up the track with the Governor alongside him. Flour all over her hands, she had stood there at a loss for a moment to think of the Governor actually coming into her house. He had greeted her politely and as she, Sarah and Ann had made their curtseys, had patted Annie on the head and called her 'my little maid'. Then he had told the child that he, himself, had five 'little maids' such as she. So overcome was Elizabeth that Matthew had needed to remind her to fetch a 'bumper' for their visitor. And when the Governor was seated at the table, Matthew had raised his tankard and proclaimed with sincerity: 'Your Excellency's very good health! And long may he remain in New South Wales.'

That had been at this table not six months since. 'How could change so quickly come?' said Elizabeth, voicing her thoughts aloud.

'It had to happen, Liz,' said Matthew, 'it had to happen. Any Governor they sent out could not do his job without running foul of the officers. If you'd seen them at Green Hills on Tuesday, burning his effigy in a great bonfire, you'd know how much they hated him and were determined to get rid of him.'

'Well, I hate to think of them getting away with it,' said Elizabeth, as she poured the tea.

'They're not, Elizabeth,' Matthew declared, 'for the wheel will turn again, you'll see. But just now we must do as the others and bide.'

They both sat there drinking their tea and thinking of what he had said until the sound of lumbering footsteps on the verandah caused them to rise. Then Matthew took down a makeshift pike from over the door, from where his musket had in former times been kept, and stood it in the corner as the hammering commenced on the other side. So quickly did he unbar the door that John Brennan, his face red and swollen from grog, was taken aback and forgot the grubby parchment in his hand so that Matthew had the advantage.

'Ye may pass me the paper, Mr Brennan and I'll sign it right enough,' he said. 'But stay on my doorstep while I do so for I'm particular who enters my house,' and here he paused to take a long look at the man who disgusted him. 'Quill, ink and sand, Mrs Everingham, if you please!'

* * *

ON JANUARY 26, 1808, the twentieth anniversary of the day on which the colony had been founded, Major George Johnston, the acting Lieutenant-Governor and commander of the New South Wales Corps found himself, by the combined actions of Bligh and Macarthur, in a position where he was forced most reluctantly to take sides and to depose the Governor, which event has ever since been called 'The Rum

Rebellion'. Despite the attempts of later historians to present the final confrontation of opposing forces as anything else, it is clear that contemporaries knew what it was all about when they named it thus.

Surprise was the element which ensured the success of the mutiny. Governor Bligh was seated at dinner in Government House when he heard the Corps and its attendant rabble approaching to the tune of 'Rule Brittania', whereupon he hurried upstairs to put on his uniform and to hide certain papers on his person. It was some time before he was found concealed in a bedroom and he later stated that he was all this while hoping that he might contrive to escape to the Hawkesbury, where he knew that he could raise a force.[224]

One of the riddles of Australian history is whether, if Bligh had escaped, the Hawkesbury would have taken arms for him. Another is whether such a raw force could have succeeded in overwhelming the Corps. A third and perhaps the most intriguing question, is whether the Corps, seeing the King's representative at the head of a group, would have engaged in conflict which might have resulted in the Governor's death and ultimately their own, at the end of ropes.

It is certain that if Bligh had in some way been reinstated to serve the ten years term for which he had originally engaged, the fortunes of Matthew and many of his neighbours would have been different. But by the time Andrew Thompson, Dr Arndell and the rest of the Hawkesburyites heard the astonishing news of the Governor's imprisonment, the moment for action had passed and the military were firmly in control. Before the settlers had time to think or to organise, their arms were taken from them.[225]

Thompson was dismissed from his post of Chief Constable and replaced by Richard Fitzgerald, Macarthur's agent at the Hawkesbury, while Arndell was dismissed from the magistracy. An officer monopoly returned to the stores which usually opened to receive wheat at the time of Bligh's deposition. While Robert Fitz and Archibald Bell were in charge, the settlers had little hope of disposing of their grain.[226]

Since Macarthur was running the colony again but was no longer officially in the military, an office was created for him, that of Secretary to the Colony. And, in an effort to make a brilliant coup appear to be the culmination of a popular movement a petition, which was the one referred to in the story as that to be signed by the river farmers, was drawn up at Green Hills.[227]

Martin Mason, who later went to England with George Suttor as a witness for Bligh at Johnston's Court Martial, testified that in the two days following the rebellion, the scene at Green Hills was one of intoxication, riot and confusion. The sergeant of the Corps detachment ordered the erection of gallows fifty paces from his door. Then cartloads of wood were brought in for bonfires and as Matthew tells in the story, Bligh's effigy and that of William Gore, the Provost Marshal, were committed to the flames.[228]

On January 28, Lieutenant Hobby and Thomas Biggers assembled their adherents, among whom were James Badgery, William Cox and John Brennan at Thompson's house-cum-inn. There Robert Fitz and Thomas Hobby drew up the petition, purportedly from the settlers, demonstrating support for the rebellion and gratitude to Major Johnston for rescuing them from Bligh's tyranny.[229]

Heated with wine and spirits, (according to Mason), they then sallied forth to solicit signatures. Mason himself was solicited three times that day and Biggers told him that, if he did not sign, he would be in gaol in Sydney within twenty-four hours. Hobby, it was claimed in evidence, swore to make five hundred people sign by nightfall. People were threatened and told in violent language that those who did not sign would be 'marked men'. Many signed from 'prudential motives', as the story suggests Matthew did, in order to prevent their indented servants being taken from them. John Brennan, who took the petition round, later wrote to Thompson and Bligh repenting his duplicity at this time.[230]

As soon as it was safe to do so, Dr Arndell wrote a letter revoking his signature and stating that he had signed 'through fear and without so much as knowing the contents' of the document; and it would have been the same with Matthew Everingham, John Cobcroft, Michael Nowland, William Addy, David Dunstan, Owen Cavanough, Thomas Dargin, Peter Hibbs and Joseph Maunds.[231]

Johnston's advisers at his Court Martial claimed that two hundred and eighty-four persons had signed, but the only extant copy shows sixty-six names. Johnston also tried to convince the Court Martial that the Hawkesbury settlers would sign an address of any import 'for the most insignificant reward, so small a matter as a glass of spirits per man' and that the pro-Bligh petitions were therefore meaningless; but the judges were unconvinced.[232]

During the period of the Macarthur regime, some of the more desperate Hawkesburyites were conspiring to assassinate him but he was warned in time. However, by April 11, everyone had had enough of Macarthur and the more respectable risked addressing Johnston to this effect. They stated that they had been 'impressed with surprize and alarm' to see John Macarthur as 'Colonial Secretary', which office he did not hold from the King. He was, they stated, 'the Last Man we would depute to represent us in any case whatever....' And they continued, while asking that he be removed from his office:

'We believe John McArthur has been the Scourge of the Colony by fomenting quarrels between His Majesty's Officers, Servants and Subjects; his monopoly and extortion have been highly injurious to the Inhabitants of every description.'[233]

By this time Johnston had already sent for Colonel Paterson, his superior officer, who had been Administrator in 1792 and who was now in charge of the colony of Port Dalrymple, (Launceston), in Van Diemen's Land. Paterson, however, was in no hurry to come to Sydney, even though he was receiving petitions from the Hawkesbury settlers who were anticipating his arrival and a return to law and order. He was still at Port Dalrymple when, on July 28, 1808, Lieutenant Colonel Joseph Foveaux arrived in Sydney from England and being superior in rank to Johnston, took command of the colony.

At Foveaux's urging, Paterson finally sailed for Sydney still uncertain whether to support Foveaux or Bligh. The receipt of a message from Foveaux that Bligh planned to arrest Paterson on arrival then decided the latter to continue Bligh's house arrest after assuming control on January 9, 1809, nearly a year after the rebellion.

Paterson finally allowed Bligh to leave for England on the *Porpoise* on March 17, 1809 on the condition that he would not call at any of the outer settlements of New South Wales. However Bligh, placing no value on this forced promise, sailed for Hobart Town where Lieutenant Governor David Collins received him once more as Captain General and Governor in Chief of the Colony of New South Wales.

The Hawkesbury settlers, Matthew among them, welcomed the easy-going Paterson with an Address and asked to be given the chance of supplying grain the next season at a fixed price. They were now hopeful that things would return to normal and that if they were fortunate enough to get a few good years without serious floods, prosperity would return. Unfortunately, as we shall see, this was not to be the case.[234]

In the meantime, during the first half of 1808, it seems likely that Matthew and his family had moved to Green Hills and that he had left his men and perhaps, young Matthew, to run the property at Portland Head or that he was letting it. For on August 23, 1808, Everingham was a juror at the Inquest held before Archibald Bell into the death of John Brazil. Since Brazil had been murdered 'on the bank of the Creek', (possibly South Creek), in the vicinity of Red House Farm and Robert Rope, one of Andrew Thompson's servants, was said to be one of the perpetrators, there is a likelihood that Matthew was at this time already involved with Thompson's affairs and living in the old part of Green Hills. Among the jurors were Martin Mason and Thomas Rickerby.[235]

In April, 1809, there occurred the first of three disastrous floods between then and July, as a result of which many settlers were distressed and had to be victualled by the Government. Though Matthew was able to place eleven bushels of wheat in the Government store at Green Hills on April 8 to aid relief after the first flood, by the time the three floods had subsided, he had sustained 'very heavy losses' from which he never really recovered.

As with so many other settlers, his problem was that the only cultivable land, (approximately eighteen acres), on his Sackville Reach property, although very rich — 'capital wheatland', as he was to term it in an advertisement, was low lying and subject to flooding. The remainder, where his house was situated, though elevated, was of rocky terrain and unsuitable for tillage. He therefore decided to petition the acting Governor, Colonel Paterson, for a grant with a greater cultivable acreage.[236]

Paterson ordered one hundred and thirty acres to be measured for him 'at the Currygong Brush lately settled' and the 'return' regarding the land was sent to Sydney for the Deed to be executed. While waiting for the grant to become available, Matthew decided to let the Sackville property for a term of three years at £30-0-0 per annum.[237]

During the floods, Andrew Thompson, though no longer a member of the police force and obliged to render service to the settlers, had again gone out in his boat and rescued a hundred people. As a reward, he received Scotland Island, (where he had moved the salt-pans formerly at Mullet Island), from Colonel Paterson as a grant — he had previously leased it; and he received a grant of 1,240 acres on the Cow Pastures (Camden) road which he called 'St. Andrew's'. However, his health had suffered as a result of exhaustion and exposure and by the end of 1809, a consumption forced him to place his affairs in the hands of that other Scot, John Howe, the *Coromandel* immigrant.

Howe was an erstwhile neighbour of Matthew's and we will presently see how his life as well as those of Matthew and Richard Woodbury were affected by connection with the affairs of Andrew Thompson; and the attention that has been paid to Thompson will now be more readily understood. With the new year came a new Governor, Lachlan Macquarie and the cumulative effect of all this will be the subject of the next chapter.

On the last day of 1809, the little township of Green Hills experienced the worst storm that anyone could remember. Over on the Sydney bank of the river at the Red House, Andrew Thompson was witnessing his last hogmanay. Outside the Heads, fierce gales had caused yet another Scot, the dour Lachlan Macquarie to wonder whether the *Dromedary* would make landfall safely. Meanwhile the inhabitants of the Green Hills, the Everinghams among them, slept snugly in their beds, little dreaming of the great changes that would take place in the decade ahead.[238]

Facsimile of a letter written by Matthew
Everingham, April 15, 1811. Original in the
Case Papers, 1811 Court of Civil Jurisdiction. [see p113]

Archives Office of New South Wales

CHAPTER EIGHT

Green Hills

'**A**NNIE, ARE YOU there?' Matthew called. 'Bring me some paper, girl, so that I can write this confounded letter!'

Sick abed for three weeks, Matthew's forced inactivity was making him querulous and giving the females of the house plenty to do. Anxious to keep the peace, his nine-years-old daughter hastened to her father with the writing materials.

'Lord! Haven't we a better quill in the house than this?' he complained and then, as she had begun to run off to the kitchen to find another, 'Never mind, it will do, it will do.'

The violence of this 'flux' had made him so weak that everything was an effort and he, who had been accustomed in childhood to copy hundreds of words in 'a good fair hand' now found it tedious to have to scribble the necessary few lines that were to accompany his Memorial to the Judge Advocate. He had not had such a bout of dysentery since the earliest days of the colony when the food had been half rotten and the Tank Stream water putrid. Momentarily, he thought of the time when the sight of a sail from the lookout at South Head had meant the difference between extinction and survival. And now, after all those years, here he lay ill, just when he most wanted to be well. If Arndell had been attending him, Matthew reflected in his prejudiced way, he would probably be on his feet by now; for the old First Fleet doctor would have known what to do better than this new fellow, Mileham.

However, once started, Matthew's hand moved swiftly over the dainty sheet of note paper and there were no painful difficulties of composition for the former scribe. Well he knew how to address his betters, to state his case clearly and to beg a favour with courtesy.

'Being very ill and Confined to my Bed — I have been Obliged to send down my wife with a Certificate from the Surgeon who attends me Stating my inability to attend the Court now...'

It was hard on Elizabeth, he regretted, to have to make the trip to Sydney when she was again big with child; but at least now there was a wagon for the sixteen hours journey and she would be able to rest at Kelly's place overnight.

'.... there is a mem! praying the Court to put the Cause back — as Mr Abbott has taken an Action ag! me for a Considerable Sum more than what is due from me....'

Damn Abbott, thought Matthew as he wrote, and those other sharks who were pressing him and the others after the floods, just so the Governor could get his due! Thompson would turn in his grave if he could see what was going on.

'There is also a mem! of my Case and Mr Fitzgerald. I should

111

be obliged to you to put them forward for her as She is a Stranger to Court Causes and when I am able to Come down to Sydney, I will remember the Obligation with gratitude. I am sir

> Your most Obedient Servant,
> M. Everingham.'

He put the pen down and settled back on the pillows to read over the letter. There was plenty of time, Elizabeth would not be leaving till the morning and he was past hurrying now — what was the good of haste anyway? It had never got him anywhere. All his industry and hopes had led only to this. Sick abed, plagued by creditors with a new baby and a new mouth to feed any day. Sometimes he felt that he was travelling in circles. What was Life about and what did the passage of time mean in a life where one was tossed about on high waves like a small splinter? Where was he, for instance, twenty years ago? And he looked at the date at the head of the letter, April 11, 1811.

His mind went back two decades to April, 1791 and he recalled that at the time, he had been at Parramatta and almost out of his 'term'. Governor Phillip had come up to see them at the Farm and had told them of his plans to set them a-farming on their own. He had been married little more than a month and Elizabeth had just become aware that she was to have poor little Mary. What a sea of troubles they had sailed through since that far off day when the child had been buried. The ways of women were strange — Elizabeth had never forgotten her firstborn and had recently said that she would like this new baby to be called 'Maria' if it were a girl.

Where would they be when the child was born? If only the floods had not come and he had had a few good years, he could have stayed on here at the *Red House* and perhaps bought it one day. For they all loved the place and had been the envy of everyone when they had moved in. But then, should he really complain? Poor Andy Thompson who had built it lay dead in yon graveyard. His eyes travelled to the window and to the distant prospect of Green Hills, to the clearing where the graveyard was and where, one day, so the Governor said, a new church would rise. It was a peaceful spot, well removed from the worldly struggles which went on in the cluster of buildings at the other end of the town. Yet Thompson had loved this bustle, had, in fact, been the means of its creation....

There was no doubt that one had a fine view of Green Hills from here at West Hill and Thompson had known what he was about when he had chosen the site, although he had had little time to sit and enjoy the view himself. Matthew's eyes continued to rest on the old centre of the town and the first buildings that he and Larry had seen when they had come to the hamlet nearly ten years ago. The three storeyed granary was still the largest building, standing near the schoolhouse-cum-church; but there were now many more dwellings encroaching on them, huddled together with barely a tree among them.

It was a good thing, Matthew reflected, that at least, this last year or

A View of the Town of Windsor *[see p118]*

Stacey/West

A. West

'The Red House Farm, Windsor in New South Wales' [see p118]

Mitchell Library

so, they had been near enough to town for the younger ones to have some schooling. Matthew Hughes was a man of good character who taught the children manners as well as their letters. Matthew smiled as he remembered George's amazement on the first day — 'He makes us bow as we go in, Father, and say: 'Your servant, sir.'' George had recounted. The boy would soon be home and Matthew looked towards the floating bridge at the bottom of the field, where he might soon expect to see him crossing.

From the bridge Matthew's eye went to the Toll House and then along the Creek where he could see the roof of the brewery and the cottage next door. Sarah would be bustling about in there as usual, never still for a moment — a good partner for the energetic Richard, who, Matthew knew, would be mending casks today and putting things right for the malting that would begin next month.

Life goes on, thought Matthew and supposed that they would all manage well enough if he were not there. So he folded the letter and addressed it on the back. Fleming would put the Case back for Elizabeth and he, Matthew, would worry about it all again next month when he could go down to Sydney himself. It would be interesting to go down and see 'the Camp' again, for it was changing so quickly. And with the anticipation of seeing the town again and looking in on old acquaintances came the realization that he was perhaps on the mend.

* * *

MATTHEW'S LETTER to William Fleming, clerk at the Judge Advocate's office, was found pinned to a memorial regarding the Suit of Thomas Abbott for Debt, in an envelope among the Supreme Court Papers in the State Archives, Sydney. Its discovery was one of those moments which make hours of sometimes tedious and unproductive research worthwhile. Indeed, it was with a feeling of awe that one held in one's hands a letter written by Matthew himself over one hundred and sixty years ago, methodically filed by some clerk and seen by few eyes since it was written.[239]

And it was natural to feel glad that illness had prevented Matthew from attending the court and resulted in its preservation.

Since the date of the letter is April 11, 1811 and the heading is 'West Hill', otherwise *Red House Farm*, Andrew Thompson's property at present day McGrath's Hill, there are the events of sixteen months to narrate betwen then and the time the last chapter ended, the last day of the year 1808. At that time we saw that Matthew, disillusioned with farming his all too small and flood prone property at Sackville Reach, had leased it and removed temporarily to Green Hills to await the issue of a grant of land at Kurrajong, which had been promised to him by the Acting Governor, Colonel Paterson.

The rent of the Sackville farm would have been insufficient to support the family and there are indications that, possibly as a result of his acquaintance with John Howe who had become Andrew Thompson's manager in December, 1809 and who was managing the store, Matthew was also engaged in some commercial way in Thompson's affairs. Being literate, he could have been working in the store and at accounts, helping in the running of the brewery or even in the rounding up of Thompson's debtors which was proceeding at this time. But now he, like every one else in the new year of 1810, would be affected by the new Governor's regime.

One of Macquarie's first acts was to voice the British Government's strong disapproval of the rebellion. Bligh's absence in Van Diemen's Land prevented his reinstatement but, upon his arrival in Sydney Cove on January 17, 1810, he was treated with every mark of respect. Though Macquarie found Bligh 'difficult', the new Governor ensured that his predecessor was farewelled with honour before he sailed for England on May 12, 1810 to see his enemies, Johnston and Macarthur, finally vanquished and discredited by the British Government, (1811). During Bligh's sojourn in Sydney, the Hawkesbury settlers had once again shown their loyalty to him by means of a Memorial.[240]

Meantime, on January 4, 1810, Macquarie had begun implementing his instructions. All the officers appointed by Johnston, Foveaux and Paterson were dismissed and the former ones restored. All trials and investigations by law, land grants and leases, pardons, etc., which had occurred since the rebellion were declared void. Since Matthew had had land promised and measured for him by Paterson, he was required to re-petition for it which he did on January 26, 1810.

Turning to his next charge, moral improvement, Macquarie began by placing a duty on spirits and ordered all public houses to be shut on the Sabbath day during divine service, on pain of the vendor losing his licence. On February 16, he reduced the number of licensed houses in order to curtail dissipation and idleness. On the following day an advertisement appeared ordering Matthew and others to collect their licences from the Judge Advocate's office. For this, his first licence, he would probably have been given a good character by Andrew Thompson, who was by now reinstated as Chief Constable at the Green Hills, or by Dr Thomas Arndell; but in a moment we will see that there was more to it than that.[241]

Returning to Macquarie's reforming campaign, we find that the Governor proclaimed it a scandal that so many couples were living in de-facto relationships and warned than an unmarried woman had no right to a man's possessions if he died intestate and would receive no favour nor help.

This admitted no toleration of Catholic opinion which deemed it worse for a member of its flock to be married by a heretic priest, (of the Protestant faith), than to live in sin. One imagines that it had been this, or perhaps the fact that one or other had a spouse in the old country, that had prevented the marriage of Thomas Chaseling and his colleen, Margaret McMahon, (McMaude), before this date. Perhaps as a result of Macquarie's attitude, they finally went to the altar in the old church-school building of St Matthew's on November 29, 1812, thereby legitimating John, born 1799, Ann, born 1802, Jane, born 1804 Thomas, born 1807, Louisa, born 1809, Charlotte, born 1811, who all but John, were baptized on the same day.

It is remarkable that Catholicism survived the early years in New South Wales for Macquarie was determined to have no recurrence of the disturbances King and Bligh had experienced and deported Jeremiah O'Flynn, a priest who arrived a few years later in 1817, before he could give any trouble.[242]

Apart from the religious consideration, there was another reason why some women preferred de-facto relationships — that of property. Until the Married Women's Property Acts later in the Nineteenth Century, a woman's property passed to her husband upon marriage. Thus Rosetta Marsh, who, seemingly as a result of Macquarie's edict, married Samuel Terry, later to be the 'Botany Bay Rothschild', saw that he signed an agreement prior to marriage securing to her 'all her own stock prior to marriage'. A more interesting case to us, because it relates to the Sackville area, was that of Elizabeth Crouch, mentioned formerly as the wife of William Addy. Elizabeth had borne a son to Stephen Tuckerman before marrying William Addy in 1807. After Addy died in 1810, she married Thomas Ivory, (1812). After Ivory died, she married Edward Churchill in 1815 but before doing so, she secured the Release, 'because of a contract of marriage about to take place', of 'one moiety', or half of Addy's farm and buildings, six head of horned cattle, a horse, two mares and household goods. Churchill's property on Addy's Creek will be a subject for discussion later on, but in the meantime, let us return to the Green Hills of 1810.[243]

With regard to the economic situation, Macquarie inherited a similar set of circumstances to that which had met Bligh on his arrival — as a result of the flood of the previous year, the stores were empty. The settlers refused to sell wheat to the Government at ten shillings per bushel until Foveaux suggested that Macquarie follow Bligh's example of appealing directly to them. Once again Thompson went round with Lieutenant Bell and the settlers responded to the call.

The next day, Thompson learnt that he had been appointed in Bell's place as Magistrate for the Hawkesbury District, (Bell having been the rebel appointee), as Dr Arndell was too old for the position. Thompson had previously acted as magistrate in times of Arndell's absence or illness and was well fitted as a result of his police work for the job. As well, it would seem that he had already become quite well known to Macquarie personally and had rendered the Governor a service in making a house in Sydney available for the new Judge Advocate, Ellis Bent.

However, when Thompson, Simeon Lord, a wealthy emancipist

merchant, and the Reverend Samuel Marsden were appointed co-trustees of the new turnpike road from Parramatta to the Hawkesbury, Marsden declined to accept, deeming it inappropriate to his position to be associated with the others who were not only ex-convicts but had mistresses and illegitimate children. The previous road had bordered the West Hill Farm on the north eastern side. Its course was now altered to run through the farm, as it has remained ever since.[244]

We saw how the decline in Thompson's health had occasioned him to appoint John Howe to manage his affairs at the end of 1809. Seemingly, it would be all he could do now to fulfil the duties of a magistrate. Whether because of his health or because it would be unfitting for him in his new position to continue his interest in the brewery and to retain the liquor licence that went with it, Thompson now, in February, 1810, leased the brewery to Henry Kable.

It was inconvenient for Kable to attend to his concerns at the Hawkesbury, for which reason he had recently appointed William Mason his agent there. For the same reason and probably at Thompson's and Howe's suggestion, Matthew received a liquor licence which would seem to have included the brewery beer. This was probably still sold at Thompson's store, although Matthew, by July, 1810, was receiving payment for Kable's debts in grain at his, Matthew's own house at Green Hills.[245]

As to the brewery itself, the practical management of it may well have been in the hands of Richard Woodbury since its commencement. It is one thing to be sold a set of brewing utensils, as Thompson was in 1806 at Governor King's direction; but it is quite another to brew beer. Woodbury was a brewer by occupation, having arrived in the colony by the *Fortune* in 1806, whereupon he had been sent to the Government Farm at Castle Hill. When Andrew Thompson went to the Farm in the capacity of bailiff to Governor Bligh to select fifteen of the best men for Bligh's Model Farm project, he possibly discovered Richard and snapped him up to relieve himself from at least one aspect of his own now very extensive concerns. Richard probably worked in Thompson's brewery from 1807 onwards as an assigned man. Partial confirmation of this comes from a reply made to one of the many thousands of questions asked by the inquisitorial Commissioner Bigge many years later, when the Macquarie regime was under investigation. On this occasion, John Howe was asked:

Question: Did Mr Thompson brew good beer?

Answer: Very good, as well as a man of the name of Woodbury.

In any case, Woodbury continued at the brewery and by September, 1811, seemed to enjoy some sort of a partnership with Kable.[246]

Matthew, apart from selling the beer, may have been involved in some activities of his own for during 1810 he issued writs against Daniel Fane, a Hawkesbury settler and Robert Sells of George's River for 'goods' and he, in his turn, was capiased by Samuel Craft of Hawkesbury and John Ritchie of Sydney for unredeemed Promissory Notes.

New South Wales society of 1810 was very litigious and the Court of Civil Jurisdiction settled a never-ending list of minor debts.[247]

During the year 1810, Thompson became ill again and died on October 22 at the age of thirty-seven, having bequeathed a quarter of his large estate to the Governor. George Howe, the editor of the *Sydney Gazette* wrote his co-emancipist's obituary — the longest yet for that paper — and the funeral was one of the largest ever seen in the colony. The new incumbent of St Matthew's Parish, the Reverend Robert Cartwright, conducted the service (Marsden was not present). Captain H.C. Antill, the Governor's Aide-de-camp and one of the executors, was chief mourner and a long procession of gentlemen, settlers, of whom Matthew would be one, and others such as Richard Woodbury, followed the coffin. Thompson was buried in the new graveyard, the first person to be buried there and Macquarie wrote his epitaph.[248]

The Executors of Thompson's Estate decided to sell the personal property and to rent the real estate until such times as they had instructions from Thompson's relatives in Scotland, who were due for a half share. (Whatever happened to the de-facto wife and children is unknown — Simeon Lord inherited the other quarter share.) At the end of December, 1810, therefore, Thompson's schooner, the *Governor Bligh* was sold, together with the effects of his hostelry, (it will be remembered that Thompson's store-cum-inn was on Crown Land.)[249]

Since we have supposed Matthew Everingham to have been the licensed vendor at the hostelry, this would have meant the end of this arrangement. Governor Macquarie had not yet ratified his Land Grant at Kurrajong, so he could not yet go there to farm. At the same time, Matthew would have been in a position to know from John Howe that Thompson's properties were to be rented and under what conditions. All this seems to have prompted Matthew to try to sell his Sackville property and to apply for the lease of the West Hill (or Red House) farm, for on the same day, December 8, as Thompson's properties were advertised for lease in the *Sydney Gazette* and immediately underneath that notice, there appeared another advertisement for the sale of the Sackville Reach farm:

> 'To be Disposed of by Private Contract, a Fifty acre Farm, most desirably situate in the lower part of the Hawkesbury River, nearly in the centre of Sackville Reach, 18 of which are in high cultivation — the whole being capital wheat land, with an orchard well stocked with fruit trees, and on the Farm is a shingled Dwelling-House, at present in the occupation of a Tenant at £30 sterling per annum, it having a Lease two years of which are unexpired. — Conditions, Six Months Credit will be given for one half the Purchase-money, or Horned Cattle will be taken at a fair valuation in exchange. For further particulars apply to Matthew Everingham, at the Green Hills, Hawkesbury, or to Mr Lamb, at Sydney,'[250]

Edward Lamb was Henry Kable's Chief Clerk in Sydney, but there was by now another of Kable's employees with whom the Everinghams had made contact during 1810. Richard Woodbury had been courting

118

Sarah Everingham, now seventeen, and they were married on December 17, 1810 at the old St Matthew's in the original part of the town. (The present St Matthew's with the churchyard containing Andrew Thompson's grave and which now seems so venerable, had not even been contemplated at this time.) The marriage register shows that Richard was literate but Sarah signed with a cross. The Reverend Robert Cartwright performed the ceremony and the witnesses were James Smith, Matthew Everingham, William Beadle(y) and Matthew Hughes, the school master mentioned in the story, whose name appears quite often in the register as a witness. While parting with one child, Elizabeth Everingham had just discovered that she was to bear another the following August.[251]

In this month of December, 1810, also, Governor Macquarie came to Green Hills as part of an inspection of the colony in general and his own inheritance in particular. The inhabitants of the Hawkesbury, once again feeling they had a champion for their cause, presented him with an Address. After visiting Thompson's grave, Macquarie went to see West Hill and Killarney Farms — 'both very good ones', of which he now owned one quarter. During this visit also, he founded the townships of Richmond, Wilberforce and Pitt Town and changed the name of Green Hills to Windsor, urging the settlers to move their homes to these townships on higher ground, an impractical suggestion for many.[252]

The Everingham family, who had anticipated Macquarie's suggestion at least a year earlier, but were still waiting for the land at the Kurryjong Hill, which Macquarie had just visited, now took the lease of West Hill and moved into the Red House. Sarah and Richard Woodbury would remain in Windsor, probably living in the house attached to the brewery on South Creek. (Incidentally Henry Kable himself now received a licence to sell spirit and a separate licence to brew beer.) The Sackville property had not yet been sold and was advertised again in the *Sydney Gazette* of February 9, 1811, Matthew now stating that he was prepared to give twelve months credit for the purchase money or for horned cattle. He seems to have anticipated that the harvests he would reap from the fertile West Hill farm would more than pay his rent to Thompson's executors.[253]

Red House, as can be seen by the drawing, was a handsome two-storeyed home where the large family could spread out in unaccustomed luxury. It must have been a dream fulfilled for Matthew and Elizabeth to live there for these two years. There was at least one other dwelling apart from the main one as well as granaries, stores, stabling, a large convenient tan yard, barn, gardens and yards. The children would surely love it and one small boy, James, was never to forget the time the family spent there.

Only a portion of the original house still exists as part of another dwelling. It is located at McGrath's Hill some distance to the right of the road going from Sydney to Windsor. The ruins behind the hotel, though of red brick and possibly, bricks from the *Red House,* are of a blacksmith's shop which formerly stood there. *Clare House,* Killarney, has also been mistaken for the *Red House,* but it was built later and in any case is located on the separate Killarney Estate. An 1816 sketch made in Windsor, referred to later, shows the position of the roof of the *Red House* as compared with the new Sydney-Windsor road. On the other hand it is impossible to see *Clare House* from Windsor as there is a hill in between.[254]

Now, in 1811, Matthew began to set up as a farmer again. At the Auction Sale on February 11, the greatest ever held in the colony and managed by John Howe for Thompson's Executors, he bought the following goods: Copperas and 24 Flints, 19/-, a pair of iron haines and a pair of traces, 13/-, a lot of shoemakers tools, £1-15-0, 24 sheets of tin, 14/-, half a gross of fruit knives, £1-1-0, a basket of tobacco, £3-7-0, a steel rat trap 8/6, and 4cwt. salt, for all of which the executors allowed six months' credit. These details show us a man self-sufficient in many ways, who could turn his hand to anything. We see him mending a roof with the tin, perhaps selling some of the knives to his neighbours and keeping some for stoning fruit to preserve or to make jam. We see him harnessing a horse to plough a furrow, checking his barn to keep down the vermin, killing his own meat and salting it and on wet days, repairing or making shoes for the family with some of the leather hides from the tannery. He would sit down in the evening with a measure of tobacco he had guillotined for a plug or to fill a pipe and then reach for his muzzle loading musket to clean it and check the flint.

On March 2, Matthew bought fifteen goats from Howe's sale of William Cox's bankrupt estate and on the same day, he informed proprietors of stock 'that having taken the West Hill Farm of the Executors of the late Andrew Thompson, Esq., all Persons having stock and in want of Pasturage (might) have the Run of these extensive paddocks at 1s. per week per head, where they (would) have the benefit of a very extensive Common with a Herdsman to attend them'.[255]

The last two actions, both calculated to provide alternate sources of income, may have been occasioned by the fact that a week after the great auction sale, on February 23, the river had again risen suddenly to a height of forty feet and of course, the West Hill wheatlands would have been flooded. It is difficult to know exactly what losses Matthew would have sustained from this flood because the growing crop may have been excluded from the lease.

Certainly he would have been affected one way or the other as far as the Sackville Reach property was concerned. There had been a drought since the last flood in August, 1809, which had destroyed the maize crops and the flood would have ruined the tenant's wheat. The tenant would have difficulty paying his rent and the property would now be more unsaleable than ever.

Directly or indirectly, this 1811 flood threw Matthew and many other settlers who owed money to the Thompson estate into debt and ultimate ruin. Yet, as Mr J.V. Byrnes points out, Macquarie did not even mention it in his home despatches at the time and it did not appear in the Government censored *Sydney Gazette* until six weeks later. The Executors sold up many debtors who might, in other times, have received official aid and the Governor, regrettably, stood to gain by their losses.

In addition to keeping goats and offering agistment, Matthew decided to let the tanyard where kangaroo skins and sealskins brought home from Bass Strait and New Zealand in Thompson's ships (and cured with Scotland Island salt) were tanned. Thus on May 4, 1811, the following advertisement appeared in the *Sydney Gazette:*

'To be Let, for a Twelvemonth certain, and entered on immediately, an extensive Tan Yard, with suitable Pits, Sheds and Buildings, situate at West Hill, late the property of Andrew Thompson, Esq., deceased, together with all sufficient Tools, Implements, and Apparatus necessary to carry on the Business on an extensive Scale. The Lesser to be furnished, at his own option, with a quantity of Hides on Six Months' Credit, on Security, and every other Encouragement that an industrious Man can wish. For particulars apply to Matthew Everingham, at West Hill Farm, Hawkesbury.'[256]

When Macquarie decided to loan stock on credit from the Government herds so that a pastoral industry could develop, Matthew borrowed on May 27, one cow, two oxen and four sheep for eighteen months, his security being James Painter and the value of the whole amounting to £92-0-0. James Painter had been a seaman on the *Sirius* and had been granted land next to the Stubbs's at Portland Head. He later married the widow, Sarah Stubbs, mother of Keturah who was later to marry Matthew's third son, George Everingham. Much of this livestock was never paid for and as late as 1842, the names of the persons who owed money to the Government, Matthew's among them, were published in *The Australian* long after he and many of the others were dead.

Through this scheme also, Richard Woodbury borrowed a cow. There is a letter extant from Richard, stating that he was unable to collect the beast because he had been injured at work in the brewery and that Henry Kable would sign as security for him; in the event it was Matthew who went bond for his son-in-law.

On June 22, 1811, Matthew advertised that a roan horse, with a black mane, tail and feet had been 'found astray on the *West Hill* (formerly called the *Red House*) at Hawkesbury' and that the owner might have the same by 'paying Expences'. At another time claiming expenses for the grass that the horse had eaten might have seemed unneighbourly but pasturage was at a premium in 1811 due to the inroads of destructive caterpillars. For this reason and during the same year, Gregory Blaxland, who had settled nearby on South Creek in 1806, set out from there with a party on his first exploratory journey to cross the Blue Mountains. He returned convinced that a crossing would be possible by keeping to the crowning ridge.[257]

The herdsman, whose services Matthew had earlier offered would probably have been young Matthew or William, now aged sixteen and fourteen. George and Ann would have attended the school at Windsor run by Matthew Hughes as described in the story. Elizabeth and James were six and four in this year of 1811 and then on August 6, another daughter, Maria was born. Thus Matthew and Elizabeth became parents again and grandparents in the same year for on September 21, Richard Woodbury the Younger was born. The two babies, Maria and her nephew were baptized on the same day, October 13, 1811 by the Reverend Robert Cartwright at St Matthew's, Windsor.

Such felicitous occasions were few for Matthew over these months for it is clear that he was badly in debt. He had managed to stave Thomas Abbott off by the assignment of two working oxen named *Boxer* and *Ranger* (hopefully not the ones he had borrowed from the Government), with a cart and harness for the same and two cows with calf, should he not pay a debt of £132-8-0 on or before 1812.

The outcome of the case between himself and Richard Fitzgerald is also unknown but the circumstances surrounding it throw some light on colonial economy and demonstrate the necessity for reformatory legislation regarding the currency and monetary transactions.

In February, 1810, Fitzgerald had allowed credit for the purchase of a mare, satisfied with shop goods and settlers' notes of hand for more than half the sum. Then he had insisted on a surety of four cattle. When, by the settlement date, these had increased to six, he had refused payment in storeable wheat, the bulk of it covered by a boat receipt from the master of Henry Kable, Junior's *Endeavour* and demanded hard cash. His object, Matthew claimed, was to keep all the cattle, of far greater value than the debt.

The economy was very much one of barter and promissory or 'currency' notes circulated or were 'current' like bank notes. The system was open to abuse by forgers, by people who issued notes they had no hope of discharging and by speculators who started rumours and consequent runs, buying up discounted notes to their own profit.

Macquarie had, in 1810 laid down rules for the issue of promissory notes, insisting on printed forms for those less than £5, proper witnessing and expression in sterling. But for years afterwards, Ellis Bent, the Judge Advocate, admitted actions on illegally-drawn promissory notes to his court. A great step forward was Governor Macquarie's establishment of a colonial bank, the Bank of New South Wales and the issue of bank notes.

Returning to Matthew — perhaps the case ended by his keeping the mare and Fitzgerald the cattle. For on October 24, 1811, he made over a bay mare and her produce to Matthew John Gibbons of Sydney in surety of a debt amounting to £150. Then as 1811 drew to a close and William Charles Wentworth, the new Provost Marshal and son of Dr D'arcy Wentworth and Catherine Crowley of the *Neptune,* sold up the goods and chattels of another twenty-three men for debts to the Thompson Estate, Matthew must have wondered when his own turn would come.[258]

In 1812, William Gaudry, the auctioneer and Kable's son-in-law, lost his house, but like Matthew and many other Hawkesburyites, he had other creditors. The intention of Captain Antill, Executor of the Estate to prosecute Gaudry and others is contained in a letter written from Government House to John Howe dated March 4, 1812, the first paragraph of which is of interest to us:

'Your letter with its enclosures I received by Dow, yesterday morning, and in answer to Mr Gilberthorpe's request, you may acquaint him that if he wishes to rent the granary from Mr Everingham he may do so without fear from me of having his grain seized as I trust Mr Everingham will pay his rent like an honest man and not put me to the trouble of distraining.[259]

The granary mentioned would be the one at *West Hill Farm;* and obviously Gilberthorpe was dubious about renting and placing his grain in this repository because he knew that Everingham was financially shakey and that the Executors were now adopting a ruthless policy towards the debtors. That Antill hoped the rent would be paid would indicate that so far it was up to date. Two months later, when it was clear that neither it nor the debt for the goods bought at auction would be received, the axe fell. Wentworth advertised that at one in the afternoon of Saturday, May 16, 51 goats and ten sheep belonging to Matthew Everingham would be auctioned in the public market place. Immediately afterwards, on the farm itself, two bullocks, one cow, one calf, eighteen pigs, a quantity of corn in stack, chaff and sundry articles of household furniture, a cart and a quantity of poultry would go under the hammer, unless the execution thereon were previously superseded.

Once more the Everingham family were to lose everything, this time not from native firebrands as in 1804, but from the combined effects of the two floods of 1809 and 1811, unmitigated as had been the case in 1806 by the interference of a sympathetic Governor. Even if Matthew's tenant had salvaged his wheat from the flood, he would have been unable to sell to the Government store and thus pay his rent unless he had been a debtor to the Thompson Estate. For the letter from Antill to Howe, quoted before, proves in other paragraphs Mr Byrnes's contention that the Government Store was being run to suit the Executors and indirectly the Governor.

In most cases there were no buyers for the goods thus sold by auction and they were usually stored. Whether Matthew stayed on at West Hill after everything was sold is unknown. He may have remained as caretaker with perhaps the use of his own furniture, if it were not brought over to Windsor to store. There remains the possibility that the sale did not take place because someone among his friends, or perhaps Richard Woodbury, may have come to his rescue in time.

There are no records of Matthew's activities in 1813 except one which indicated that he did not return to his Sackville Reach holding. The lease on the property would have expired at the end of 1812 but apparently the tenant had defaulted in the meantime because in July, 1812, a new lease was made out in favour of Matthew James

Everingham, the Younger, now seventeen. Probably because of the claim that the Thompson Estate had over the property, the lease was formally registered. It was for a term of three years from July, 1812, at £30 per annum and Matthew, Senior agreed to furnish Matthew, Junior with one man until December, 1812 to assist him in putting in his crop. The witnesses were Thomas Buchanan and Lawrence Burns, the assigned servant who had been with the family since their first days on the river, who would probably be the one to help the young master in putting in his crop.

So here we have young Matthew back on the old plot as tenant and neighbour again to the Chaselings, a circumstance that would have interesting consequences over the next three or four years. But in May, 1813, there was a severe drought and then a flood, so poor young Matthew was not to find farming the block any easier than his father had done.

At the end of 1812, two years had passed since Thompson's death and as no one had come from Scotland to claim the inheritance, it was decided to sell the real estate, including *West Hill Farm* and the brewery. There seems to have been no buyer for *West Hill* and the first record of any part of it being sold is on January 17, 1815 when a quarter only (thirty acres of one hundred and twenty) was sold to James McGrath for £130-0-0. As the years went by, McGrath was unable to meet the terms of sale and the property fell into the hands of the Governor's Secretary, Mr J.T. Campbell, but not before the hill on which the *Red House* had stood had earned the name by which it has ever since been known, McGrath's Hill. It was ironic that the humbler man's memory should thus be perpetuated and that few of the travellers who now speed along the road have ever heard of Thompson or of the mansion's existence. McGrath also had the contract for the new bridge over South Creek, adjacent to *West Hill* that was to replace Thompson's old floating one. When he was unable to carry on, John Howe completed it on November 10, 1813, it being named Howe's Bridge. The only connection the Everingham family now has with the *West Hill Farm* at McGrath's Hill is that the grave of James's first wife, Cologne Everingham, (nee Goddard) is located in the tiny and much overgrown Wesleyan cemetery alongside McGuire's Hotel.[260]

At the same time as *West Hill* and the other Thompson real estate were offered for sale, October, 1810, an offer for £300 for the brewery by Mr George Palmer was passed over; and it was decided to let it for another year at the cheaper rate of £100 to Richard Woodbury. Just at this time, also, Richard and Sarah became parents again of a daughter, called for her grandmother and her aunt, Elizabeth. This girl was born on December 3, 1812, baptized on April 25, 1813 and in later years married William Hibbs.

The day after Elizabeth's birth, Richard Woodbury bought a horse called *Snapper* and a fortnight later bought the house of John Austin from Andrew Thompson's Executors, so that Richard, at least, seems to have been prosperous during this time and may have assisted his wife's family.

Not so Matthew James II, and the rest of the farmers, for with a bountiful harvest in December 1812, the Governor decided to reduce the price of wheat to 8/- per bushel, two shillings under the level at which it was profitable to grow. On New Year's Day, 1813, therefore, the settlers sent Governor Macquarie an Address congratulating him on his pro-emancipist policy but complaining of a lack of a market for surplus grain; and they protested at the new order for supplying the stores by tender which would effect a disadvantage to the lower classes of settlers. To this Macquarie, who had seen two hundred and forty people sold up so that he could get his inheritance, replied that there was no need to worry and that the interests of the lower and poorer classes of settlers would continue to be promoted.

May 1813 saw a severe drought and it was suddenly discovered that the Government stores had only two weeks supply of grain. The settlers had been forced to sell to someone else, Garnham Blaxcell, who had bought grain to export it to Rio, but now offered to sell it back to the Government as bread.

How Matthew Senior was affected by these agricultural fluctuations is not known, but the Windsor Muster of 1814 shows that he was still able to afford one convict servant, who would have been John Stapleton, who arrived on the *Providence* in 1811.

During 1814, on July 29, the last Everingham child was born, a son called John. It was twenty-three years to the month from the time that Matthew and Elizabeth had moved on to their first grant at The Ponds at Rydalmere and the time when Elizabeth had been pregnant with her first baby, Mary. Elizabeth was now forty.

Three months later, the third Everingham grandchild, William Woodbury, was born, on October 24, 1814 and once again, the two babies, child and grandchild, uncle and nephew, were baptized on the same day seven months later, May 21, 1815. The cause of the delay is not known — perhaps this day had special significance for the whole family.

The family seems still to have been in Windsor in 1815 when an advertisement regarding a Promissory Note to John Johnson for Matthew, witnessed by Richard Woodbury, appeared in the *Sydney Gazette* of May 6, 1815.[261]

Earlier the same year, 1815, the Executors of the Thompson Estate had decided to sell the brewery and it passed into the hands of the Government, with John Howe as dummy purchaser, to be used as a barracks for the military and eventually as much needed hospital. The brewing utensils were sold for £65-0-0, probably to Richard Woodbury, for he continued to brew in premises in Macquarie Street, opposite the New Market Place which he had bought from James Richards. Matthew had witnessed the sale of this property in April 1816, so was probably in Windsor at this date also.

The year 1816 also saw another enormous flood, which certainly would have affected Matthew Junior down at Portland Head. During this inundation, an unknown artist took up his position on an eminence in the centre of the town of Windsor and sketched four views, which are of considerable value to the historian seeking the location of houses and properties at that time. The complete drawing is too large to reproduce in whole; but a sketch has been made of the section which shows the Toll House, the new road to Parramatta and the position of the *Red House* on *West Hill Farm* in relation to the road, giving some idea of the extent of the waters. The complete diagram also shows 'Woodbury's'.

Throughout 1816 and despite the flood, the debtors to the Thompson estate continued to be sold up. Two of these were James Ruse, the First Fleeter and Australia's first farmer and William Bladdey, both of whom had been Thompson's good friends and witnessed his will. Thompson had once paid a debt for Ruse to enable him to go on a sealing voyage. Ruse eventually lost his home.

At long last, in the middle of this year 1816, Matthew's Land Grant at Kurrajong was issued, nearly six years after Macquarie's arrival. But it seems unlikely that Matthew ever lived on this property and possible that William, now eighteen, may have farmed it.

For by the following year, 1817, Matthew had gone back to Portland Head or Sackville Reach and was renting a small property directly opposite the Chaselings' and very close to his original Hawkesbury block that Matthew Junior was farming. This land was to have been granted to John Palmer but was never properly deeded. It later became *Elizabeth Everingham Farm*. Family legend has it that, in early times, the Everingham boys used to swim the river to meet the Chaseling girls and vice versa. A glance at the map will show that such a thing would have been quite practical while the Everinghams lived on this property.

Perhaps through the auspices of John Howe, who had stepped into Andrew Thompson's shoes in many ways and was now Chief Constable at Windsor, Matthew was now appointed District Constable at Portland Head, (William Addy, constable from 1810 having died). Here we will leave the family temporarily, down river again where the final chapter of Matthew's life was to be lived out.[262]

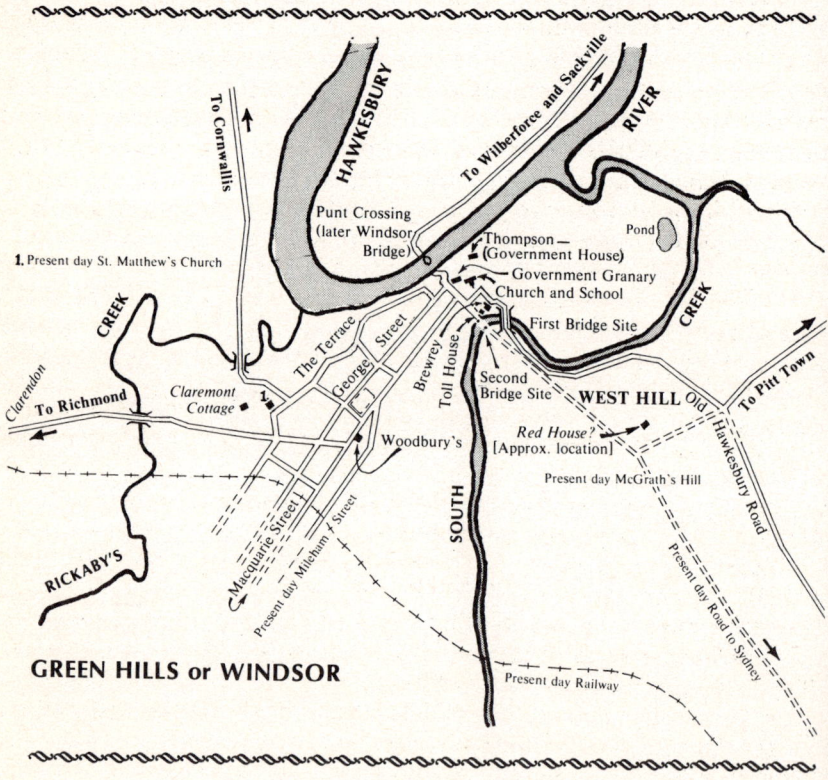

To Cornwallis

HAWKESBURY

RIVER

To Wilberforce and Sackville

Punt Crossing
(later Windsor
Bridge)

Pond

1. Present day St. Matthew's Church

Thompson —
(Government House)

Government Granary
Church and School

CREEK

First Bridge Site

CREEK

The Terrace

George Street

Brewery

Toll House

Clarendon

To Richmond

Claremont
Cottage

Second
Bridge Site

WEST HILL

Old Hawkesbury Road

To Pitt Town

1

Woodbury's

Red House?
[Approx. location]

SOUTH

Present day McGrath's Hill

Macquarie Street

Present day Mileham Street

Present day Road to Sydney

RICKABY'S

GREEN HILLS or WINDSOR

Present day Railway

CHAPTER NINE

Yule-Tide

'NOW LET ME see,' said Elizabeth, 'how many are there of us?' as she washed the last potato, cut it and began counting with her knife. 'I've allowed three pieces of potato for young Dick, Sally, do you think that will do?'

'It will be plenty, mother,' said Sarah. 'I'll be surprised if he can eat anything, the way Father has been feeding him sugar sticks. I declare he was never like that with us as children,' she added, not really chiding.

'Well, he could never give you older ones treats, dear, so he makes up for it now. Let him have his pleasure — he spoils our John too,' said Elizabeth.

'There's no spoiling John though, Mother, he's such a gentle child,' said Sarah, 'You really are blessed with him.'

'Well, dear 'God tempers the wind to the shorn lamb' said Elizabeth. 'It's just as well, at my age, to have an easy child.'

Just then, as if to convince Elizabeth how fortunate she really was to have a quiet child, the two older Woodbury children burst into the room. 'Mother,' said Elizabeth Woodbury, 'Dick said I can't sit next to James though I asked Grandma first!'

'Just a minute, then, till we sort it out,' said Sarah, taking them into the main room of the house. 'Now, let's have a look. It's a matter of how we can best fit at the table, so stop making a fuss.'

'Look at the box I'm going to sit on! It's marvellous fun! See how it wobbles!' said Richard, as he bounced about on the wooden box that had been brought in to supplement the overpressed seating capacity of the Everingham house and wrinkled the tablecloth in the process.

'That's enough!' said Sarah, who was beginning to sound harassed. 'All out of the house for a while or there'll be no Christmas pudding!' and she hunted them out through the kitchen door.

'Oh, that reminds me,' said Elizabeth, hearing this last threat, 'Take a look in the boiler, Sally and make sure there's still plenty of water around the pudding, will you, dear.'

The pudding was boiling away on an outside fire, the open fireplace of the kitchen being almost entirely filled by the young pig that had already been partially cooked the day before, in order to keep the house cooler today. 'It's right, mother,' said Sarah, as she replaced the lid, 'steaming away beautifully. What a whopper it is!'

'Yes, and Ann was worried it wouldn't be big enough,' said Elizabeth. 'It's the first one she's ever made, you know and she was so proud when she brought it over last night as her contribution to the dinner.'

'What time are they coming, Mother?' asked Sarah, referring to her brother and sister-in-law, Matthew and Ann.

'About two o'clock, I told her,' said Elizabeth, 'for she wanted Young Matt to take her over to see the family this morning.'

'And how are the Chaselings?' asked Sarah. 'Very well, dear, we hear almost daily, with our Will courting Jane and young John Chaseling always here with some excuse to see Ann. Our Ann has gone over there, too, with Matt and Annie.... Now there's the men coming back,' said Elizabeth, as she glanced out the window. 'I must get your father to sharpen the knife, to be ready to carve.'

It was, indeed, the men, Matthew looking older but kindly as his fifties approached and the robust, lively Richard Woodbury, whose presence seemed always to fill a room. They had been visiting the neighbours and were thoroughly enjoying the day.

'Now, Matt,' said Richard, 'I've something very special for you that has just come up from Sydney Town. Some glasses, Sally! Try a drop of this and tell me if it's not like velvet!'

'He's been trying a drop already, Richard, if you ask me,' said Elizabeth, 'I suppose you've had a drink with everyone.'

'Couldn't help it, Mother,' said Matthew, ''Tis Christmas, you know,' which information was perhaps a trifle unnecessary, 'and the neighbours wouldn't let us go without we shared a dram.'

'Shared a dram!' said Sally, laughingly, 'We were stopping all the way from Windsor this morning. It's just as well that *Snapper* knows his way so well or I'd have to drive home,' and she went to fetch the glasses.

Very soon Young Matthew and his bride of eleven months, Ann, arrived, together with William and Ann Everingham, who had been with them for the morning at the Chaseling house. 'Now you sit down, Annie,' said Elizabeth to her daughter-in-law, who was very close to the time for bearing her first child. 'Our Ann will help me while you and Sally have a chat.'

So the Christmas proceeded until somehow seventeen people were seated at the two tables which had been placed together and were covered with bed sheets, now almost invisible under the simple but hearty food that was placed on them. Yesterday Matthew had gone into the bush with young James and cut some foliage from a vivid red-flowering tree which they called 'Christmas Bush'. On the way he had told James of the holly that was used in 'the old country', he never called it 'home' now, for 'home' was here in this noisy bush where cicadas shrilled and you had to watch out for black snakes. Ann had put a big bunch of the Christmas Bush in a stone demijohn on the sideboard and Maria, now six, had arranged smaller pieces on the table this morning by way of decoration.

By now it was three and the dinner was in full swing. Down at the far end of the table, where the children had been placed by choice, the excitement and noise were hard to control. The dramatic collapse of the

a The Red House
b Road to Parramatta
c Toll House
d A   House
e Old Burying Ground
f   Mr Allcorns Farm
g   Mr Aspinalls Farm
h   Mr Marsdens Farms
i   Mr Fitzgeralds Farms
k   Mr Tebills Farm (Mr Marsdens
l   Rochesters Farm

The dotted line is nearly the course of the South Cre

Mitchell Library

'A Sketch of the Inundation of 1816', artist unknown.   Retouched section of original
showing the position of the *Red House* compared with the new Sydney-Windsor Road
[see p119]

130. Acres.

BY HIS EXCELLENCY LACHLAN MACQUARIE, ESQUIRE, CAPTAIN GENERAL AND GOVERNOR IN CHIEF OF HIS MAJEST[Y]
TERRITORY OF NEW SOUTH WALES and its DEPENDENCIES, &c. &c. &c.

WHEREAS full Power and Authority for GRANTING LANDS in the Territory of NEW SOUTH WALES is vested in His Majesty's Capt[ain]
General and Governor in Chief (or in his Absence the Lieutenant Governor for the Time being), in and over the said Territory and
Dependencies, by His Majesty's Instructions under the Royal Sign Manual, bearing Date respectively the Twenty-fifth Day of April, One thousand se[ven]
hundred and eighty-seven, and the Twentieth Day of August, One thousand seven hundred and eighty-nine.

IN PURSUANCE of the Power and Authority vested in me as aforesaid, I DO BY THESE PRESENTS GIVE and GRANT [to]
Matthew Everingham His Heirs and Assigns, to HAVE and to HOLD FOR EV[ER]
One hundred and Forty Acres of LAND, lying and situate in the Distric[t]
Richmond Hill, Bounded On the South side by a West line of Forty One Chains, On the West by a line North [*]
Degrees East Sixty three Chains, On the North by an East line of Sixty One Chains, And On the East by [a]
line South Twenty Degrees East Twenty three Chains.

To be HAD and HELD by H[im] the said Matthew Everingham His Heirs and Assigns free f[rom]
all Taxes, Quit Rents, and other Acknowledgments for the Space of Five Years from the Date hereof (Provided always, and it is hereby expressly to [be]
understood, that the said Matthew Everingham the Grantee in these Presents named, shall in no wise ei[ther]
directly or directly Sell, Alienate, or Transfer any Part or Parcel of the Land hereby Granted, within the said Term of Five Years; And also, provi[ded]
always, that the said Matthew Everingham shall Clear and Cultivate, or cause to be Cleared and Cultivated within the s[aid]
Term of Five Years, the Quantity of Twenty two Acres of the said Land hereby Granted: Otherwise the Whole of the said L[and]
shall revert to the Crown, and the Grant hereby made thereof shall be held and deemed NULL and VOID), and saving and reserving to Government the R[ight]
of making a Public Road through such Part of the said Land, as may at any time be required; such Timber as may be growing, or that may grow herea[fter]
upon the said Lands, which may be deemed fit for Naval Purposes to be Reserved for the Use of the Crown, and paying an Annual Quit Rent of Three [*]
after the Term or Time of Five Years before-mentioned.

IN TESTIMONY whereof I have hereunto set my Hand, and the Seal of the Territory, at Sydney, in New South Wales,
Eighth Day of October in the Year of Our Lord One thousand eight hundred and Sixt[een]

Signed and Sealed in our Presence,

H. C. Antill

Joseph Cowgill

L. Macquarie

Matthew Everingham Grant
One hundred Forty acres &c.

Mitchell Library

Facsimile of Land Grant to Matthew Everingham, 1816. In the John Norton Papers,
1817-1868. [see p125]

box, after one wobble too many on young Richard's part and its replacement with a taller one, on which he now sat perched like a monkey, had been a high spot in the festivities for the young fry.

The dinner had commenced quietly enough, with Matthew at the head of the table saying Grace. Then, as Annie, his daughter-in-law, seated on his left, had passed plates to him, he had ceremoniously carved the pork, passing the plates on to Sally, who served the vegetables out of two dishes. Now all ceremony was over and little of the table's earlier pristine appearance remained. Though the giant carving board had been removed to make way for a smaller one on which the remains of the pudding stood, it had been impossible to clear the table entirely. Little sprigs of Christmas bush mixed with fragments of pork crackling and pudding crumbs and there were wet patches on the cloth from spilt ale and other beverages.

But it didn't matter, thought Elizabeth, as she regarded the table — it had all gone very well and the sheets would be boiled tomorrow. Then she looked over to her husband, a veritable patriarch, with the baby of the group, little Jeremiah on his knee, who was now growing tired from the merriment.

Her eyes moved to Annie and young Matthew, tall, lean but broad-shouldered, with a long face, heavy brows and big hands, now toying with a spoon as he talked, almost a replica of his father twenty years before. Elizabeth enjoyed the pleasure of having her eldest son beside her once more. She herself was seated on the side of the table today, near the door to the kitchen for convenience and had Richard Woodbury on her other side. Capable, resourceful Richard, thought Elizabeth, much older than Sally and well able to take care of her. He had been a help to them all these last years.

Alongside Richard was Ann Everingham, who could also be helpful, when she was not in front of the looking glass. At the moment she was wiping pudding off young William Woodbury's face; and he was protesting because the delay meant that his young uncle John and sister, Elizabeth, were getting ahead of them with the fruit, nuts and other good things. At the end of the table and opposite her grandfather, sat Elizabeth Woodbury, five years old and copying everything that her Aunt Maria, a more mature six years, was doing.

Then, down the long side of the table were Richard Junior, also six, as lively as his father, James and Elizabeth Everingham, now ten and twelve, and George, a serious young man who had had his eighteenth birthday only three weeks before. Next to him was William, twenty years old, who resembled George in that his face was not so lean as Matthew's — but all the boys had their father's brows and deep set eyes. So back to Sally, in whom Elizabeth saw herself as a girl.

'Well, that's all, is it, Mother?' asked Matthew, Senior, jokingly, 'There's no more to come?'

'That's all and enough,' said Sally, 'and we'll be lucky not to have the young ones ill tonight after the way they've hoed into Ann's pudding. Come on, let's clear the dishes away.'

'Not so fast, Sal,' said Matthew, 'it's not often all the family are gathered at one table.' (What he didn't speak of, but merely reflected upon, because he knew the young ones did not like him doing so, was a Christmas thirty years before — and meagre rations on a storm-tossed ship at the bottom of the world, as they had approached Van Diemen's Land and they knew not what. To see this family about him, healthy, well-fed and hopeful was more than he could have wished for on that yule-tide so long ago.)

'Well, we'll have to set out back to Windsor soon,' said Sarah, 'so we'd best get on with it.' And the women rose to clear the table.

'Bring me the tobacco box, Will,' said Matthew, 'and we men shall have a quiet pipe.'

'And a drop more of the brandy, Matt, for Christmas cheer,' said Richard, 'though Annie's pudding was pretty well laced, I'll admit.'

The men betook themselves to the cool verandah which overlooked the river, the children went off to play, the baby was put down to sleep and the women got on with their job of clearing the table.

Presently the men saw a row-boat approaching the Everingham landing and made out the form of the Lower River Constable, John Williams, making fast at the wharf and heading up the track towards them.

'No rest for the wicked, Matt, even on Christmas Day,' Williams greeted them. 'A message has come through from Hobby on the sloop, *Ann Maria,* I was telling you about. They're still selling spirits by the gallon down at Maun's so we're to go aboard and seize her.'

'Trust Hobby to expect us to do that today,' said Matthew, 'I'll wager his Christmas is not disturbed! Why couldn't it wait until tomorrow when he comes down for the Inquisition on Pollard?' The settlers' dislike of Thomas Hobby went back exactly ten years to the time of the Rum Rebellion, when he had supported Macarthur and been a party to the venomous petition they had been forced to sign. Now he was 'jumped up' to Coroner, although Matthew had to admit that he did the job well.

So he knocked his pipe on the rail and went inside to get his coat and to tell the women. They all came out onto the verandah and waved him off, Elizabeth a little anxious, because she knew he would be tired and that, not knowing he would be called out, had already had a generous share of Richard's brandy.

When they got down to the boat, Williams took the oars and they skimmed off round the bend into the Sackville Reach, where the family lost sight of them. The tide answered so Matthew let the other man row. The bush was hazy with heat and they saw no one as they went down Kent, Boston, Cambridge and Sussex Reaches. Everyone is asleep, thought Matthew and we should be too. Then at last they came round to Maun's and saw the sloop anchored. Young William Maun who was on board, caught their painter and helped them up.

'Captain Irwin is on shore at our place, Mr Williams,' he said, 'and the crew are off in the bush somewhere.'

'Well, let's take a look,' said Williams and they climbed into the hold. He levered off the lid of a cask and dipped in a pannikin. 'Good spirits alright,' he said, passing the tin to Matthew. 'Well, we'll have to stay here until Hobby comes down.'

'Then we may as well make ourselves comfortable,' said Matthew as he settled himself on the sweeps at the stern of the boat where he could get a breeze and at the same time hear anyone approaching.

At that moment they heard the sound of voices raised in quarrel come over the water and, at the same time, saw two men, obviously drunk, fighting on the shore. 'Some of the crew, I suppose,' said Williams, 'Too tipsy to have the sense to get off and away. I'll have to go and see what they're up to. Matthew, you stay here and look after the boat. But for the Lord's sake, man, come in off the sweeps, you know you can't swim!'

'It's too hot down the hatches,' said Matthew, 'I want to stay here where I can get a breath of air.'

His head was swimming from the draught of spirits he had had from the cask. After the food he had eaten, the pudding and Richard's brandy, all he wanted now was to sleep, if only this feeling of nausea would go. Even out here on the water, it was still hot.

As a fresh wave of giddiness came over him, he grasped a line to steady himself. But it was not secured and came away in his hand so that he lost his balance and, before he knew what was happening, had toppled into the water. He struggled and rose to see, not twenty feet away, a glimpse of Williams' horrified face as the man quickly turned the head of the skiff to come back to him.

Then the waters closed about him, yet it seemed an age before he knew that it was the end and that Williams would not reach him in time; and he thought many things. How wry it was that but an hour since, he had been at home, part of a scene so happy and secure. 'Boast not of tomorrow', the Scriptures said, how true it was! For the river, at once old enemy and old friend, had been waiting to take him at last.

The river, and his struggles with the river and with the land — the whole of his past life now swept through his consciousness. He saw a vision of himself as a young man, a farmer in a smock, rough casting his seed. And the words of a verse imperfectly remembered came back to him: 'Then I looked on the works that my hands had wrought and on the labour that I had laboured to do and all was vanity.' Then the face of the sower came closer and it was not his own face but that of Another....

* * *

T HE   of Matthew's drowning is based on the Coroner's
Inquest into his death, held the following day, December 26, 1817,
facsimile of which is reproduced. A week later, the *Sydney Gazette* of
January 3, 1818, carried the following report:

'On Friday last, Mr Matthew Everingham, settler and District Constable at Portland Head, fell overboard from a Hawkesbury Boat and was
unfortunately drowned. On the finding of the body an Inquest was convened who returned a verdict Accidental death. He leaves a large family
to deplore his premature death.'[263]

It will be remarked that there is no suspicion of foul play either in
the Coroner's Inquest or the newspaper report. Nearly a century was to
pass before the suggestion that Everingham had been murdered
appeared in print for the first time. This was contained in one of a series
of articles by 'Chris', or J.T. Christie, in the *Hawkesbury Herald* of
1905, under the heading *A Bit of River History*. Christie's information
was demonstrably hearsay — he confused Matthew with his second son,
William — and was corrected by a grandson, Stephen Everingham. Mr
J.C.L. Fitzpatrick in *Those Were the Days,* published in 1922, repeated
the article without the correction. Here is the relevant passage:

'William held some official position on the river in his time, that of
chief constable, I believe... He met his death by drowning in the year
1859 at Lower Portland, immediately opposite where Peacock's house
stands. It appears that a boat was engaged in the illicit rum-selling business, and Mr Everingham, with several other gentlemen, all holding official positions, went on board to investigate matters. After taking an
inventory of the boat's cargo, Mr Everingham's colleagues went to
Peacock's to have dinner, and, on their return made the appalling discovery that Mr Everingham had been drowned in their absence. Many
advanced the opinion that he met his death by foul play, but this is one of
the many mysteries of old times on the river which must forever remain
unsolved.[264]

Then, in the *Windsor and Richmond Gazette* of February 2, 1932,
there appeared under the heading, *Murdered?-Romantic Hawkesbury
Story,* an article of which this is an extract:

'Most I know about the Everingham affairs', says Mr [Matthew M.]
Woodbury, 'I got from my grandmother. She told me that her father
(Matthew James Everingham, the pioneer) was District Constable at the
Hawkesbury (Sackville) when there was trading on the river between
Windsor and Sydney which was suspected of smuggling grog. 'The
pioneer was an exciseman and went on board a vessel to conduct a
search. Whilst engaged in looking over the ship he was knocked on the
head and his body thrown overboard and drowned, so he was really murdered. 'One of Betsy Everingham's [his daughter's] husbands was on
board at the time and saw him 'knocked overboard', but would not tell
the authorities. They had him arrested and tried to make him disclose the
names of those who had done the deed, but he refused to do so. So the
judge put Betsy Everingham's husband in the murderer's place and sentenced him to be hanged. Then he began to tell but the judge told him it
was too late, as he had taken the other man's (the murderer's) place.[265]

This story, then, was said to have come from Matthew

Everingham's eldest daughter, Sarah Woodbury, who had been twenty-four at the time of his death. But whatever credence the first part of it deserves for that reason is negated by the embellishment regarding Sarah's brother-in-law, Betsy Everingham's first husband, Charles Butler. There is no evidence of Butler being either on the boat or nearby when Matthew was drowned: he was neither a witness nor a juror. He was certainly in the colony at the time, having arrived in the previous April, but the earliest date placing him with Matthew Everingham, the Younger, as an assigned servant is the muster of 1820. He did not become Betsy's husband until 1822. The penalty for Contempt of Court was not hanging and though Butler was hanged in 1826, it was for a far more serious crime which must have brought shame to his family. Perhaps her grandson's queries about the latter affair had led to an invention on Sarah's part which, though understandable, was to have quite unforeseen results.

There has been a tendency in nearly every old Australian family, perhaps because of ignorance due to the long unavailability of official records, to romanticize the past of its founder. A not uncommon story will concern the loss through misfortune of money or property in the old country. In our case, the story of a disinherited heir, combined with the rumour of his murder, were to culminate in a fortune hunt this century known as 'The Everingham Millions' which is the subject of another chapter. Any remnants of the belief that Matthew was a disinherited heir or that an unclaimed fortune existed will therein be disproved. This is discussed in *A Hawkesbury Story*.

Here it is only relevant to point out that Everingham can never have believed that he had financial expectations for, if he had, it is unlikely he would have died intestate. And that neither his family nor his creditors believed him to be entitled to an English inheritance at the time of his death. And that neither they, nor the Coroner, jury, witnesses, nor neighbours had anything to gain by his death. And that while Matthew may, like any man, have had enemies, there is no evidence to support the rumour that he was murdered for any reason whatsoever.

A by-product of a discussion focused on these matters will be a measure of general social history — for the work of the Justices of the Peace and constabulary are partially examined — and appropriately, local Hawkesbury history, an intrinsic element in **Book Two**.

Aptly, the location of the drowning will first claim our attention. And the article by 'Chris' was close to the truth in stating that Matthew was drowned near Peacock's at Lower Portland, that is, on the Maund-Cross peninsula, then known as Maun's Point. It would have been more accurate to say 'opposite to where Peacock's house later stood'; for although Maun would have had a dwelling there, Peacock did not acquire the land until 1819 and the earliest we can date his house, still extant and the subject of a full description in **Book Two**, is 1826.[266]

The legend that Matthew was drowned near 'Berry Hill' at Leet's

Vale, that he had lived there and had there been attacked by natives, following which he is said to have crawled into the reeds to hide for two days, is proved false by the Inquest and the fact that 'Berry Hill' was not granted to his son, Matthew, until 1831. However, on the opposite promontory, John Llewellyn's servant had in 1805 suffered this experience, which may account for the legend.[267]

It was at Maun's Point, Lower Portland, then, that Matthew was drowned and the 'Inquisition' into his death held. And it is with the manner of this Inquisition and with justice at the common level that we now have to deal.

Probably due once again to a lack of information, there has formerly existed in the mind of the general public a view that 'anything went' in the administration of justice in the early days of the colony. This has been referred to as the 'Court House Cave Predilection', because stories propagated regarding certain caves on the route of the Great North Rock offer an extreme example of the syndrome. This will be expanded in the following chapter. Here let it be said that the ideas that 'people just disappeared' or that 'they strung you up for anything in those days' are disproved by a perusal of Court records and Coroners' Inquests for the period. It is evident that the law was remarkably well kept under existing circumstances.

In charge of law enforcement at the Hawkesbury and in other country centres were the Justices of the Peace, appointed as either Magistrates or Coroners. The English system of appointing Coroners goes back to the reign of the absentee Richard I (Lionheart), when his Archbishop of Canterbury, Hubert Walter, governed in his stead and began a policy of trusting the middle classes of town and country and of using them as instruments of government, the Crown thus depending on the amateur services of local gentry to enforce the King's Peace. The next step by which the Mediaeval Kings of England forced the English to acquire the habits of self government was the appointment of Justices of the Peace in reign of Edward III. This ultimately led to a strong House of Commons and to the British system of representative government as we know it.[268]

Thus, as Mr J.K. McLaughlin remarks in his study of the magistracy in N.S.W. from 1788 to 1850, the institution or office of Justice of the Peace arrived with the First Fleet and their role was an important one in colonial society. The Justices of the Peace were involved in a very real manner with just that, the meting out of justice or judgements or law and the maintenance of peace and order. Thus the functions of both Mediaeval 'J.P.'s' and Hawkesbury 'J.P.'s' of the early Nineteenth Century contrasted with the restricted duties of those persons today holding that office alone.[269]

When appointed magistrates, they exercised both criminal and civil jurisdiction, dealing summarily with and sentencing less serious offenders and holding inquiries on persons charged with serious crime. The object of such inquiries was to decide not whether the accused were guilty but if there were enough evidence to justify putting him on trial at a superior court in Sydney.

Justices of the Peace who were appointed Coroners held jurisdiction only within the boundaries of their districts. They also had a common law right to preserve general order, but their main function was to hold inquests on the bodies of persons dying in institutions or by causes considered unnatural. They were empowered to commit for trial persons judged criminally responsible for a death.[270]

Trevelyan says of the English office holders, and it applies to the Hawkesbury:

'Justices of the peace.... like the Coroners, were not bureaucrats but independent country gentlemen.... the magistrate who expounded and enforced the law for ordinary people in ordinary cases may not have known much law but he knew his neighbours and was known of them.[271]

A study of the backgrounds of Hawkesbury Justices of the Peace – Magistrates and/or Coroners — shows them to have been engaged in one or more of the following occupations prior to their appointments: surveyor, settler, clergyman, surgeon, roadbuilder, military officer, naval and commercial pursuits. Though educated and reasonably substantial men, none seem to have had any legal training. Most had been in the colony for some time before their appointment and Dr Thomas Arndell, Reverend Samuel Marsden, Andrew Thompson, Surgeon James Mileham, John Howe and Thomas Hobby knew the Hawkesbury well before commencing duty. Charles Grimes, (1800), Andrew Thompson and John Howe had previous experience in police work.

In a case which occurred early in the Macquarie era, we have at once an example of the work-a-day magistracy and the transplantation of English common law and custom to colonial soil.

It was 11 o'clock on the night of April 17, 1810, when an old couple, George and Ann Cox, came to the house of James Paynter next door, when only his servant, James Cobb, was at home, with a 'Hue and Cry' that they had been robbed.[272]

When later the clerk who recorded evidence capitalized the nouns 'hue' and 'cry', he was not merely adhering to common literary practice. The Coxes, contrary to our interpretation of the expression, were not merely making a fuss about their experience. For a Hue and Cry was the old legal name for the official outcry made when calling for assistance in the pursuit of a criminal escaping from justice. (The derivation is from the Old French, 'huer', meaning 'to hoot or shout'.) Under Mediaeval law, every Englishman was a policeman. Persons failing to respond when the hue and cry was raised were liable to penalties and indeed, the law of hue and cry in New South Wales has never been repealed. Thus the Hue and Cry had its place with the call of 'Stop Thief!' or 'Murder!' in the era which preceded non-personal methods of communication.[273]

Accordingly, Cobb went eight miles down river with Cox the next morning to William Addy's, the latter being District Constable for Portland Head and living where the Sackville punt is today located. With William Jacklyn, James Kelly and John Williams also assisting, Addy now set off fifteen miles down river to the house of Edward Flynn — believed to be one of the assailants — examined a whaleboat and was shown the stolen and now butchered sow by a black woman. Flynn, James Davis and John Harris, his partners in the crime, were next taken to the magistrate, Mr (Andrew) Thompson's, who duly held an inquiry and took sworn evidence. Upon the basis of this, the prisoners were then sent to Sydney and charged with Burglary in a Dwelling House before the Judge Advocate, Ellis Bent, in the Court of Criminal Jurisdiction. Because of the early English veneration of the sanctity of the home, this crime was always regarded much more seriously than theft so that, when judged Guilty, the three were sentenced to be hanged. Flynn and Harris were later granted conditional pardons but Davis was actually sent back to be hanged at Portland Head, attended by the Reverend Samuel Marsden.

The fact that D'arcy Wentworth, Simeon Lord and Henry Kable all spoke for and knew Flynn, who had been in the colony for seventeen years, is indicative of the smallness and close-knittedness of colonial society in 1810 before large numbers of transportees augmented the population.

Returning to the 'hue and cry' aspect, one here sees concerted action for the maintenance of law and order and the defence of property. To what extent the neighbours' response was one of outrage at the offence or recognition of a legal obligation, we cannot know. John Williams, later to be a constable himself, went so far as to shoot the prisoner, Harris, when the latter had attempted to escape. Yet victims, pursuers, the constable, yea, even the magistrate, were all ex-convicts. They were now, with the exception of Cobb, free and landholders, living their lives alongside those who had come free. And as we note this welding of society and the disappearance at the common level of differences between the ex-bond and the always-free, we remark also the assimilation of the Irish. Flynn, the malefactor, was spoken for by four Protestants. On the other hand, Kelly, one of his pursuers, was an Irishman.

Let us now look at the work of the Coroners. And in expanding an earlier point — their familiarity with the district and people over whom they had jurisdiction — we return to our central argument that there was nothing irregular about the Inquest into Matthew Everingham's death nor any suspicious circumstances.

Thomas Hobby, Coroner for Everingham's Inquest, though he had been against Bligh in the Rum Rebellion, had been Lieutenant in charge of the military at the Hawkesbury as early as 1799, so that he knew the area and its people. Time after time he was called out to cases of drowning, to find bodies swollen from immersion, mutilated by native tomahawks or to such unusual cases as when an infant was suffocated in bed by being lain upon by a drunken mother. When he was too ill to officiate Surgeon Mileham, also of the military and a Justice of the

Peace, stepped in and did the best he could, probably with the advice of whomever recorded the cases and wrote to the Judge Advocate to apologise if anything were out of order. Windsor was too far from Sydney to wait if an inquiry had to be held before a corpse could be buried. The Judge Advocate, Ellis Bent, had personal knowledge of the characters of the District Coroners as had Governor Macquarie.[274]

If there were any doubt about a verdict, as we saw in the case of William Yardley, as early as 1805 and though the case occurred right in the middle of the native attacks, one doubtful neighbour could prompt exhumation. Even during the Rum Rebellion and though his appointment by the rebel government was actually illegal, Archibald Bell as magistrate held Inquests on the bodies of persons who had suffered unnatural deaths.

Coroners journeyed many miles in the course of their duties. John Howe was later to write of travelling all the way to remote Mangrove Creek and collecting jurors on his journey, who had to take their food with them, in order that the accidental death of the humblest man might not go uninvestigated.[275]

The Coroner was assisted to a large extent by the District Constable, who went as far as he could to prepare things beforehand for such 'Inquisitions'. Let us have a look at Matthew Everingham at work as District Constable of Portland Head in November, 1817, a month before he died, to see what used to happen.

On November 10, at 5 o'clock, Patrick Conway was cleaning corn on the riverbank when he discovered a corpse. He called John Everett and the rest of the neighbours and they determined to call the District Constable, Mr Everingham. Everingham immediately accompanied them to Fitzpatrick's Wharf and went to view the corpse with Everett 'but could not find either pocket or papers about it so as to ascertain the person', nor did he know of anyone being missing; nor were there any marks of violence on the body. He immediately sent word into Windsor to the Coroner, Thomas Hobby, who came down the next day and held an Inquest with the body of the man 'lying then and there dead' before him and the jury, whom Matthew would have assembled.[276]

The Jury who now agreed on the verdict of Accidental Death was composed of: John Everett, the neighbour whom Conway had first called: James Dunn, who appears to have been Headman and whose grant was adjacent to Henry Lamb's; Patrick Burn, who had come on the *Rolla* and who had married Dunn's daughter, Ellen in 1816; William Bayley and his eighteen years old son of the same name, who would marry a Margaret Jones in 1820; Humphrey Taylor, a landholder at Lower Portland Head by 1828; Charles Thorp, who is hard to trace because there are two in the Windsor Muster of 1820; Hugh Dogerty, ex the *Queen,* 1791, a landholder in the 1814 Muster; Lawrence Byrne, Matthew Everingham's servant; William Green and Joseph McGloghlin. These appear to have been the neighbours who had seen the body and others who lived or worked near Fitzpatrick's Wharf, almost opposite what would become *Elizabeth Everingham Farm,* where Matthew was now living.

Fitzpatrick's Wharf, like Maun's Point, seems to have been a local name only and is not shown on any map. It is presumed to have been on Henry Lamb's grant for the following reasons. In 1812, Lamb sold thirty acres of his seventy to Thomas Clarkson of Sydney, having sold the balance of forty to John Jones. It is thought that Clarkson also acquired this land from Jones because on December 19, 1817, he assigned forty acres to James Fitzpatrick, who was already in occupation. Fitzpatrick had come from Cork, Ireland in 1803 on the *Rolla* the same ship as Andrew Doyle, who appears in Part Two. (Doyle had bought Bartholomew Morley's grant in 1809 and Fitzpatrick had witnessed an agreement regarding this land between Doyle and his son Cyrus, in 1811.)[277]

Though the sale of part of Lamb's property to Fitzpatrick may never have been completed — because by the time old John Turnbull died in 1834, his wife and son, Ralph had bought Lamb's seventy acres from Clarkson — still Fitzpatrick was long enough in occupation for the landing place to bear his name.

As Patrick Conway, who had found the body, is shown in 1822 as renting thirty acres, it may be that he was renting the other portion of Lamb's from Clarkson. In any case, Conway, who was the first witness, put his mark to his evidence and then Matthew, the only other witness, gave his testimony and signed it.[278]

Six weeks later on Christmas Day, 1817, Matthew himself was drowned and Coroner Hobby held an Inquest into his death on Boxing Day, December 26, 1817. At the same time and place he held an Inquest into the death of John Pollard which we will consider first because it throws some light on Matthew's death.

John Pollard, who seems more likely to have been a labourer, ex the *Duke of Portland,* rather than the ex-soldier of the same name who held land next to Matthew in 1803, had died on the previous Monday, December 22, 1817. On that day he and Edward Griffiths (an expiree from the *Admiral Barrington* according to the 1814 Muster) had been drinking on board the ship, *Anna Maria,* which 'laid alongside of a large tree' at Maun's Point. 'On leaving the vessel, Pollard was assisted to get on to the tree by William Chapman, but was in so much of a hurry to get on shore and was, in any case, intoxicated, so that he jumped into the water.' He got 'intangled in the weeds' and was drowned. John Irwin (the master of the vessel) jumped into the water to save Pollard but was not able to do so. In about a quarter of an hour, James Sutherland (an expiree from the *Albermarle,* Third Fleet, 1791) found the body but there was no appearance of life.[279]

It is interesting that Pollard, like William Stubbs in 1805, got 'intangled with the weeds' or reeds, which must have edged the river for a considerable length at this time.

Of the twelve men who decided that Pollard had died accidentally, six would serve on the jury for the Inquest into Matthew's death. They were: Michael Lamb, about forty-one at the time, who had been transported on the first of the Irish Ships, the *Queen* in 1791 and who, at least by 1828, had acquired James Sherwin's property opposite Maun's Point; Joseph Maun and John Cross, the original grantees on the promontory and John Cross's son, William; James Kelly and James Levello, (ex the *Aeolus,* Life, 1809). The other six were: John Brown, the grantee on Maun's north; Peter Ibbs and George Ibbs, (Hibbs father and son), their names spelt phonetically, who were next door to Michael Lamb; Joseph Maun's son, William Maun, Henry Sergeant and Jacob Williams, who had bought twenty acres more or less of Maun's grant, bounded by the rocks on John Brown's side and by the creek on Maun's on the other. Thus we see that nine of the twelve lived on or near Maun's Point.[280]

The Inquest into Matthew's death was probably held directly after that on Pollard, and John Williams, District Constable, who then or later had land down the river on Liverpool Reach, was the chief witness. Williams told how the *Anna Maria* had been seized by the direction of the Coroner for selling and retailing spirituous liquors and how he and Everingham had been on board at five o'clock the previous day, Christmas Day, when the accident occurred. The preceding story, 'Yule-tide', shows Williams and Everingham going on board on Christmas afternoon but they may have seized the vessel earlier.[281]

The *Anna Maria's* official activities during the years 1817-1818 are listed as carrying ballast to the Hawkesbury and returning with cargoes of maize. On this trip she had sailed from Sydney on November 29, three and a half weeks earlier carrying 'ballast' but evidently had a considerable quantity of spirits on board. While she was tied up at Maun's ostensibly loading maize for the return trip, she seems to have been a floating pub. John Irwin, her master, who had dived unsuccessfully to rescue Pollard, had already been in trouble over an illicit still. What we know of her owner, Robert Waples, indicates a character similar to that of Sam Terry, 'the Botany Bay Rothschild,' but on a smaller scale. He had been transported on the *Morley* in 1816 and married in 1817 Sarah Packer, widow of William Packer. In the Bigge Enquiry, three years later, it was said that she had kept a 'flash house', the *Adam and Eve* in Pitt Street. At least two farmers seemed to be the worse for the *Anna Maria's* visits. Waples already held a mortgage over fifty acres of Maund's land and was to sell him up in January, 1819, the buyer being John Jenkins Peacock. Jacob Williams, who had bought Maund's other twenty acres on October 4, 1811, a sale which incidentally, had been witnessed by Richard Woodbury and William Everingham, assigned his plot to Waples on March 27, 1818, just prior to the ship's return trip to Sydney, where she arrived on March 30.[282]

So it is hardly a matter of surprise that Williams, the Constable, had heard quarrelling on shore that Christmas afternoon, to which disturbance he had set out rowing in 'a boat which was at the sloop's head'.

The whereabouts of the Captain and crew are unknown but they cannot have been far away and may have been involved in the quarrelling. Williams went on to testify that before going, he had cautioned Matthew not to sit in so dangerous a place as the 'sweeps'. This could mean on the sweep oars, those used for steering or propelling the boat when it was becalmed, or a 'sweep' could also mean a semicircular plank fixed under the beams near the fore-end of the tiller, which it supported. Either way, the 'sweeps' would be at the after-end of the boat, whereas the row-boat in which Williams had left the vessel had been at the sloop's head. 'Scarcely had he done so and proceeded but a very few yards when he heard a splash and saw Matthew struggling under water about a foot'. He tried to save Matthew but was too far away. Then he 'immediately gave an alarm but as not any other person was on board not any assistance could be afforded him.'[283]

William Maun then stated that he had seen Matthew sitting on the sweeps and had heard Williams caution him about sitting in so dangerous a place and request him to remove to the hatches. Maun said that he was on board when Williams gave the alarm — and here there is a discrepancy between his evidence and Williams's — and that when Williams gave the alarm, he, Maun immediately went to the spot but could not see the body. He thought the deceased had been intoxicated.

As with Pollard's body, Matthew's was brought up by James Sutherland who was also one of the jurors. We have already treated with six of the others, Michael Lamb, Joseph Maun, John and William Cross, James Kelly and James Levello, who were on the jury in the Pollard Inquest. The other six were James Dunn, evidently Headman, Hugh Docherty, who had served on the jury which Matthew had assembled for the Inquest on the body of the unidentified man, John Burton, who was living on the promontory, having bought the eastern part of Cross's Farm in 1815, Edward Morton and George Walford, who may have been one of Cross's servants, for by 1828 he was with David Cross. Once again they were all quite obviously disinterested locals with nothing to gain or lose by Matthew's death or the Coroner's verdict.[284]

James Dunn had been a neighbour of Matthew's since 1803. He now owned land closer to the place where Matthew was drowned, that is thirty acres of Smith's Farm on Cumberland Reach. Smith had advertized his farm for sale as early as 1807 when he had been a debtor in the County Gaol at Sydney at which time Dunn may have acquired it; but in any case, Dunn sold thirty acres of Smith's Farm to Michael Napthali in 1822. James Dunn's daughter and granddaughter were to marry Everingham's son and grandson, an unlikely consequence had Dunn been involved in covering up any foul play to do with Everingham's death. (Dunn, himself was drowned in Boston's (Cumberland) Reach in 1837).[285]

Quite apart from the jury which had been called, it is likely that a crowd of people would have assembled to watch the proceedings. While it is perhaps unlikely that Matthew's widow, Elizabeth would attend, it is highly probable that Matthew James Everingham, the Younger, a young married man of twenty-two years would be there, also William, aged twenty and George aged eighteen. Quite probably Richard Woodbury, Thomas Chaseling, now related to Matthew by marriage and his son, John Chaseling would attend. If any of these people were dissatisfied with the verdict, they had every chance to protest. The body was lying 'then and there' in front of them. It had been brought up on the same evening that Matthew had drowned and since he had fallen into the water at five o'clock, had there been any marks of violence on the corpse, they would still be distinguishable.

In fact there was no more reason to suspect that Matthew Everingham had been murdered than to imagine that John Pollard, who had met his death in much the same way or the unidentified man, the Inquest into whose death Matthew had acted in, had been the victims of foul play. As will be seen in Part Two, there was no suggestion whatsoever that Matthew Everingham had been murdered throughout the rest of the Nineteenth Century and until 1905, almost ninety years later. The Coroner's verdict, guided by the Jury was 'Accidental Death'.

Within a week, Governor Macquarie had directed his Secretary, John Thomas Campbell to write to John Piper, who held the lucrative position of Naval Officer for the Port of Sydney, as follows:

'.... It has been represented to (His Excellency) that owing to the large quantities of spirits which have been lately conveyed into the Interior and particularly by water, to Windsor, much of the recent scenes of extraordinary intoxication attended by fatal effects in several instances are to be attributed. His Excellency is anxious to prevent a recurrence of such scenes of disappation [sic] and desires you will not grant permits for passengers or others to convey spirits to Windsor.... or elsewhere by water carriage and refer people to apply in future to Mr Jones, who is the person authorized to grant permits for the removal of spirits.[286]

Matthew's body was released to be buried on the day after the Inquest, December 27, 1817, being brought most likely by boat from Maun's Point up river to a landing place convenient to the Wilberforce schoolhouse and the burial ground that had been laid out there on Macquarie's orders. There was as yet no church at Wilberforce, the present St John's not having been built until 1859. At this date the district came under the Parish of St Matthew, Windsor, and the service was performed by the Reverend Robert Cartwright. The details he recorded in the Parish Register are those which are supplied to anyone applying for Matthew's Death Certificate from the Registrar General's Department. Compulsory registration of Births, Deaths and Marriages did not commence until 1856. Following the Clergy Returns Act of 1878 as many Parish Registers as possible were called in to form what could only be a partial or incomplete bank of records for the earlier period. On application the writer received the following details, which omit even details that appear in the Church Register:

142

Number 3920   Vol. 2

Name: Matthew Everingham	When buried: 27 December 1817
Abode: —	Where ceremony performed: —
Age: 48 years	Where registered: —
Quality: —	Clergyman officiating: —

Note: It will be seen that names of Matthew's parents were not given, if indeed they were known. When Registration became statutory, such details were required.

Regarding Matthew's grave one assumes that, because of the time involved in cutting the inscription, the headstone must have been placed there some time afterward. The epitaph must have been ordered by someone who was familiar with Matthew's life history. The philosophy of the verse, that is, the uselessness of a life which has as its centre worldly things or 'vanity' had been a favourite one since Puritan times — one thinks of 'Vanity Fair' in Bunyan's *The Pilgrim's Progress.* Spelling mistakes have occurred by omissions by the stone-cutter, who may not even have been able to read or understand what he was transcribing. While Matthew may have known of the verse, its subsequent adoption was not a deathbed request because he had no idea he was going to die so soon. The grave next to that of Matthew, that of Elizabeth Everingham, *is not that of his wife* but of his grand-daughter whom he never saw, an infant child of Matthew Everingham, the Younger. The two stones might have been cut at the same time, when the family had five years to reflect on Matthew's death and life.

While no Will is recorded in the Register of Wills, 1817-1824 in the State Archives, Sydney, neither is the Estate recorded by N.S.W. Curator of Intestate Estates, nor is there evidence of Letters of Adminstration being granted. However in a Lease of *Everingham Farm* dated August 9, 1819, which can be seen in the Howe Papers in the Mitchell Library but which was never officially registered, Matthew James Everingham was named as the son and heir-at-law of Matthew Everingham deceased. The lease, for the original Hawkesbury grant of fifty acres was between Matthew, the Younger and Colden Antill, Executor of the Thompson Estate. On August 14, 1820, this land was sold to Andrew Doyle and the Recital in the transaction reveals that the land had been sold to Henry Colden Antill as Executor of the Estate of the Late Andrew Thompson, in settlement of a debt. *Everingham Farm* later came into the possession of the Tuckerman family and now belongs to Sackville Ski Gardens.[287]

That young Matthew was his father's heir is also borne out by the fact that it was he who sold the one hundred and thirty acres at Kurrajong, which had been granted to his father by Macquarie in 1816, to George Howe on August 1, 1818. It would appear that this conveyance had already been begun in September, 1817, prior to the death of Matthew, the Elder. To sum up, it is unlikely that either Antill or Howe would have received the possession of property from other than its legal owner. On the one hand, Antill was the Executor of an Estate and Howe was paying good money to purchase. The point that Matthew, the

Younger was officially recognized as his father's heir is here stressed because of the spurious will naming all five sons as beneficiaries, which was produced at the time of the 'Everingham Millions'.[288]

After her husband's death, Elizabeth continued to rent the farm on which they had been living. It is unknown how long Matthew had been District Constable at Portland Head but the *Windsor Ration Book* shows that they and two children were drawing stores, (as part of Matthew's salary) during 1817. Elizabeth was taken off the stores in 1821 and was at this time receiving her support from eight acres of land contiguous to the farm she was renting. She explained all this and also that she had cleared and fenced the land, when she applied to have it Deeded to her on January 17, 1825. Her Memorial was addressed to Governor Brisbane, Macquarie having gone home after the Bigge Enquiry into his administration. The petition, in which Elizabeth stated that she had 'reared a large Family to habits of Industry' breathes with the energy and resilience of this remarkable woman. The same year, Lewis Jones evidently laid claim to this land. There exists a note in the handwriting of the Surveyor General, John Oxley, headed 'Portland Head' and dated August 22, 1825 in which he certifies that 'Jones has not any claim whatever to the land situated between Mr Johnstones and Mr Palmer's (formerly Cheshire's) and that the same will not be granted to him it not being the intention of the Government to disturb or remove the Widow Everingham or Dennis Kirwan from the lands they at present occupy at the pleasure of His Excellency.' The land, measured by Assistant Surveyor Felton Mathew on April 25, 1833 was finally granted to 'Elizabeth Everingham' in 1838. She then lived at George Street, Windsor and gave the intended name of the property as *Glen Everingham*. By this time she had already resided on the farm for well over twenty years and earlier in the year had sold it to her son, George. It is now known as *Elizabeth Everingham Farm* and will be referred to as such throughout Book Two.[289]

Though the Deed was made out to Elizabeth 'Everingham', she had in 1827 married an Irish convict aged twenty-five, Patrick McGahy, with the Governor's permission. All persons, even though free, if they had formerly been convicts, were intending to marry a convict or were the child of a convict, were required to obtain permission to marry at this period. The *Permission to Marry Book* lists all persons applying, whether permission were granted and if not, for what reason. The most common reason for refusal was evidence in a ship's convict indent that an applicant was married. The applications reflect the pathetic desire of many to regularise a union with a new partner with whom they now had ties and perhaps offspring. Many had no hope of ever seeing their English spouses again nor even of determining whether their former mates were still alive — particularly where illiteracy existed.

Permission for Elizabeth to remarry was applied for by the Rev. Matthew Devenish Meares, the first incumbent of the new Parish of Pitt Town. Her age was given as fifty-three and McGahy's as twenty-five. Permission was granted on July 14, 1827 and the couple were married on August 20, probably in the Macquarie Schoolhouse, Wilberforce (built 1820), near where her former husband was buried in 1817. Elizabeth signed with a cross and the witnesses were William Gow, the teacher and parish clerk and Thomas McQuestion.[290]

Patrick McGahy signed his name and was partly literate, according to the Indent of the *Sir Godfrey Webster* on which ship he had arrived from Cork on January 3, 1826. His full description is: 'Reads and writes a little. 23. Roman Catholic. Single. Sentenced to seven years. From County Mayo. Occupation Pedlar. Convicted of Highway Robbery. Tried March 24, 1825. No former convictions. Height 5'3". Dark, ruddy complexion, dark brown eyes and hair. Remarks: Quiet. Small scar under left eye. How disposed of: Joseph Owen (Ovens?) Richmond.' There was now much more information on the Indent papers of the convict ships which were bringing an average of 2,700 convicts per year to New South Wales and Van Diemen's Land until Transportation (to New South Wales) ceased in 1840.[291]

The English surgeon's report for Patrick's ship, *Sir Godfrey Webster* is preserved. Obviously a humane man, he wrote that when the ship arrived in Ireland to collect 196 male convicts, he had to insist on leaving behind two men, one blind and one a cripple who could not perform the calls of nature. The convicts had received no animal food, had been victualled on the hulks for three pence per day and were not well enough to withstand the voyage. The old could not chew and were seasick in bad weather. Ailments prevalent were diarrhea, spongy gums, dysentery and constipation, for they had been living on gruel, bread and oatmeal. His medical knowledge being so limited, it is remarkable that his patients survived in spite of treatment. Cases of pneumonia he treated by blood letting, blisters, aperient medicines, diaphoretics, (to make the patient perspire), and a spare diet, 'to which treatment they yielded without any concommittant symptoms'.[292]

That the quiet man, Patrick McGahy was happy to settle into comfortable domesticity with the widow Everingham soon after his arrival in New South Wales is understandable. The 1828 Census shows Elizabeth and Patrick living at Portland Head, with eleven of fifteen acres cleared and cultivated. John Everingham, aged fourteen was 'with Elizabeth McGahy'. All the other children were by now married but we will take up their stories separately in Book Two.

Elizabeth outlived Matthew Everingham by twenty-four years. Fifty-eight grandchildren, five of whom were called Elizabeth, and several great-grandchildren were born before she died early in December, 1841. She was buried at Knight's Retreat, Matthew Everingham, the Younger's property, in the private cemetery laid out by him. George Reeve, the historian, saw her grave there when he visited Robert Everingham sometime in the late 1920's. The headstone bore a verse describing her as 'a loving wife' and was said to be 'erected by her loving grandchildren'. The funeral service was conducted by the

Facsimile of an extract from the Inquest of the body of Matthew Everingham, Judge Advocate, Report of Coroners' Inquests, 1796-1820. *[see p132]*

Attributed to *G.W. Evans*   Mitchell Library

'The Settlement on the Green Hills, Hawkesbury, 1809 [?]' *[see p115]*

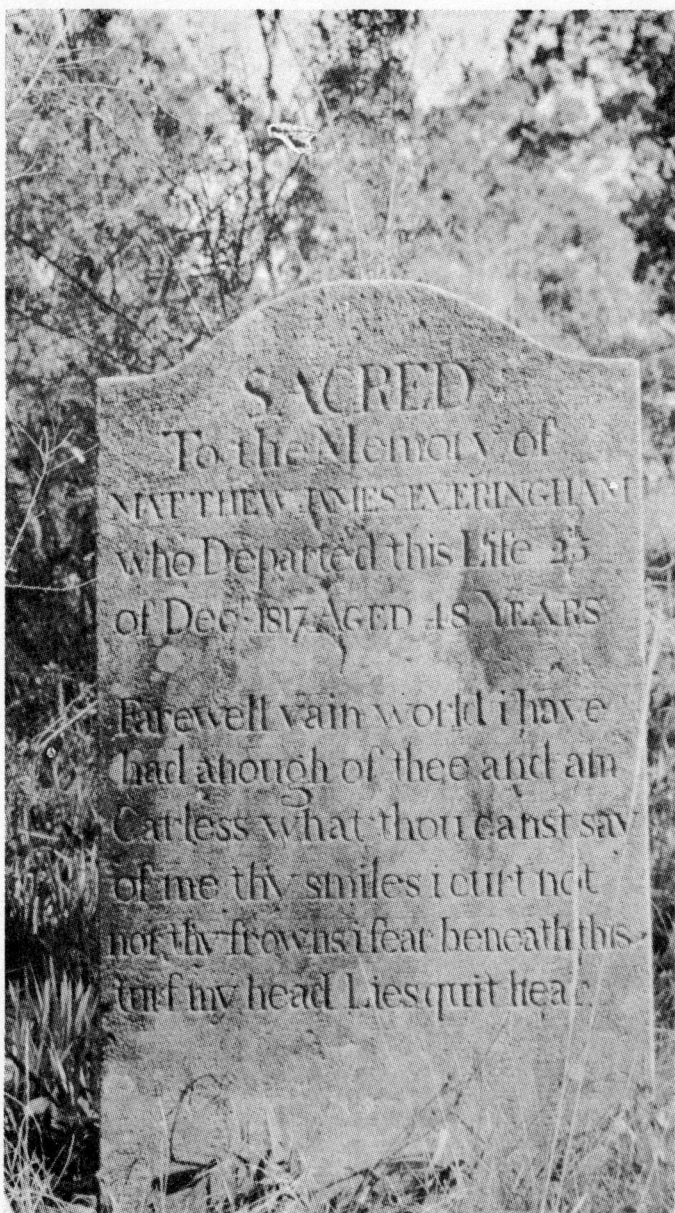

SACRED
To the Memory of
MATTHEW JAMES EVERINGHAM
who Departed this Life 23
of Dec. 1817 AGED 48 YEARS

Farewell vain world i have
had ahough of thee and am
Carless what thou canst say
of me thy smiles i cort not
nor thy frowns i fear beneath this
turf my head Lies quit hear

Frank Everingham

Headstone on Matthew Everingham's grave. *[see p142]*

Reverend John Weatherstone, a Minister of the Wesleyan Church. The 1841 Census of Householders shows Patrick McGahy as a householder with a wooden house at Knight's Retreat, Matthew Everingham, the Younger's property, so perhaps Elizabeth had lived here in her old age, having left the farm for George to work. What happened to McGahy is unknown.[293]

Before leaving the first part of our story, it will be interesting to see what happened to those who, though background figures in the tale of Matthew Everingham, had major roles in the wider area of the nation's early history.

Phillip regained his health after his return to England, rose in the Navy to Admiral of the Blue, remarried and retired to Bath, always taking an interest in the Colony. One of his last acts before he died in 1814 was to recommend the services of the convicted architect Francis Greenway to Governor Macquarie. Hunter, who also was promoted to the rank of Vice Admiral, continued to be interested in the colony, despite the anguish it had caused him and finally died in London in 1821. King, who after Phillip, had done more for the settlement than any other Governor, died in London in 1808, before his work had been recognized. Bligh died in London in 1817, now a Rear Admiral of the White. His name was long remembered on the Hawkesbury, at least two families naming sons after him. Macquarie, though granted a pension, was never able to clear his name of the charges laid against him as a result of the Bigge Enquiry and died embittered in 1824.[294]

The Reverend Richard Johnson lived on in anonymity in England from mid 1801 until 1827; but Marsden remained in the colony to acquire wealth and to bedevil Governor Brisbane, to send missionaries to New Zealand and finally to die while on a visit to Windsor at the Rectory of St Matthew's in 1838.[295]

John Macarthur, the perturbator whose dynamic character had so influenced the fortunes of Elizabeth and Matthew, was finally allowed to return from exile in 1817, a month before Matthew's death. In the meantime, his wife, Elizabeth, had built on the foundations he had laid for Australia's wool industry. As a result of Bigge's Enquiry, the advice given by Macarthur and with the final crossing of the Blue Mountains, Australia became a land of squatter dominance. Ironically, the happiness of the Macarthur family was marred during later years by the mental illness of its founder, who died in 1834. Elizabeth Macarthur lived on until 1850.[296]

William Charles Wentworth, son of Dr D'arcy and Catherine Crowley, co-passengers with the Macarthurs and Elizabeth Everingham on the *Neptune,* was to be the champion in the thirties of 'Native' Australia and Australian independence from England. As the years went by, he pressed for an autonomy to be directed by wealthy pastoral leaders such as himself, a 'Bunyip aristocracy'.

Sarah Bellamy, the spirited redhead(?)who had uttered the 'cry of Murder' in those far off First Fleet days, bore seven children to James

Bloodsworth, their descendants still living near the town of Sydney for which their forbear did so much. A builder by trade, Bloodsworth was the first man to make bricks in the colony. In October, 1790 he was pardoned by the Governor for, as Collins wrote, there was not a house or building in the settlement that did not owe something to him. He was the builder of the first Government House, (1788-1846), to be seen in so many early drawings. From here Phillip governed in the finest sense of the word. Here he summoned his officers in the desperate days after the wreck of the *Sirius,* when they must decide to send their last small ship away. Here, to the tune of *Rule Britannia* came the rebels as Bligh sat at dinner. The site, on the corner of Phillip and Bridge Streets is now vacant and one wonders whether the suggestion to rebuild this structure in time for the Bi-Centenary will be adopted. Bloodsworth had the first Government House up in just on twelve months.[297]

Since Elizabeth Everingham did not die until 1841, she saw many of the changes mentioned earlier. The year before her death, as a result of protests by the ordinary classes of people, many of whom were the children of convicts, transportation ceased. 'Australia', the name suggested by Flinders and which had come into general use in the twenties, had been born; and the new generation and free immigrants resented the country being a dumping place for Britain's unwanted criminals. By then, Elizabeth had been here fifty-one years and barely remembering the slums of Spitalfields, would count herself an 'Australian'.

We will be seeing Elizabeth again in Part Two but Matthew's story is told. Had he lived another month to January 26, 1818, he would have seen the thirtieth anniversary of the Colony. He had know five Governors and four Acting-Governors. There had been thirty exciting years and a floodtide of events, parallelling the great floodtides of the Hawkesbury which had ruined him.

At the time of his death and after the end of the Napoleonic Wars, (1815), the number of convicts transported would begin to swell to a torrent and the 'system', incorporating the features generally but mistakenly associated with convictism as a whole and exemplified by Sarah's Story which follows, would commence in earnest. For these people, a different experience entirely from those who had been here in the first years.

Matthew's children, proud of being 'native born' would call themselves 'Currency' Lads and Lasses to distinguish themselves from the 'sterling' or English imports. It is their story we now have to tell because it too, like Matthew's has been largely forgotten. There would come a time when the family could number eight generations Australian born which, had he foreseen it, would surely have been a source of pride to Matthew Everingham, the First Fleeter. ༄

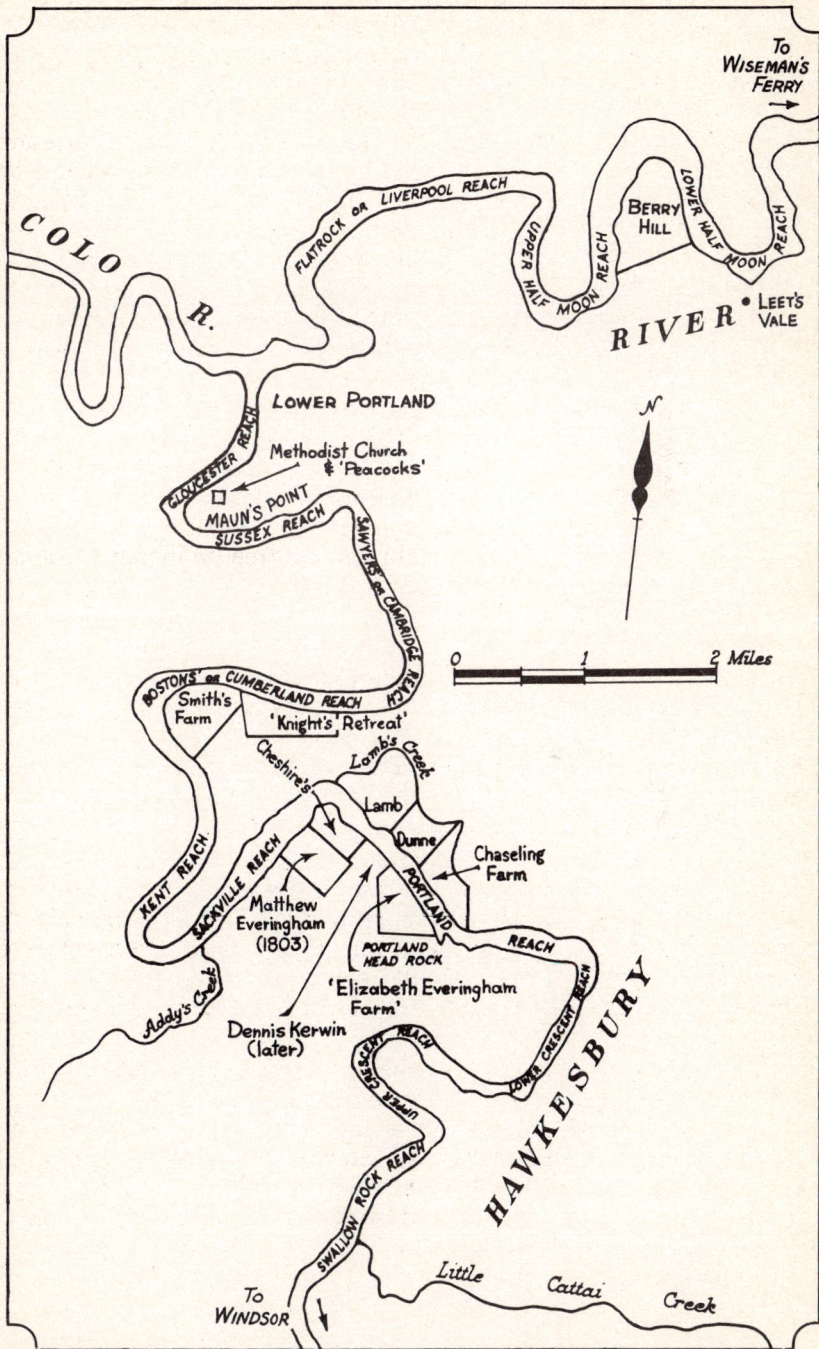

To WISEMAN'S FERRY

FLATROCK or LIVERPOOL REACH

UPPER HALF MOON REACH

LOWER HALF MOON REACH

BERRY HILL

COLO R.

RIVER

LEET'S VALE

N

LOWER PORTLAND

GLOUCESTER REACH

Methodist Church & 'Peacocks'

MAUN'S POINT

SUSSEX REACH

SAWYERS or CAMBRIDGE REACH

0   1   2 Miles

BOSTONS' or CUMBERLAND REACH

Smith's Farm

'Knight's Retreat'

Cheshire's

Lomb's Creek

Lamb

Dunne

Chaseling Farm

KENT REACH

SACKVILLE REACH

Matthew Everingham (1803)

PORTLAND

PORTLAND HEAD ROCK

REACH

Addy's Creek

'Elizabeth Everingham Farm'

Dennis Kerwin (later)

LOWER CRESCENT REACH

UPPER CRESCENT REACH

SWALLOW ROCK REACH

HAWKESBURY

To WINDSOR

Little   Cattai   Creek

ABBREVIATIONS

A.O. or
 A.O.N.S.W. ... Archives Office of New South Wales.
B.T. .... Bonwick Transcripts.
C.S. or Col. Sec. Colonial Secretary.
Col. Sec. re
 Land. .... Letters to the Colonial Secretary regarding Land.
H.O. .... Home Office.
HRA. .... Historical Records of Australia.
HRNSW .... Historical Records of New South Wales.
J.R.A.H.S. ..... Journal of the Royal Australian Historical Society.
ML .... Mitchell Library.
O.B.S.P. .... Old Bailey Sessions Papers.

REFERENCE NOTES

1 Sessions Minute Book, no 150, 1783-1785. Gaol Delivery, 7th July 1784, Records Office, Guildhall, London; *Old Bailey Sessions Papers, 1783-1784.* Sixth Session, Trial No. 775, p.1028, Q.343. 1/L, Mitchell Library, Sydney. 'Everingham Millions' See *A Hawkesbury Story*
2 Letter of Rev. R.C.P. Milburn, Master's House, Temple, London, dated January 18, 1974; letter from Rev. Peter Thornton, Rectory, Everingham, Yorkshire, dated February 8, 1974.
3 Letter from Matthew Everingham dated April 11, 1811 accompanying Memorial to Ellis Bent in Capiases for Debt, 1811, Supreme Court Papers, No 2292 Archives Office of N.S.W.; Letter of Abel Everingham dated April 2, 1924, Letters Hawkesbury Descendants to George Reeve, Vol.1, A1602 Mitchell Library, Sydney; *An Encyclopaedia of London,* Ed. William Kent, (London, 1937), p.492.
4 Letter dated October 19, 1973, Keeper of Manuscripts, Guildhall Library, London; letter dated April 8, 1975, D.H. Barron, regarding research at Borthwick Instiue of Historical Research, University of York.
5 *Blue Guide to London,* pp.96-97.
6 R.L. Sharpe, *Memorials of Newgate Gaol and the Sessions House,* (London), p.264, M.L. 365.942/ 1A1.
7 *Richards' Topical Encyclopaedia,* Vol.13, (New York, 1945), p.243.
8 L.L. Robson, *The Convict Settlers of Australia,* (Melbourne 1965), p.7.
9 *Ibid.;* A.G.L. Shaw, *Convicts and the Colonies,* (London, 1966), pp. 158-159, quoting the *Taunton Courier* of 1828.
10 J. Cobley, 'The Crimes of the First Fleeters', *Journal of the Royal Australian Historical Society,* Vol. 52, Pt. 2, June, 1966.
11 *O.B.S.P., 1783-1784.*
12 Letters dated May 23, 1972, Librarian of the Law Society, London; letters dated April 26, August 8, 1973, Librarian and Keeper of the Records, The Honourable Society of the Middle Temple, London.
13 Newgate Calendar of the Sessions File, September, 1784, Records Office, Guildhall, London; W. Branch-Johnson, *The English Prison Hulks,* (London, 1957); Class P COM 2—171, P.R.O. Kew.
14 Ibid., pp.4-5.
15 Ibid., pp.5, 33; Article, 'Remarks on the Convict Act', *The London Magazine,* May, 1777, M.L. 052/13.
16 Branch-Johnson, *op.cit.,* pp.7-14.
17 *Ibid.,* p.14.
18 *Ibid.,* pp.25,16.
19 *Ibid.,* p.3.
20 C.M.H. Clark, *A History of Australia,* Vol.I, (Melbourne, 1962), p.64, quoting A.E. Smith, *Colonists in Bondage. White Servitude and Convict Labour in America,* 1607-1776, (Chapel Hill, 1947), pp.123-124; Charles Dickens, *Great Expectations,* (London, 1945), pp.38-39.
21 James Bonwick, *Australia's First Preacher, The Reverend Richard Johnson,* (London, 1898), p.42.
22 Trials Nos. 850,852, *O.B.S.P. 1783-84,* pp.1187, 1191; John Easty, *Memorandum of the Transactions of a Voyage from England to Botany Bay,* 1787-1793, (Sydney, 1965), pp.7-8.
23 Richard's Returns, p.264, H.O. 11/1, p.2, Archives Office, N.S.W.; Indent of *Scarborough,* A.O. Reel 392.
24 G.B. Barton, *History of New South Wales from the Records,* (Sydney, 1889), p.38; M. Barnard Eldershaw, *Phillip of Australia; An Account of the Settlement at Sydney Cove 1788-1792,* (London, 1938), p.37.
25 Lieutenant William Bradley, R.N., *A Voyage to New South Wales,* reproduced in facsimile as *The Journal of Lieutenant William Bradley, R.N., of H.M.S. Sirius, 1786-1792,* (Sydney, 1969), p.9; Easty, *op.cit.,* p.3; John Cobley, *The Crimes of the First Fleet Convicts,* (Sydney, 1970), *passim.*
26 Charles Bateson, *The Convict Ships,* 1787-1868, (Glasgow, 1959), p.116, quoting Journal of Arthur Bowes, pp.57-58.
27 Barton, *op.cit.,* pp.67,49; Easty, p.4; Barnard Eldershaw, *op.cit.,* p.43.
28 David Collins, *An Account of the English Colony in New South Wales,* (Adelaide, 1971), Vol 1, p.iv.
29 *Ibid.*
30 Watkin Tench, *Sydney's First Four Years,* (Sydney, 1961), p.13.
31 John Cobley, *Sydney Cove, 1788,* (London, 1962), pp.14-16.
32 Barnard Eldershaw, pp. 30-31.
33 Barton, pp.22, 7-8, 30, 485, 40.
34 *Ibid.,* pp.40-41; Bateson, *op.cit.,* p.117 quoting a letter from Lieutenant Ralph Clark, dated Nov. 8, 1787.

35 Easty, pp.5, 12, 31-32; Barnard Eldershaw, p.63, quoting Clark's journal, pp.23-27; Easty, p.7; Barnard Eldershaw, p.31.
36 Barton, p.60; Bateson, p.100.
37 *Ibid.*, pp.95-96, 112.
38 Barton, p.489, quoting Lieutenant King's journal.
39 Collins, *op.cit.*, p.iii.
40 Tench, *op.cit.*, p.65; Barton. pp.67, 489; Cobley, *loc,cit.*, 135; Collins, p.iv.
41 Charles H. Brown, *Meteorology for Masters and Mates*, (Glasgow, 1942), p.63; Bradley, *op.cit.*, p.18.
42 Easty, p.20; C.S. Forester, *Hornblower and the Hotspur*, (London, 1962), pp.80-81 and passim.
43 Easty, p.11; Collins, p.vii.
44 Easty, pp.11; Barton, p.39; Barnard Eldershaw, p.48.
45 Easty, pp.12-15.
46 Collins, p.xiii.
47 Easty, p.18; Cobley, *loc.cit.*, p.135, quoting letter from Daniel Southwell to his mother.
48 Easty, pp.18-21; Bradley, p.29; Barton, p.67.
49 Easty, p.19; James Scott, *Remarks on a Passage to Botany Bay, 1787-1792*, (Sydney, 1963), p.4.
50 Collins, p.xv.
51 Easty, pp.27-29.
52 Compilation, *The Voyage of Governor Phillip to Botany Bay*, Ed. James J. Auchmuty, (Sydney, 1976), p.13, hereafter referred to as 'Phillip'; Easty, p.30; Bradley, p.37.
53 Collins, p.xiii; Easty, p.33.
54 Collins, p.xviii; Easty, pp.30-31.
55 *Ibid.*, pp. 36-37.
56 *Ibid.*, p.48; Collins, p.xxv.
57 Easty, p.56; Collins, pp.xxiii-xxxi.
58 Phillip. pp.19-20.
59 Easty, pp.66-67, 73-74.
60 Easty, p.76; Collins, p.xxxv; Bateson, pp.112-113; Collins, p.xxv; Easty, p.79.
61 *Ibid.*, pp.80-82.
62 *Ibid.*, p.88; Collins, p.21.
63 Bench of Magistrates, Minutes of Proceedings, February 1788 — January, 1792, Case of Sarah Bellamy, pp.210-217. 1/296, Mitchell Library.
64 Phillip, pp.105, 107; Cobley, *Sydney Cove, 1788*, p.138 quoting Bradley's Journal; *ibid.*, quoting Surgeon Worgan's Journal, M.L. C.830; *ibid.*, p.248, quoting letter from a female convict.
65 *Ibid.*, p.114, quoting Collins Account, March.
66 *Ibid.*, p.251, quoting Reverend Richard Johnson; Map of the Cove dated March 1, 1788, in Bradley's Journal; Cobley, *loc.cit.*, p.244, quoting Collins Account, October, 1788.
67 *Ibid.*, p.248, quoting letter of a woman convict.
68 *Ibid.*, p.20, quoting Hunter; *ibid.*, p.31, quoting Phillip's despatch of May 15, 1788; Easty, pp.93.94; Collins, *op.cit.*, p.6.
69 Easty, p.94; Collins, p.6; Cobley, *loc.cit.*, p.48, quoting Clark's Journal.
70 *Ibid.*, p.54.
71 *Ibid.*, pp.58-59, quoting Bowes's Journal.
72 Collins, p.7; Cobley, *loc.cit.*, pp.60-63; C.H. Currey, 'An Account of the Ceremony at Sydney Cove, February 7, 1788', *J.R.A.H.S.*, Vol.43, pt.4, pp.31-32.
73 Phillip, p.30; Collins, p.28; Cobley, *loc.cit.*, p.113, quoting Collins; *ibid.*, p.174, quoting Surgeon White; Cobley, *Sydney Cove, 1789-90*, (Sydney, 1963), pp.31-32.
74 Cobley, *Sydney Cove, 1788*, p.135.
75 Clark, *op.cit.*, Vol. 1, p.113; Cobley, *loc.cit.*, pp.113-114, quoting Collins, pp.24-25; Phillip, Chapter x.
76 Cobley, *loc.cit.*, p.53, quoting Capt. Campbell's Orders for the Day, February 3, 1788; Tench, pp.191-192; Collins, p.58; Cobley, *loc.cit.*, pp.178-179, quoting Phillip.
77 Cobley, *Sydney Cove, 1789-90*, p.161; Cobley, *Sydney Cove, 1788*, p.186; Collins, p.100; Cobley, *loc.cit.*, p.188, quoting letter from John Russell to his mother; Tench, p.115, note 14, quoting White, p.196.
78 Bradley, pp.181-184; Tench, p.65; Phillip, p.353, note 4; Cobley, *Sydney Cove, 1789-90*, p.165.
79 Tench, p.220; Cobley, *loc.cit.*, p.137.
80 Collins, p.43; Tench, p.166.
81 Tench, p.72; Cobley, *Sydney Cove, 1788*, p.116, quoting Bowes Journal; Bradley, pp.97, 105; Tench, p.165.
82 Bradley, pp.181-184; Barton, p.121, quoting Tench.
83 Collins, p.45; Cobley, *loc.cit.*, p.230, quoting Phillip's despatch to Lord Sydney.
84 Cobley, *loc.cit.*, pp.207, 228, *Sydney Cove, 1789-90*, p.158; Bonwick, pp.56,100.
85 Bench of Magistrates, Minutes of Proceedings, 1788-1792, p.139, 1/296, M.L.
86 Cobley, *Sydney Cove, 1788*, pp.165, 91.
87 Easty, pp.98, 111; Barton, p.424, quoting letter from Governor Phillip to Major Ross, August 26,

1789.

88 Collins, pp.56, 68.

89 See note 1; Hunter, p.53, (6th May, 1788).

90 Cobley, *Sydney Cove, 1789-1790*, p.56, quoting Hunter; Collins, pp.79, 85.

91 Collins, pp.68, 72.

92 Cobley, *Sydney Cove, 1788*, quoting Collins. (December).

93 Cobley, *loc.cit.*, p.57, quoting Scott; Collins, pp.82, 101.

94 See note 1; Cobley, *Sydney Cove, 1791-1792*, (Sydney, 1965), p.275.

95 Cobley, *Sydhey Cove, 1788*, pp.225, 262.

96 Easty, *passim;* Collins, p.29, Cobley, *Sydney Cove, 1789-1790*, p.7; Cobley, *Sydney Cove, 1788*, p.158.

97 Easty, *passim;* Cobley, *loc.cit.* p.74.

98 Collins, p.40; Cobley, *loc.cit.*, pp.259.,67 quoting Bowes; *ibid.*, p.259; Tench, p.73.

99 Collins, pp.34, 77-78; Cobley, *Sydney Cove, 1789-90*, pp.136-137.

100 Cobley, *Sydney Cove, 1788*, pp.65, 176-177.

101 See note 1; Cobley, *Sydney Cove, 1789-1790*, p.190; Collins, p.105.

102 Collins, pp.105-6; Barnard Eldershaw, pp.165 ff.; *ibid.*, p.169, quoting H.R.N.S.W., Vol.2, p.770; Tench, pp.164-165; Cobley, *loc.cit.*, pp.165, 188, 191; Tench, pp.162, 169-170.

103 Although in her trial and marriage record, Elizabeth's name is spelt 'Rymes', research in London Parish records show that the name was more usually spelt 'Rimes'. I am deliberately inconsistent about this and other variously spelt names such as Paynter, (Painter), Maun, (Maund). Surgeon William Gray complained in a letter dated April, 13, 1790 that the convicts under his care were dying of scurvy through poor victualling, Mitchell Library, Sydney; Tench, pp.170-172; Collins, Vol.1; p.118.

104 Collins, Vol.1, pp.122-123, Letter from a woman convict from the *Lady Juliana*, *H.R.N.S.W.*, Vol. 2, p.768; *H.R.N.S.W.*, Vol. 1, Part 2, pp.354-355; Letter Rev. R. Johnson to H. Fricker, August 21, 1790, (original in St Paul's Cathedral, Melbourne, *H.R.N.S.W.*, Vol.1, Part 2, pp.386-389; ibid., pp.366-368.

105 See Chapter Three; Bateson, pp.127-130; Collins, Vol.1, p.124.

106 Collins, Vol.1, p.123; Bateson, pp.127-130.

107 Denton Prout and Fred Feely, *Petticoat Parade*, (Adelaide, 1965), p.28; Clark, Vol.1, p.124; *ibid.*, Vol.2, p.42, quoting Norfolk Island Victualling Book.

108 Cobley, *Sydney Cove, 1791-1792*, p.18, quoting Phillip to Grenville, March 4, 1791; Collins, pp.125, 132; Tench, p.246; James Jervis, *The Cradle City of Australia — A History of Parramatta*, (Parramatta, 1961), pp.6, 28.

109 Elizabeth Rimes signed with a cross for two marriages. In the Register of St John, Parramatta, the cross is almost in the spine of the book. See also Register of St John, Wilberforce; 1828 Census, Mitchell Library, Sydney; Copy of an entry in the register of Presbyterian burials at Sackville Reach, Registrar General's Department.

110 Boyd's Marriage Index, Guildhall Library, London; Register of St George, Hanover Square, London.

111 Letter of R.J. D'Arcy Hart, Genealogist, Jewish Museum, London.

112 *O.B.S.P.*, 1789, Trial 763, pp.916-917, M.L., Sydney; For general background, L.L. Robson, *The Convict Settlers of Australia* and A.G.L. Shaw, *Convicts and the Colonies,*

113 Robson, pp.10-11.

114 Harold P. Clunn, *The Face of London*, (Spring Books, London), p.301; *ibid.*, pp.300-1; Robson, pp.12-14.

115 *O.B.S.P.*, 1818, Trial No. 511, pp.174-175, M.L. Sydney; Clunn, *op.cit.*, pp.301-2.

116 *O.B.S.P.*, 1791, Trial No. 155, pp.270-1; Charles Dickens, *Oliver Twist*, (London, 1945), pp.70-1; Robson, pp.15-16.

117 P.M. Cunningham, *Two Years in New South Wales*, (London, 1828), Vol.2, pp.52-3; Clark, Vol.1, p.149.

118 M.H. Ellis, *John Macarthur*, (Sydney, 1955), p.17; *ibid.*, quoting Macarthur Papers, Journal of Elizabeth Macarthur, p.1, A.2906, Mitchell Library, Sydney; *ibid.*, quoting letter of Elizabeth Macarthur to mother, October 8, 1789, Macarthur Papers, A.2908, No. 1. M.L. Sydney; *ibid.*, pp.50-1.

119 *Ibid.*, pp.18-25.

120 *Ibid.*, pp.30-38.

121 Phillip to Secretary of State, Despatch, November 5, 1791, 4/1634, Mitchell Library, Sydney; Collins, Vol. 1, p.169; *ibid.*, p.158; Tench, pp.220, 239; Clark, Vol.1, p.137.

122 Phillip to Grenville, Nov. 5, 1791, A.O. 4/1634; J.F. Campbell, 'The Dawn of Rural Settlement in Australia', *J.R.A.H.S.*, Vol. XI, pp.94, 112.

123 Eris O'Brien, *The Foundation of Australia* (1786-1800), (London, 1937), p.296.

124 Phillip to Grenville, Nov. 5, 1791; *H.R.N.S.W.* II, p.75, quoting Phillip to Dundas, Oct.,26, 1793.

125 Collins, Vol.1, p.178.

126 *Ibid.*, pp.252-254, 265.

127 O'Brien, pp.294, 300, 329.
128 *Ibid.*, p.294.
129 Cunningham, *op.cit.*, Vol. 2, p.70.
130 Tench, p.259; Cobley, *Sydney Cove, 1791-1792*, pp.325-326.
131 Easty, p.126.
132 Campbell, *J.R.A.H.S.* Vol. XI, p. 119.
133 Tench, p.246; Jervis, *op.cit.*, pp. 6, 28
134 *Ibid.*, pp. 7, 63.
135 Cobley, *Sydney Cove, 1789-1790*, pp.153, 313; Cobley, *Sydney Cove, 1791-1792*, pp.27, 111, 117, 343.
136 Cobley, *loc.cit.*, pp.121-122, quoting Johnson's letter to Fricker; *ibid.*, p.235, quoting letter to Rev. William Morice.
137 Collins, Vol. 1, p.198.
138 *Ibid.*, p.148; Cobley, *loc.cit.*, p. 211; *ibid.*, p.10.
139 Collins, Vol. 1, p.493.
140 *Ibid.*, p. 359
141 Jervis, p.63; Chateau Tanunda 'Historical Firsts', No.166, *Sydney Morning Herald*, December, 1973. This article states that 'The Mason's Arms' was later called 'The Woolpack', and the present 'Woolpack' on the opposite corner retains its licence.
142 Phillip to Grenville, Nov. 5, 1791; Cobley, *loc.cit.;* p.90, quoting Hunter.
143 Tench, p.253, Tench is here describing Prospect, but later says that the same terms of settlement applied at the Ponds.
144 *Ibid.*, pp.253-254.
145 *The Shorter Oxford English Dictionary,* Third Edition, (Onions), 1967, Vol. II, p.2137.
146 Tench, pp.253-254.
147 *Ibid.*, Phillip to Grenville, Nov. 5, 1791.
148 Cobley, *loc. cit.*, p.221, quoting David Burton's letter to Phillip.
149 *Ibid.*, p.228; Cobley, *loc. cit.*, p.152, Collins, Vol.1, p.204.
150 Cobley, *loc.cit.*, pp.155,261.
151 *H.R.A.* Vol. 1, pp.401-402, Return of Lands in Cultivation; O'Brien, p.262.
152 Tench, pp. 237-238; Collins, Vol.1., p.257; *ibid.*, Vol.11, p.100; Cobley, *loc.cit.*, p.348.
153 **Indent** of Royal Admiral, A.O., 4/3998, C.O.D.9; Robson, p.14.
154 Reports of Coroner's Inquests, 1796-1820, A.O. 2/8286, p.223.
155 Collins, Vol.1, p.237; Chateau Tanunda 'Historical First', No.166., S.M.H., December, 1973.
156 Collins, Vol.1.., p.241.
157 Collins, Vol. II, pp.142, 121;
158 *Ibid.*, Vol.1, p.222; Cobley, *loc.cit.*, p.327.
159 Collins, Vol. 1, p.225.
160 *Ibid.*, p.240
161 *Ibid.*, p.422; Court of Criminal Jurisdiction, July 20, 1795. A.O. Reel 45; David Collins, *An Account of the English Colony in N.S.W.*, Ed., B.H. Fletcher, (Sydney, 1975), Vol. 1, p.354.
162 Collins (Adelaide 1971) Vol. II, p.25. Note the use of the word 'brush' for 'bush', which was a later South African importation.
163 Clark, Vol. 1., p.133.
164 Collins, Vol. 1., p.301.
165 *Ibid.*, p.311; Indent Sugar Cane, A.O. Reel 392.
166 Collins, Vol. 1., p.417.
167 *Ibid.*, pp.455-456; Indent, Marquis of Cornwallis, A.O. 4/3998. C.O.D. 17; Robson, pp.26-28. Enquiry into Mutiny A.O. 1/296 C.O.D. 17.
168 O'Brien, p.314.
169 *H.R.N.S.W.*, Vol.III, p.188-189.
170 Collins, Vol. II, pp.82, 92.
171 Hunter to Portland, Despatch 32, Enc. No. 1, H.R.A. Series 1, Vol. II, p.136-140. C.O. 201/14 is a copy. No names of signators.
172 Macarthur Papers. M.L. A2908, Elizabeth Macarthur to Kingdon, Sept. 1, 1798.
173 Hunter to Portland, Despatch 52, Encs.Nos. 1, 2. C.O. 201.
174 Muster Book, Parliamentary Library, Sydney.
175 King's Return, 1802 Muster, Mitchell Library, Sydney.
176 Register of Arms, April 10, 1802. 4/1719, p.82, Mitchell Library, Sydney; Clark Vol.1. pp.169-170.
177 *Australian Dictionary of Biography,* (Ed. Douglas Pike), (Carlton, Vic., 1966), Vol. 1, Article A.J. Gray. p.161; *Sydney Gazette*, April 1, April 8, 1804. A.O. 1167 Miscellaneous Quit Rent Papers, 1797-1815, bracketed with others in Oxley's notes as 'supposed to belong to Hannibal Macarthur'.
178 The *Sydney Gazette and New South Wales Advertizer*, Sunday, June 3, 1804 (henceforth referred to as '*Sydney Gazette*').
179 *Ibid.;* Collins, Vol. 1, p.416; 1806 Muster, M.L. A/4404.

180 Harold C. Field, editor, *The British Empire*, Time/Life/B.B.C., (Norwich, 1972), 'Guns That Won the Empire', No. 35, pp.970-1; James E. Serven, editor, *The Collecting of Guns*, (Harrisburg, Pennsylvania, 1964), p.96; Ian D. Skennerton, *Australian Service Longarms*, (Margate, Qld., 1976), pp.66-7; Anthony D. Darling, *Red Coat and Brown Bess*, (Ottowa, 1970), p.11; general information, Mr K.W. Luker; *Sydney Gazette*, June 3, 1804.

181 Memorials 1810, A-K, 4/1821, p.104, A.O.N.S.W.

182 *Sydney Gazette*, April 8, 1804; Collins Vol. 2, p.78; *Sydney Gazette*, March 11, 1804.

183 J.V. Byrnes, 'Andrew Thompson, 1773-1810', Part 1, *J.R.A.H.S.* Vol. 48, Pt. 2., p.113. I am greatly indebted to Mr Byrnes's work on Thompson for the background of the next two chapters.

184 A.J. Gray, Article on Matthew James Everingham, *Australian Dictionary of National Biography*, ed. Douglas Pike, (Melbourne, 1966,); *Sydney Gazette*, April 1, 1804.

185 D.G. Bowd, *Macquarie Country*, (Melbourne, 1969), p.6.

186 Return of Lands granted in N.S.W. from 1800-1803, Bonwick Transcripts, Box 88, p. 56, M.L. Sydney. In this 'I' means 'Industrious' as opposed to 'W.L.' meaning 'Worthless and Lazy'; *Sydney Gazette*, October 21, 1804.

187 *H.R.A.* Series 1, Vol. 5, p.166; *Sydney Gazette*, September 16, September 9, October 7, 1805.

188 *Ibid.*, April 21, 1805.

189 *Ibid.*, May 19, 1805.

190 *Ibid.*, June 2, 1805.

191 *Ibid.*, June 2, 9, 23, 1805.

192 *Ibid.*, July 7, 1805.

193 *Ibid.*, Supplement, September 8, 1805; *Ibid.*, September 15, 1805.

194 *Ibid.*, December 8, 15, 1805, March 9, 1806.

195 *Ibid.*, January 12, 1806.

196 *Ibid.*, December 8, 1810.

197 C. Grimes, Diary, 1802-3. S.Z. 81, M.L. Sydney.

198 Dr. T.G. Parsons has informed the writer that the original recruiting papers for the N.S.W. Corps are lost; John T. Christie, *A Bit of River History*, Chapter XIV, p.32, 991 3/C, M.L. Sydney; Charles Swancott, *The Brisbane Water Story*, Part 2, (Gosford, 1953), p.112.

199 I am doubtful about Jones, Macdonald, Bradley and Smith there being so many persons of the same name in the colony at the time; *Sydney Gazette*, July 7, 1805.

200 *Ibid.*, June 3, 1804.

201 *Ibid.*, July 6, 1806, *Ibid.*, February 2, 1806.

202 Rev. George R.S. Reid, *The History of Ebenezer*, (Gosford, 1964), pp.1-3; Bowd, *op. cit.*, p.136; *Sydney Gazette*, June 3, 1804; Collins, Vol. 2, p.78; Reid, *op. cit.*, pp.4-6.

203 Bowd, p.129.

204 Byrnes, *op.cit.*, pp.105-107.

205 *Ibid.*, p.117; *Sydney Gazette*, August 12, 1804; Byrnes, p.111; Bowd, p.66.

206 *Sydney Gazette*, June 3, 1804; Reid, pp.7,9.

207 Byrnes, pp.120, 121; Brian H. Fletcher, 'The Hawkesbury Settlers and the Rum Rebellion', *J.R.A.H.S.*, Vol. 54, Pt. 3, September 1968, p.218, quoting King to Castlereagh, July 27, 1806, Enc. 8, *H.R.A.* Vol. V., pp. 759-760; Letters from Dr T. Arndell to Governor King, March 9, 22, 23, King Papers, pp.155-184, M.L. A.1980-2.

208 Bowd, p. 17, quoting *H.R.N.S.W.*, Vol. VI, p.826, Marsden to King; Marsden to King, March 28, 1804, King Papers, p.184, M.L. A.1980-2.

209 1806 Muster, M.L., Indent of Atlas II. 2/8243, A.O.N.S.W.

210 *O.B.S.P.*, 1801, Trial 37, Q.343.1, Rimes then lived at No. 1, Queen's Head Court, Strand; Additional Papers, Fortune, 2/8259, p.273, A.O.N.S.W.

211 Byrnes, p.114, quoting G. & G.O. May 11, 1806, *H.R.N.S.W.*; Vol. VI, p.72.

212 Clark, *op.cit.*, Vol. 1, p.212. Bank's first suggestion had been the site of Botany Bay for penal colony as he had accompanied Captain Cook on the 1770 discovery voyage; *ibid.*, p.72; *ibid.*, p.213.

213 *Ibid.*, p.164; *ibid.*, pp.199-200; M.H. Ellis, *John Macarthur*, pp. 266, 267.

214 *Ibid.*, C.O. 201/46, A.O.N.S.W. pp.187, 188, Address of Sydney Inhabitants, headed S. Lord; Address Hawkesbury Inhabitants, C.O. 201/46, pp.183, 186. Texts of the two Addresses, Also *H.R.A.* Vol. VI, pp.568-572.

215 Bligh to Windham, H.R.A., Vol. VI, p.149; Fletcher, p.221.

216 Fletcher, pp.218-219.

217 *Ibid.*, pp.221-222.

218 *Ibid.*,

219 Enc. No. 25, Bligh to Castlereagh, Address of Hawkesbury Settlers to Governor Bligh, January 29, 1807, Text *H.R.A.* Vol. VI, p.577. Also Banks Papers, Vol. 22, p.178, M.L. A.85.

220 *H.R.A.* Vol. VI, pp.578-579, Banks Papers, Vol. 22, p.201.

221 *H.R.A.* Vol. VI, p.373, Banks Papers, Vol. 22, p.43.

222 Essays of Reverend S. Marsden concerning N.S.W., 1806-1818, M.L. M.SS.18.

223 Marsden Papers, Vol. 9, p.9.

224 Proceedings of a General Court Martial - Held at Chelsea Hospital — for the Trial of Lieutenant Colonel George Johnston on a charge of Mutiny, Reported by Mr. Bartrum, (London, 1811),

hereinafter referred to as 'Bartrum', M.L. 344/4A1 section reproduced in M. Clark, *Sources of Australian History*, (London, 1957), p.106. Bligh says he knew 'the whole body of people (in the country adjacent to the Hawkesbury) would flock to my standard'.

225 Bligh to Castlereagh, June 30, 1808, *H.R.A.* VI, p.535.

226 Bigge Report, B.T. Box 5, pp.2162-2164, evidence of Palmer re Stores; Byrnes, pp.135, 136.

227 *Ibid.*, p.136; *H.R.N.S.W.*, Vol. VI, pp.458-9 and pp.534-535; Banks Papers, Vol. 22, p.359, for loyalty to Johnson Address, signed by Matthew Everingham.

228 Bartrum, pp.122-124. M.L. 344/4A1.

229 *Ibid.*,

230 *Ibid.*, p.126; John Brennan to Thompson, April 28, 1808, Banks Papers, Vol. 22, p.357.

231 Dr T. Arndell to Edward Griffin, Esq., Secretary to Governor Bligh, April 11, 1808, *H.R.A.*, Vol. XI pp.564-5.

232 Bartrum, p.145. An interesting discussion of all these Addresses is in Brian Fletcher's article previously quoted.

233 Banks Papers, Vol. 22, C.O. 201/46, p.192 ff. Text *H.R.A.* VI pp.573-574.

234 *Ibid.*, p.199, ff, Address of Settlers to Lieutenant Governor Paterson, signed by M. Everingham and others.

235 Coroners' Inquests, 1796-1820 p.29, 2/8286, A.O.N.S.W.

236 Hawkesbury District Storekeeper's Weekly Return, April 8, 1809, 7/2673, p.10; Memorials 1810 , A-K, 4/1821, p.104 A.O.N.S.W.; *Sydney Gazette*, December 8, 1810 February 9, 1811.

237 *Ibid.*, The advertizement of sale of Sackville Reach property stated it was on lease, two years of which were unexpired.

238 Byrnes, pp.138-9.

239 Letter and Memorial from M. Everingham to Ellis Bent, Certificate from Surgeon Mileham, Supreme Court Papers, Case Papers for 1811, A.O.N.S.W. 2210.

240 Macquarie to Castlereagh, March 8, 1810, *H.R.A.* Vol. VII, p.219; *H.R.N.S.W.*, Vol. VII, p.78.

241 Clark, *A History of Australia*, Vol. 1, p.268, quoting *Sydney Gazette*, Jan. 7, 14, and Feb. 4, 1810; Memorials 1810, A-K, 4/1821, p104, A.O.N.S.W., *Sydney Gazette*, February 24, 1810; *ibid.*, February 17, 1810.

242 *Ibid.*, February 24, 1810; Thomas Kenneally, *Bring Larks and Heroes*, (Sydney, 1967); Parish Register of St Matthew's Windsor; Clark, *op.cit.*, pp.320-1.

243 Gwyneth M. Dow, *Samuel Terry — The Botany Bay Rothschild*, (Sydney, 1974), p.59 quoting Old Registers, 4/32/369, R.G.; Mutch Indexes to Births, Deaths & Marriages, M.L., Sydney; Registers of Assignment, 6/101/1495, M.L.

244 Byrnes, pp.162-4.

245 *Ibid.*, p.172; *Sydney Gazette*, November 26, 1809; *ibid.*, July 14, 1810.

246 1806 Muster, M.L. Sydney; Byrnes, p.129, quoting Blaxland to Windham, October 16, 1807, *H.R.N.S.W.*, Vol 7, p.305; Bigge Report, B.T. Box 2, p.725; *Sydney Gazette*, September 28, 1811.

247 Supreme Court Papers, 1810, Capiases, A.O.N.S.W. 2292.

248 Byrnes, pp.165-6.

249 *Ibid.*, p.172.

250 *Sydney Gazette*, December 8, 1810.

251 *Ibid.*, October 29, 1809; Parish Register of St Matthew's Windsor; Bowd, p.183.

252 L. Macquarie, Journal of Travels, 1810-1818, A.778, p.28 M.L.; Byrnes, pp.170-1.

253 *Sydney Gazette*, March 16, 1811; *ibid.*, February 9, 1811.

254 Sketch of the Inundation of 1816, XVLBWIND/1, M.L., Sydney; Commentary in History and Prospects of Hawkesbury District, 1910 Centenary, Ferguson, M.L. Q991.3/N.

255 Sales by Auction by John Howe of Windsor, 1811, C.197, pp.7,11,13,15,16,23, Mitchell Library; *Sydney Gazette*, March 2, 1811.

256 .Byrnes, pp.176,179; Sydney Gazette, May 4, 1811.

257 List of persons indebted to Crown for Government Stock, C.S.I.L., 1813, p.155, 4/1728, A.O.N.S.W.; *The Australian*, February 26, 1842, p.2; Letter from R. Woodbury, June 3, 1811, C.S.7, p.231, A.O.N.S.W.; *Sydney Gazette*, June 26, 1811; Clark, **p.277, quoting** *A Journal of a tour of Discovery Across the Blue Mountains in New South Wales*, (London, 1823).

258 Registers of Assignments, A.3611, No. 546, M.L.; Supreme Court Papers, 2293, A.O.N.S.W.; Capias Book, 1811, M.L. 1130; Supreme Court, Capias Papers, 1811, Vol 8A, Causes 1-305, No. 148, A.O.N.S.W.; Byrnes, pp.179-80.

259 *Ibid.*, p.181; Letter from H. Antill, reproduced in *Windsor and Richmond Gazette*, April 15, 1927, p.8.

260 *Sydney Gazette*, May 9, 1812; Byrnes, p.180; Register of Assignments, A.3612, Book 5, second part, Entry 967, July 1, 1812; Byrnes, pp.183,197,201; Letters from J. Campbell to James McGrath, February 4, 1828, on display Argyle Centre, Sydney; Official Papers of J.E. Manning, January 27, 1832, Norton Smith Papers, A.5350-2, M.L.

261 Byrnes, pp.185-90; Supreme Court Case Papers, 2294, A.O.N.S.W.; 1814 Muster, M.L.; *Sydney Gazette*, May 6, 1815.

262 Byrnes, pp.198-200; Register of Assignments, A. 3613, Book 6, p.161, Entry 43; Sketch of the Inundation of 1816, see Note 16; Original of Land Grant in Norton Smith Papers, A.5328-9,

M.L.; *H.R.A.* Vol.X, p.561; Memorial of Elizabeth Everingham, January 17, 1825. In this she stated that at the time of her husband's death, she rented the land, 4/1841B, A.O.N.S.W., Reports of Coroners' Inquests, 1796-1820, 2/8286, A.O.N.S.W., Depositions of Hawkesbury before A. Thompson, April 20, 1810, Evidence of W. Addy, Constable at Portland Head, Box 1151-2, A.O.N.S.W.

263 Judge Advocate, Reports of Coroners' Inquests, 1796-1820, pp.223-8, 2/8286, A.O.N.S.W.; *Sydney Gazette,* January 3, 1818.
264 J.T. Christie, 'A Bit of River History', published in The *Hawkesbury Herald* c.1905, bound copy, M.L. 991. 3/c. Chapter XVIII; J.C.L. Fitzpatrick, *Those Were the Days,* (Sydney, 1927), p.142.
265 *Windsor & Richmond Gazette,* February 2, 1932.
266 Letter dated December 8, 1829, from J.J. Peacock, Letters to the Colonial Secretary regarding Land, henceforth called 'Col. Sec. re Land', 2/7947, A.O.N.S.W., See also Chapter Twelve; Letters from Clergymen, Catechists and Schoolmasters, Colonial Secretary, 4/320, p.165, A.O.N.S.W.
267 Col. Sec. re Land, 2/7853; A.O.N.S.W., Parish Map of Cornelia, Co. Cumberland, Portion 119; see Chapter Six, Part One.
268 G.M. Trevelyan, *A Shortened History of England,* (Harmondsworth, Middlesex, 1959), pp.144, 159.
269 J.K. McLaughlin, 'The Magistracy in N.S.W., 1788-1850', qualifying thesis for Master of Laws, University of Sydney, M.L. M.S.S. 2670, p.11.
270 J. Baalman, *Outline of Law in Australia,* Second edition (Sydney, 1955) pp.35-38.
271 Trevelyan, *op.cit.,* pp.144,159.
272 Court Criminal Jurisdiction, Miscellaneous Criminal Papers 1788-1816, pp.387-389, 1152, also Court Criminal Jurisdiction, March 1810 — August, 1811, 1119, A.O.N.S.W.
273 Brewer, E.C., *A Dictionary of Phrase and Fable,* New Edition, (London, n.d.), p.573; Baalman, op.cit., p.281.
274 *Sydney Gazette,* May 19, June 2, 16, 23, 30, 1810; Col. Sec. re Land 2/8286, A.O.N.S.W. passim.
275 *Sydney Gazette,* August 4, 1828. McLaughlin, *op.cit.,* p.106.
276 Col. Sec. re Land, 2/8286, p.195 A.O.N.S.W.
277 Judge Advocate, Registers of Assignment, Book 5 — 127 — 749, Book 7 — 32 — 253; *Sydney Gazette* June 16, 1810; Windsor Muster, 1814, M.L.; Registers of Assignment, Book 5 — 149 — 797, M.L.; Arndell, p.252.
278 Col. Sec. re Land, 2817; Mutch Indexes to 1820 Muster, Windsor and 1828 Census, M.L. Sydney.
279 Windsor Muster, 1814, M.L.; Col Sec re Land, 2/8286, p.219, A.O.N.S.W.
280 1828 Census; Windsor Muster, 1820, M.L. Sydney.
281 See Portion 10, Parish of Hawkesbury, Co. Hunter.
282 J.S. Cumpston, *Index to Shipping,* 1788-1825, Q.656,509 Mitchell Library; Colonial Secretary 4/4521, A.O.N.S.W.; Bigge Returns of Births, Deaths and Marriages, A.2130; Evidence of D. Wentworth, Bigge Enquiry, B.T. Box 2, p.579; B.T. Box 12; *Sydney Gazette,* January 30, 1819; Col. Sec. re Land, Letter of J.J. Peacock, November 7, 1831, 2/7916, A.O.N.S.W.; Col. Sec. re Land, 2/7947, A.O.N.S.W.
283 *The Shorter Oxford English Dictionary on Historical Principles,* Vol. 2, Ed. C.T. Onions (Oxford, 1967) p.2100.
284 1814 Muster, M.L.; Judge Advocate, Registers of Assignments, Book 6 — 48 — 1387/8, M.L.
285 *Sydney Gazette,* March 8, 1807; Registrar General's Dept., A.3619, Book 9, p.15, No. 17.
286 Colonial Letter Book, Letters to Miscellaneous Persons, August, 1817 to January, 1818, 4/3497, p.271 A.O.N.S.W.
287 Ecclesiastical Jurisdiction of the Supreme Court of N.S.W. Registers of Wills Proven and Letters of Administration Granted, 1817-1824, 7/2582, A.O.N.S.W.; Supreme Court Curator of Intestate Estates, M.L. F.M.4/589.
288 Howe Papers, M.S. 106, p.31ff. M.L.; Registrar General's Dept., Series 3, p.105; Series 6, Book 9, p.57; R.G. Register of Assignments, Book 7, p.140. See *A Hawkesbury Story*
289 Windsor Government Stores, Ration Book, 1812-1818, M.L. A.803, pp.219, 221, 225; Bigge Appendix, B.T. Box 25, p.5396; Col.Sec. re Land, 2/7853, A.O.N.S.W. Petition of Elizabeth Everingham dated August 25, 1829, letter dated July 24, 1838; Memorial of Elizabeth Everingham, dated January 17, 1825, 4/1841B, p.709, A.O.N.S.W.
290 Marjorie Wymark, *The History of The Macquarie Schoolhouse, 1820 and Saint John's Church 1859,* (Granville, N.S.W., 1970).
291 A.O. Reel 397, (4/4011), Indent of Sir Godfrey Webster, 1826, Patrick McGahy, No.97.
292 Reel 3210 A.D.M. 101/68, Surgeon Superintendents'Journals, Evans, 1825-1826.
293 Everingham File, 7/179, Reeve Records, Society of Australian Genealogists, Sydney.
294 C.M.H. Clark, *A History of Australia,* Vol. 1, p.131; M.H. Ellis, *Francis Greenway,* (Penrith, 1972), p.15.
295 Clark, *loc.cit,* p.159.
296 M.H. Ellis, *John Macarthur,* (Penrith, 1972), pp.443, 530-1, passim.
297 *Australian Dictionary of Biography,* Ed. Pike, (Melbourne, 1968), Vol. 1, p.122; David Collins, *An Account of the English Colony in N.S.W.,* Vol. 1, Ed. B.H. Fletcher, (Sydney, 1975), p.115.

BIBLIOGRAPHY

1. BOOKS OF REFERENCE

An Encyclopaedia of London, Ed. William Kent, (London, 1937).
Australian Dictionary of Biography, Ed. D. Pike, 2 vols., (Melbourne, 1968).
Blue Guide to London, no date.
Brewer, E.C., *A Dictionary of Phrase and Fable,* New Edition, (London no date).
Cumpston, J.S., *Shipping Arrivals and Departures 1788-1825..* (Canberra, 1964).
Richards Topical Encyclopaedia, 15 vols., (New York, 1945).
The Shorter Oxford English Dictionary, Third Edition, (Onions), 1967, 2 volumes.

2. PRIMARY SOURCES

A. PRIVATE PAPERS, LETTERS, JOURNALS, MANUSCRIPTS.

Banks Papers, Vols. 9,22, M.L., A.85, C.O. 201/46.
Grimes, C., Diary and Field Book, 1802-3, M.L., S.Z.81.
Howe Papers, M.S. 106.
King Papers, M.L., A1980-2.
Macarthur Papers, M.L., A2908.
Essays of Rev. S. Marsden concerning N.S.W., 1806-1818.
Macquarie, L., Journal of Travels, 1810-1811, M.L., C.Y.A.778.
Norton Smith Papers, A.5350-2, M.L.
Letters of Hawkesbury Descendants to George Reeve, 2 Vols., M.L., A.1602.
Reeve Records, Everingham File, 7/179, Society of Australian Genealogists, Sydney.
Sketch of the Inundation of 1816, XVLB/WIND/1, M.L., Commentary of this located in History and Prospects of Hawkesbury District, 1910 Centenary, Ferguson, M.L., Q991.3/N.
The Missionary Register, Dec. 1818., Vol. 1, M.L.
Sales by Auction, Windsor, 1811, John Howe, M.L., C.197.

B. ARCHIVES

English Archives

Newgate Calendar of the Sessions File, 1784, Records Office, Guildhall, London.
Boyd's Marriage Index, Guildhall Library, London.

Archives Office of New South Wales.

Governor's Despatches Phillip to Secretary of State, 1790-1792, 4/1634.
Colonial Secretary.
Letters Sent to Miscellaneous persons, 4/3497.
Memorials, 1810, 4/1821-2; 1825, 4/1841.
Letters received regarding Land, 2/7853, 2/7916, 2/7947, 2/8286.
Letters received from Clergy, 4/4521. Letters from Clergymen, Catechists and Schoolmasters, 1825 +, 4/320.
Register of Arms, 1802, 4/1719.
List of Persons indebted to the Crown for Government Stock, 1813, 4/1728.
Hawkesbury District Storekeeper's Weekly Return, 1809, 7/2673.
Convict Indents, Musters and Additional Papers. Bound copies by Ship, 4/3998+, alphabetically, 4/4003+, on microfilm, A.O.392+.
Indents Scarborough and other ships of the First Fleet, Neptune and Marquis of Cornwallis.
Second Fleet, Third Fleet, Royal Admiral, Marquis of Cornwallis, Sugar Cane, Atlas II, A.O. Reel 392.
Fortune, A.O. Reel 393.
Sir Godfrey Webster, A.O. Reel 397.
Additional papers, Marquis of Cornwallis, Enquiry into Mutiny, A.O. 1/296, C.O.D., 17. Sir Godfrey Webster, Reel 3210, A.D.M. 101/68.

Judge Advocate
Reports of Coroners' Inquests, 2/8286-7.
Miscellaneous Quit Rent Papers, 1797-1815, 1167.
Registers of Assignments and other Legal Instruments, 1794-1824, 11 volumes, photo-
  copy, Mitchell Library, A3 609-619.
Index, M.L. A3620. Also T.D. Mutch Card Index.
    Benches of Magistrates
County of Cumberland, Bench Book, Minutes of Proceedings, February 1788-January
  1792, 1/296.
Court of Criminal Jurisdiction, papers 1795, A.O. Reel 45.
    Supreme Court
Capiases for Debt, 2210, 2291-2, 1811.
Curator of Intestate Estates, Index 1818-24, Microfilm, M.L., F.M. 4/589.
Ecclesiastical Jurisdiction, Registers of Wills Proven and Letters of Administration
  granted, 1817-1824, 2/2582.
Holders of Land formerly Convicts, District of Hawkesbury.
Bonwick Transcripts, Box 24, M.L.
Return of Land Granted in New South Wales, 1800-1803, Bonwick Transcripts, Box 88,
  M.L.
Bigge Report, Bonwick Transcripts, Box 2, M.L.
Bigge Appendix, Returns of Births, Deaths and Marriages, A.2130 M.L.
Windsor Government Stores Ration Book, 1812-1818, M.L., A.803.
    Other Archives
Records relating to Land at the Land Titles Office of the Registrar General's Department
  and the Land Department.
Wills examinable at the Probate Division of the Supreme Court of New South Wales and
  on microfilm at the Society of Australian Genealogists.
Church Registers at the Churches themselves, Copies of Registers of St Philip's Sydney,
  A.4372 and D.364, M.L.
T.D. Mutch Indexes to Births, Deaths and Marriages, compiled from early registers,
  Mitchell Library.
T.D. Mutch card indexes to Convict Indents, by ship and biographical; to ship's Musters,
  1816-1821; to Musters; to Land Grants; to 1822 Sydney Constables Round Book.
1828 Census, Mitchell Library and Society of Australian Genealogists.

C. PUBLISHED JOURNALS, DIARIES, MEMOIRS, etc.

Bradley, W., *A Voyage to New South Wales, The Journal of Lieutenant William Bradley R.N.
  of H.M.S. Sirius, 1786-1792*, Sydney, 1969.
Collins, David. *An Account of the English Colony in New South Wales,* first published T.
  Cadell, Jnr. and W. Davies, London, 1798.
Both the fascimile edition in two volumes published Adelaide, 1971 and the edition pub-
  lished Sydney, 1975, edited Brian H. Fletcher have been used. Extracts from the
  Fletcher edition are so designated.
Cunningham, P., *Two Years in New South Wales*, 2 vols., (London, 1828).
Easty, J., *Memorandum of the Transactions of a Voyage from England to Botany Bay, 1787-
  1793,* Sydney, 1965.
Hunter, J., *An Historical Journal of Events at Sydney and at Sea 1787-1792.,* ed. J. Bach,
  Sydney, 1968.
Phillip, A., *The Voyage of Governor Phillip to Botany Bay,* Introduction and Annotations by
  J.J. Auchmuty, (Sydney, 1970).
Scott, J., *Remarks on a Passage to Botany Bay, 1787-1792,* Sydney, 1963.
Tench, W., *Sydney's First Four Years, being a reprint of a Narrative of the Expedition to
  Botany Bay and A Complete Account of the Settlement at Port Jackson,* Introduction and
  Annotations by L.F. Fitzhardinge, Sydney, 1961.
*Proceedings of a General Court Martial.... for the Trial of Lieutenant-Colonel Geo.
  Johnston.... on a Charge of Mutiny.* Reported by M. Bartrum, (London, 1811). M.L.
  344/4A1.

D. COLLECTIONS OF SOURCES

Historical Records of Australia, Series 1, Volumes I, II, V, VI, VII, X, XV, XXIII.

Historical Records of New South Wales, Volumes I, II, VI.
Old Bailey Sessions Papers, (The Whole Proceedings of the King's Commission of the Peace, Oyer and Terminer, and Gaol Delivery for the City of London; and also Gaol Delivery for the County of Middlesex held at Justice Hall in the Old Bailey), (1782-1833).
Clark, M. editor, *Sources of Australian History,* (London, 1957).
Gooden's 1814 Muster. A.1942.
1820 Muster.
1828 Census.
1806 Muster, A/4404.

E. NEWSPAPERS AND PERIODICALS
The Australian, 1842.
The Sydney Gazette, 1804-1829.
Windsor and Richmond Gazette, 1927, 1932. M.L.

3. SECONDARY SOURCES
A. PRINTED BOOKS
Baalman, J., *Outline of Law in Australia,* (Sydney, 1955).
Barnard Eldershaw, M., *Phillip of Australia: An Account of the Settlement at Sydney Cove 1788-1792,* (London, 1938).
Barton, G.B., *History of New South Wales from the Records,* (Sydney, 1889).
Bateson, C., *The Convict Ships 1787-1866,* (Glasgow, 1959).
Blainey, G., *The Tyranny of Distance,* (Melbourne, 1966).
Bonwick, J., *Australia's First Preacher, The Reverend Richard Johnson,* (London, 1898).
Bowd, D.G., *Macquarie Country,* (Melbourne, 1969).
Branch-Johnson, W., *The English Prison Hulks,* (London, 1957).
Brown, C.H., *Meteorology for Masters and Mates,* (Glasgow, 1942).
Burke's Peerage, Baronetage and Knightage.
Christie, J.T., *A Bit of River History,* a collection of articles published in the Hawkesbury Herald, c.1905, of which there is a bound copy in the Mitchell Library, 991.3/C.
Clark, C.M.H. *A History of Australia,* Vol. I, (Melbourne, 1962).
Clunn, H.P., *The Face of London,* (London, nd.)
Cobley, J., *Sydney Cove 1788,* (London, 1962), *Sydney Cove 1789-1790,* (Sydney, 1963), *Sydney Cove, 1791-1792,* (Sydney, 1965), *The Crimes of The First Fleet Convicts,* (Sydney, 1970).
Darling, Anthony D., *Red Coat and Brown Bess,* (Ottawa, 1970).
Dickens, Charles, *Great Expectations, Oliver Twist, Bleak House,* (Nelson ed., 1945).
Dow, G.M., *Samuel Terry — The Botany Bay Rothschild,* (Sydney, 1974).
Ellis, M.H., *John Macarthur, (Sydney, 1955), Francis Greenway,* (Penrith, 1972).
Fitzpatrick, J.C.L., *Those Were the Days,* (Sydney, 1927).
Forester, C.S., *Hornblower and the Hotspur,* (London, 1962).
Jervis, J., *The Cradle City of Australia — A History of Parramatta,* (Parramatta, 1961).
Josephson, *History of Floods on the Hawkesbury River,* (1886) M.L.
Kenneally, T., *Bring Larks and Heroes,* (Sydney, 1967).
Martin, E.G., and Irving, J., *Cruising and Ocean Racing,* Vol. XV, Lonsdale Library, (London, 1935).
O'Brien, E., *The Foundation of Australia (1786-1800),* (London, 1937).
Prout, D., And Feely, F., *Petticoat Parade,* (Adelaide, 1965).
Reid, G.R.S., *The History of Ebenezer,* Sixth Edition, (Gosford, 1964).
Robson, L.L., *The Convict Settlers of Australia,* (Melbourne, 1965).
Serven, James E., editor, *The Collecting of Guns,* (Harrisburg, Pennyslvania, 1964).
Sharpe, R.L., *Memorials of Newgate Gaol and the Sessions House,* (London, n.d.) M.L. 365.942/1A1.
Shaw, A.G.L., *Convicts and the Colonies,* (London, 1966).
Skennerton, Ian D., *Australian Service Longarms,* (Margate, Queensland, 1976).
Swancott, C., *The Brisbane Water Story,* in three parts, (Gosford, 1953).
Trevelyan, G.M., *A Shortened History of England,* (Harmondsworth, Middlesex, 1959).
Wymark, M., *The History of The Macquarie Schoolhouse, 1820 and Saint John's Church 1859.* (Granville, 1970.)

B. PERIODICAL ARTICLES

Byrnes, J.V., 'Andrew Thompson', *J.R.A.H.S.,* Vol. 48, Pts., 2 and 3, 1962.
Campbell, J.F., 'The Dawn of Rural Settlement in Australia', *J.R.A.H.S.,* Vol. XI.
Cobley, J., 'The Crimes of the First Fleeters', *J.R.A.H.S.,* Vol. 52, Pt. 2, June 1966.
Currey, C.H., 'An Account of the Ceremony at Sydney Cove, February 7, 1788', *J.R.A.H.S.,* Vol. 43., Pt. 4.
Fletcher, B.H., 'The Hawkesbury Settlers and the Rum Rebellion', *J.R.A.H.S.,* Vol. 54, Pt. 3, September, 1968.
The London Magazine, 1777, M.L. 052/13.
The British Empire, Time/Life/B.B.C., (Norwich, 1972), editor Harold C. Field, No. 35.

C. THESES

McLaughlin, J.K., *The Magistracy in N.S.W., 1788-1850,* qualifying thesis for Master of Laws, University of Sydney. M.L. MSS.2670.

D. PARISH MAPS

Lands Department — current.
Mitchell Library — superseded.

INDEX

p.13 '...for it was crystal clear that the lad was guilty...' Matthew himself later admitted his guilt in a letter to Sir Samuel Shepherd, who had become his benefactor. See V. Ross, *The Everingham Letterbook.*

p.18 For Shepherd as prosecutor, see *Letterbook*

p.19 It is now known that Everingham was on the *Censor* hulk, see *Letterbook* Delete last paragraph and substitute:
'After his trial, Matthew was returned to Newgate Prison where he was lodged in the Master's side until September 6, 1784 . He was then delivered out of the custody of Richard Akerman, the Keeper of Newgate to the *Censor* hulk at Woolwich.'

p.37 For escape of cattle, see *Letterbook* pp.45,91ff.

p.38 John Ramsay, fellow *Scarborough* transportee and Everingham's settler companion in exploration, later claimed to have helped to saw the ridge pole, (defined as the horizontal pole for a long tent), for the Government House built in the colony, see *Letterbook* p.102

p.41 Everingham later claimed that he had been overseer of the 'pitt sawyers and measured the work' *Letterbook* pp.35,48

pp.44,45 Re Matthew as servant to Charles Parker, Master Carpenter of the *Sirius.* Matthew was particularly interested in shipbuilding timbers, *Letterbook* p.56

p.55 Matthew actually became friendly with Elizabeth as soon as she entered the colony. He supervised the 'women at their needle' while attending Henry Edward Dodd, Superintendent of Agriculture in the first days of the settlement at Rose Hill. *Letterbook* p.48

p.59 It is suspected that Macarthur may have fostered the Everingham expedition to the Blue Mountains in 1795.

p.60 For Matthew's decision to 'turn settler' and his farm, see *Letterbook* p.35

p.65 Matthew writes of this period and the monopolies in the *Letterbook*

pp.67,68 It is now believed that Everingham was at Parramatta for about two years prior to having taken up his land and was servant to Dodd until the latter's death. The baby, Mary Everingham may have been buried on Everingham's property though the death was recorded in the register of the Parish of St John.

p.68 Par.4, Line 2, Following '...Everinghams' baby, Mary,' insert and read 'born Dec 23 1791, would have been...'

p.69 Par.1, Line 9, After 'born' insert 'Nov 7, 1802...'

pp.71-73 This is all corroborated in the *Letterbook.* He had one servant in 1792 and hoped soon to have two.

p.94 Matthew was familiar with the Hawkesbury as early as 30 October 1795. See *Letterbook*

p.106 For 'Rule Britannia' read *The British Grenadier.*

p.120 Re Blaxland and the crowning ridge. Everingham had already enunciated the 'ridge method' of exploration. Blaxland knew Ramsay, Everingham's companion and almost certainly would know of their earlier attempt. See *Letterbook*

p.134 In Par.3, for 'Great North Rock' read 'Road...' The reference to the 'following chapter' indicates it is dealt with in *A Hawkesbury Journey.*

p.146 For 'Rule Britannia' read *The British Grenadier.*
'Sarah's story' is covered in *A Hawkesbury Story*
For 'eight generations' read 'nine...'